International Perspectives on Contemporary Democracy

DEMOCRACY, FREE ENTERPRISE, AND THE RULE OF LAW

This series is sponsored by the Cline Center for Democracy, which is devoted to the study of democracy throughout the world, of institutions that sustain and extend it, and of forces that perpetually challenge and endanger it.

Series Editor
Peter F. Nardulli, University of Illinois

A list of books in the series appears at the end of this book.

International Perspectives on Contemporary Democracy

Edited by

PETER F. NARDULLI

UNIVERSITY OF ILLINOIS PRESS
Urbana and Chicago

Manufactured in the United States of America
1 2 3 4 5 C P 5 4 3 2 1
∞ This book is printed on acid-free paper.

Library of Congress Cataloging-in-Publication Data
International perspectives on contemporary democracy /
edited by Peter F. Nardulli.
p. cm. — (Democracy, free enterprise, and the rule of law)
Includes bibliographical references and index.
ISBN-13 978-0-252-03335-3 (cloth : alk. paper)
ISBN-10 252-03335-3 (cloth : alk. paper)
ISBN-13 978-0-252-07544-5 (pbk. : alk. paper)
ISBN-10 0-252-07544-7 (pbk. : alk. paper)
1. Democracy.
2. Democratization—International cooperation.
I. Nardulli, Peter F.
JC423.I586 2008
321.8—dc22 2007030914

To Richard G. and Carole J. Cline,
whose vision and generosity
made this undertaking possible

Contents

II. Globalization and Democracy

Preface

As a form of government, democracy enjoys unparalleled prestige at the beginning of the twenty-first century. The most prosperous nations in the world were democracies. Moreover, democracy's "third wave" had generated an unprecedented number of new republics in southern and eastern Europe as well as Latin America. Reflecting on these developments, some see the "end of history." They argue that democracy has vanquished its competitors, and that it is the only legitimate form of government in the modern era. Others are more cautious. Mindful of the challenges to democracy in the new century, as well as its ebb and flow throughout history, they envision a more problematic future.

Several salient challenges confront democracy's durability and portability: the increasing racial, ethnic, and religious diversity of many societies; the rapid diffusion of innovations in information and communication technologies; and the emergence of global forces and institutions. While these developments present new possibilities for democratic governance, they also have the potential to disrupt its formulation and implementation. Moreover, in conjunction with the demise of the cold-war era in the 1990s, these developments give rise to barriers that could affect the diffusion of democracy beyond its current frontiers. In the twenty-first century the joint effects of these developments could:

- affect the ability of individuals to discharge the responsibilities of democratic citizenship;
- undermine the commitment and identification of citizens to their domicile;

- affect the structure, operation, and legitimacy of institutional mechanisms for linking elite behavior to mass preferences;
- place extraordinary burdens on democratic political and civic leaders;
- limit the legitimacy of traditional conceptions of democratic institutions in non-Western settings; and
- constrain and curtail the actions of democratically elected governments in historically unprecedented ways.

The confluence of two milestone events on the Urbana-Champaign campus of the University of Illinois made it possible to organize a set of activities around these important concerns. One was the centennial of the university's Department of Political Science; the second was the inauguration of a newly endowed center within the College of Liberal Arts and Sciences, the Cline Center for Democracy. To mark these events the college, the department and the center hosted a week-long conference.

In preparation for this conference, the editor initiated a wide-ranging consultative process to clarify the implications of increasing social heterogeneity, Information Age innovations, and globalization for the health and practice of democracy in the twenty-first century. Once these topics were clarified, he used them in conversations with leading political scientists to identify a wide range of accomplished scholars (comparativists, theorists, political economists, communication scholars, law and society students, etc.) who were equipped to make original and important contributions to the topics. Discussions with these scholars led to new insights and further refinements in the topics to be addressed.

These scholars were then commissioned to prepare original essays that focused on assigned, clearly developed themes for a general academic audience, refraining from excessive jargon and focusing on "the big picture." These essays were initially presented in October 2004 in a leisurely collegial setting, and exchanges among the participants were lively and enlightening. The reflective atmosphere was due in large part to the fact that the conference brought together scholars from a variety of subdisciplines, scholars who seldom interact with one another.

A set of discussants was also commissioned to prepare detailed reviews of the papers, which were supplemented by a review written by the editor. The essayists then revised their papers in light of the reviews and the insights gained from the conference. The result is a collection of wide-ranging essays that make original and important contributions to issues facing democracy at the beginning of the twenty-first century. This volume examines two cross-national phenomena: the prospects for a fourth wave of democratization and the challenges that globalization poses for democratic governance. The companion volume, *Domestic Perspectives on Contemporary Democracy* deals with two issues that affect mass-elite linkages within democratic societies: social heterogeneity and Information Age challenges.

International Perspectives on Contemporary Democracy

1

International Perspectives on Democracy in the Twenty-first Century

BRIAN J. GAINES AND
PETER F. NARDULLI

This volume touches some truly profound and fundamental questions about the future of democratic governance in the upcoming century. One subset of questions derives from matters that cloud the prospects for continued democratization (i.e., Will a fourth wave of democratization emerge?). The nations yet to embrace democracy include some of the poorest and socially most heterogeneous nations in the world (i.e., those in Central Asia and Africa). Others have cultures and traditions that will make the emergence of democracy challenging, to say the least (i.e., Arab states in the Middle East, China). If democracy is to spread beyond the reaches of the third wave, what will drive it?

The literature on democratization has traditionally placed a great deal of emphasis on intranational factors (level of economic development, the structure of class alignments, cultural factors, elite motivations, etc.). But it is hard to see intranational factors driving democracy movements in the existing set of nondemocratic nations. Thus, if a fourth wave is to emerge, it is most likely to be driven by extranational factors. This extranational scenario, however, raises a set of difficult questions. Can extranational influences have enduring effects on domestic governance structures? What types of extranational influences are most likely to effect domestic changes? Are some extranational strategies for fostering democratization more effective than others? Under what conditions are these strategies most effective? Are these conditions likely to exist in the twenty-first century?

The second subset of questions addressed in this volume derives from the political implications of globalization. The globalization of various forms of human activity has the potential to produce both profound and ironic effects on democratic governance in the twenty-first century. Globalization's potential effects on democracy are profound in two ways. First, globalization can erode the political dynamics that make it possible for democratic citizens to hold elites accountable for their stewardship. Second, globalization can undermine the capacity of governments to address domestic concerns and priorities. These two effects are ironic because the extranational forces that are most likely to power democracy's fourth wave may well undermine the capacity of democracies to do what makes them attractive forms of government: respond to the needs and desires of its citizens.

At the core of democratic responsiveness is a set of mass-elite linkages that rests on a foundation of electoral institutions and mechanisms. Empiricists, however, have lately questioned the capacity of citizens to fulfill the expectations of democratic citizenship—even the reduced expectations embodied in a Schumpeterian model of democracy. If citizens were too uninformed, apathetic, and inattentive to cast their votes responsibly when times were simpler, how will they perform after globalization has added a layer of issue complexity to the democratic milieu? Compounding the challenges facing democratic citizens is globalization's impact on national identities and civic commitments. Can a form of government that depends so greatly on citizen involvement remain viable in an era in which citizens are increasingly detached from their political domiciles?

Raising even more profound questions are the constraining effects that international institutions and global economic forces have on the policy choices of government officials. Of what importance is the effectiveness of mass-elite linkages if democratic stewards in the global era do not have the capacity to respond to domestic needs and desires? But is the encroachment of global forces really inexorable? Or do societies have alternatives—viable choices they can make to enhance a democratic government's responsiveness to its citizen's desires and needs? If so, what are they? What are their tradeoffs? How can these costs and benefits be identified, given the diversity of the existing community of democratic nations?

Part I: Democratization on the Frontiers of the Third Wave

Larry Diamond (chapter 2) adopts an expansive view of the forces and circumstances surrounding the third wave of democratization. This provides him with a decidedly optimistic view of democracy's future in the twenty-first century. Examining a broad array of data, and drawing from a variety of examples, he argues that cultural, historical, and economic barriers do not rule out democratization. On the contrary, what matters most is the willingness of national elites to entertain democratization and their commitment to democratic norms, values, and processes. Hence, the necessary conditions for the emergence of new democratic states include sustained pressure from both civil society and international actors.

Sustaining democracy in the face of unfavorable cultural, economic, and historical factors is not automatic but requires that democratic reforms perform robustly. Mature regimes are attractive governance models only insofar as they continue to thrive, generating more prosperous, just, and humane societies. Because Diamond views democratic, accountable, and transparent government as a precondition for sustained development, he has a largely optimistic outlook on the future. That future includes the wide dissemination of democratic regimes, rooted in human dignity and liberty, that will enhance global peace and prosperity.

Zachary Elkins (chapter 3) and Bruce Russett (chapter 4) shift attention from outcomes to mechanisms, addressing how democratization occurs. Both Elkins and Russett focus on extranational factors, a domain that is increasingly important but is also theoretically underdeveloped. But while Elkins focuses on uncoordinated extranational influences, Russett's focus is on the concerted, and often organized, efforts of international actors.

Elkins begins by noting that while the "wave" metaphor has been widely embraced by democratization scholars, the dynamics underlying it have been under-theorized. Empirical analyses of democracy indicators confirm that the post–World War II era has, indeed, seen temporally clustered democratic shifts. But it is unclear what factors account for these clusters. Temporal clustering could reflect coincidental changes, as multiple nations react similarly to some external force (including pressure from external actors). Elkins, however, argues that democratic reforms are consistent with the wave metaphor because they diffuse across nations.

He views diffusion as a process by which uncoordinated external influences affect the choices and decisions of domestic elites. He points to two mechanisms that are central to the diffusion process: adaptation and learning. Thus, the probability that a nondemocracy will adopt democratic reforms is affected by the success of democratic reforms in neighboring countries. In this respect, Elkins's analysis, like Diamond's, underscores the importance of the performance of established democracies. If established democracies do not perform well, they can retard diffusion processes that feed on the attractiveness of neighboring democracies.

Russett's chapter is also concerned with the role of extranational factors on democratization. Historical review of the influence of international actors on democratization informs speculation about the future impact of similar campaigns. His review leads him to focus on carrot-and-stick mechanisms. The primary stick mechanism is, of course, imposition of democratic regimes following the overthrow of nondemocracies by military force. Carrot mechanisms, on the other hand, include peacekeeping initiatives; organizing, monitoring and legitimizing elections; and economic and political sanctions. Russett's analysis leaves him encouraged about the future, chiefly because recent history has seen a steep increase in dyadic IGO memberships and also the gradual domination of these IGO's by stable, prosperous, and powerful democracies. This latter trend increases the likelihood that these IGO's will attempt to promote democracy. Moreover, it enhances their ability to affect the cost-benefit analyses of domestic elites, as well as the balance of power among competing domestic elites.

Diamond's optimism for democracy in the twenty-first century is mostly reinforced by the implications of the Elkins and Russett chapters—provided that democracies perform well. The values, principles, and norms of high-performing democracies can diffuse to neighboring states, as their example strengthens the position of domestic democracy advocates while undercutting the credibility of autocrats. As these same nations come to dominate IGO's they can, in turn, use their resources to strengthen and support fledgling democracies. And diffusion of democratic reforms can then continue throughout the developing world.

This mutually reinforcing process is appealing and encouraging to democracy advocates everywhere. But others are more skeptical of the optimism, indeed triumphalism, of democratic "Tinas."[1] A common error is to assume that historical events could only have turned out as they did. But had the Luftwaffe developed the ME-262 in time to win the Battle of Britain, might not we all be living under a German-based fascist world empire today? Back in the present, more sober voices point to possible scenarios other than the spiraling global diffusion of democracy. Globalization, for example, could generate such severe economic hardships in some fledgling democracies that they could be destabilized, truncating diffusion processes and stemming the democratic tide. To the extent that these economic hardships were imposed by IGO's determined to reform domestic economic and political institutions, backlashes against external actors could emerge. This could both undermine the credibility and influence of external actors and empower demagogues promising better times through nondemocratic measures—as may be currently happening in some Latin American nations.

Similar backlashes could be fueled by negative developments in the fledgling free states established by American military force in Afghanistan and Iraq. It must also be noted that even if democratic nations do not experience disastrous times in the near future, there is no guarantee that their experiences will always be worthy of emulation, as in the case of some Eastern European and African democracies. Finally, democracies in the twenty-first century will have to compete with China and other Asian tigers. Their development models will surely be attractive to some domestic elites in some developing nations, thereby muddying and clogging diffusion processes and providing competition for international democracy advocates.

Lisa Anderson (chapter 5) is skeptical about the "spiraling diffusion of democracies" scenario, but she offers a very different argument to support her skepticism. Anderson's analysis focuses on the attractiveness of democracy to recipient nations rather than on the ability of democracy's advocates to foster democratic regimes. At the core of her work is a formidable critique of a notion that is embedded in the paradigmatic Western perspective on democratization: that democracy is the natural expression of universal values. According to Anderson, only insofar as democracy embodies natural human aspirations does it deserve to be treated as the default form of government, making all other nations "holdouts." The notion that democracy is the default form of government, she argues, fails to be disinterested, ignores the history of Western civilization, and underestimates the roots of local traditions, values, and institutions in "holdout" nations. Anderson reminds us of the myriad debates—as well as the chronic ambiguity, skepticism, and ambivalence—that have surrounded democracy for most of its relatively brief modern history in the West. She then presents non-Western perceptions of liberal democracy and suggests that it might be naive to expect a democratic transition in regions such as the Middle East any time soon.

Part II: Globalization and Democracy

In this section scholars from a number of subdisciplines (political behavior, political economy, political theory) articulate and assess the implications of challenges posed by globalization for democratic governance. James Kuklinski, Paul Quirk, and Buddy Peyton (chapter 6) and Wendy Rahn (chapter 7) examine these challenges from the perspective of democratic citizens; they consider how globalization may affect citizens' ability to discharge their political duties and responsibilities. Beth Simmons (chapter 8) and John Freeman (chapter 9) examine the impact of globalization on the discretion of democratic nation-states. They question whether the emergence of supranational governments and global capital markets can erode the linkage between mass preferences and domestic policies, a linkage that is at the heart of democratic theory. Finally, Melissa Orlie (chapter 10) broadens the conventional debate over globalization and democracy and questions its inevitability, arguing that nations have choices and that there are viable alternatives that should be considered.

The promise of democracy is that it permits citizens to take part in deciding their own fates. One can be outvoted and never see one's preferences enacted, but there are always new opportunities to express a preference and to attempt to win over others to one's side. But even before the emergence of a markedly more interdependent and complex world, much empirical research questioned the capacity of most citizens to discharge capably their democratic duties and responsibilities. The potential impact of information overloads generated by the complexity of issues inherent in a globalized world casts a dark pall over the viability of traditional forms of mass-elite linkages in the twenty-first century.

Kuklinski, Quirk, and Peyton (chapter 6) argue that a globalized setting does not pose fundamentally new challenges for the theory and practice of democracy. On the contrary, they argue, globalization—increased integration of people and communities all over the globe—produces policy questions that confront citizens with tasks similar in character to those generated by domestic politics in any democracy. Of course, to say that coping with a rapidly shrinking and uniform world does not require unique skills is not to say that democracy is problem-free. On the contrary, the authors use surveys about the Iraq war and its aftermath to demonstrate that citizens' attitudes can be intractable, surprisingly resistant to updating as events unfold. Moreover, contrary to some popular theories about how electorates cope with complicated life, the less knowledgeable members of the public are often, by virtue of being less attached to particular partisan camps, better able to make use of the new information that comes forth each day.

Many prominent theories of how publics cope with the complexity of evaluating governance in modern democracies emphasize the gap between a smaller, better-informed and adept segment of the population, and a larger segment whose members are generally inattentive, ideologically unconstrained, and uninformed. As long as the former group is not too small, all is well, many observers argue. Kuklinski, Quirk, and Peyton show that this contrast misses the mark—the more informed are often poor guardians of responsible citizenship insofar as they are determined resisters of information that contradicts their firmly held prior beliefs. If theories emphasizing the supply side of public opinion are flawed, the dominant demand-side explanations of information flows are profoundly, even shockingly, antipopulist. They emphasize how little impact on governance anyone except true elite insiders ever has, and thus undercut most of the promise of popular self-determination. Hence, the authors caution that zeroing in on globalization is missing the point: mass democracy does not face new threats so much as old, but underappreciated, ones.

While Wendy Rahn (chapter 7) also focuses on citizens, her concern is the effect of globalization on national identities and civic commitment. She roots this concern in a growing body of literature suggesting that global influences may be fraying the ties that bind citizens to their own nations. Globalization has led to greater immigration in many democratic nations. However, unlike in prior eras, the greater availability of affordable transportation and communication has made it easier for immigrants to maintain homeland ties and identities. This allows them to resist assimilation into the cultures and polities in which they reside. Technological advances have also made accessing reference groups outside of national boundaries progressively easier—for natives and immigrants alike. This is a boon for global integration, but it poses subtle risks for national unities. The long-term effect of these developments on citizens' commitments to local entities is potentially troubling because citizen engagement is essential for a democracy to function effectively.

Rahn peeks into the future by examining a cross-national sample of high school students. While globalization and civic commitment are broad, amorphous concepts, she casts a wide net by considering multiple, alternative measures of each. More than one-third of the coefficients measuring globalization effects on citizenship commitments are negative and significant. Hence, her analysis suggests that the problem of a disengaged population effectively living in exile at home is genuine. In addition, she demonstrates that one can predict detachment in teens surprisingly well using measures of the extent to which their home nations are open and globally integrated. Rahn concludes that maintaining popular commitment to, and engagement in, local polities in the face of ever-expanding global integration is an issue of some import for democracy's future and is, consequentially, a task that democracies must face head on. To do otherwise risks the collapse of democratic societies as tomorrow's adult citizens simply shrug off the weight of civic duties and responsibilities.

Beth Simmons (chapter 8) focuses on the internationalization of political authority and its implications for democratic governance at the nation-state level. Simmons's concern with this issue stems from three important empirical observations. Her essay documents: (1) the exponential growth of international organizations with governing authority during the 20th century; (2) the propensity of democratic governments to delegate governing authority to these organizations; and (3) the tendency of international "agents" to operate in ways that are inconsistent with democratic norms and principles. Thus, just as democracies are diffusing throughout the globe, there is a marked tendency for them to delegate their authority to politically insulated international bureaucracies whose operations lack transparency. Compounding this situation is the fact that these entities are dominated by powerful nations. Thus, her analysis suggests that the real losers are emerging democracies that are least likely to have their interests reflected in the decisions of these organizations. In short, she re-injects classic power politics and realpolitik theory into sunny scenarios of liberal theorists, who imagine that international coordination must always entail Pareto-improving cooperation.

John Freeman's analysis (chapter 9), like Simmons's, is concerned with the tension between globalization and democratic governance at the nation-state level. While Simmons frets over the abdication of authority by national governments to undemocratic international organizations, Freeman sees a different threat. There is, he fears, a seemingly inexorable migration of political authority to global capital markets, which are both private and unaccountable. This migration of authority is largely ignored, or viewed as inevitable, by technocrats who are temperamentally and vocationally indifferent to democratic concerns. Freeman argues that the failure to acknowledge the explicitly political nature of many "technocratic" economic issues could produce a scenario that undermines the foundation of democratic government. As the operation of global capital markets constrains the ability of democratic nations to provide for the welfare of their constituents, citizens' recognition of their national governments' limited capacities will lead them to view their elected officials as unaccountable for their welfare. Once this happens, the mass-elite linkages that are at the core of democracy will begin to uncouple, disengaging mechanisms that provide for a uniquely democratic form of governmental responsiveness. Freeman is particularly critical of the failure of political economists to address these concerns. Consequently, he outlines a research agenda that will bring these issues into the mainstream of political economy research.

Melissa Orlie (chapter 10) speaks to the very concerns that Freeman delineates, but from a very different intellectual tradition. Her chapter begins by appraising the current state of political debate about economic globalization and democracy. Her assessment is that advocates and critics of economic globalization, when they acknowledge the other's point of view at all, are too quick to dismiss it. This is lamentable because the failure to engage a broader array of perspectives impoverishes the debate. One important cost of this truncated political discourse is a loss of awareness of the range of competing human goods that democratic nations must balance. Correspondingly, policy issues relating to markets and democratic governance are too often treated as nonpolitical matters to be decided by the very technocrats who cause Freeman such angst.

Depoliticizing these issues obscures the fact that defenders and critics of economic globalization have different conceptions of human welfare and make basic assumptions and philosophical commitments that are often incompatible. Orlie argues that there is no empirical or normative perspective that can provide definitive answers to such basic questions as who we are, what we value, or how we should govern ourselves. Rather, these matters require vigorous public debates that will necessarily touch upon the future course of economic globalization and its consequences for democratic governance and human welfare. Such debates, she believes, will underscore the fact that nations have alternatives to the rule of global markets. They will also help identify those alternatives in ways that comport with the preferences and desires of different democratic communities.

The chapters included in this volume will not conclusively resolve the questions with which this chapter began. But, in at least some instances, common themes and responses are apparent in very different chapters prepared by very different scholars. Perhaps the most obvious theme is the importance of democratic performance for the health and spread of democracy in the twenty-first century. At the core of Diamond's optimistic forecast is his belief that free societies will perform better than others, thereby shoring up democratic experiments. Governmental performance is also at the heart of Elkins's argument about the central role of diffusion in democratization; neighbors are unlikely to emulate poorly performing governance models. Finally, performance is equally important to Russett's analysis. Weak, faltering nations will not dominate international organizations and direct their resources to aid the spread of democracy.

A second common theme is the importance of extranational factors for understanding issues related to democratic governance in the modern era. Diamond sees these factors as important for both supporting domestic democracy advocates and convincing democratic skeptics that "there is no alternative." Both Elkins and Russett are concerned with outlining ways in which these extranational factors affect democratization. With the exception of chapter 6 (Kuklinski, Quirk, and Peyton), which suggests that globalization is a red herring, the contributors to this globalization section underscore the centrality of extranational factors for the future practice of democracy. Moreover, these globalization chapters reveal a chilling picture: distracted, detached, and disengaged citizens; powerful, insulated international organizations dominated by a handful of major powers; emasculated national governments; domestic policy making dominated by indifferent technocrats; and truncated public debates that fail to engage the full range of issues that affect human welfare.

While a distillation of these observations recalls the dismal science of Malthus and other Cassandras of past political economy, the relatively brief history of modern democratic rule suggests that the future is not as bleak as it may appear. Malthusianism never seems to go out of style, but its namesake clearly overlooked the ability of ingenious people to solve resource problems. One of the remarkable strengths democratic regimes demonstrated throughout the twentieth century is the ability to muddle through difficult issues and challenges (wars, depressions, fascism, totalitarianism, terrorism) with remarkable consistency. Indeed, it is the very success of these regimes that powered democracy's third wave. Few would depict the process by which democracies engaged these challenge as poetry in motion—analogies to sausage making are more common. But the solutions that have emerged have been workable, more often than not, even if they have not been optimal. Citizens are important components of democratic feedback mechanisms that constrain elected officials, so democracies will continue to fashion workable solutions, even in a globalized milieu. Perhaps the greatest threat to the emergence of democratic responses to globalization's challenges is the failure to engage those challenges in open and far-ranging dialogues.

Note

1. The sentiment embodied in the "end of history" rhetoric has also found its way into the political lexicon: so effective was Margaret Thatcher's repeated use of the assertion "There is no alternative," that her opponents nicknamed her "Tina." The world's democracy advocates have increasingly taken to mimicking Thatcher's rhetoric. They bluntly announce to "holdout" nations that there is no alternative to democratic governance in the modern world.

PART I

Democratization on the Frontiers of the Third Wave

2

Democratization in the Twenty-first Century

The Prospects for the Global Diffusion of Democracy

LARRY DIAMOND

One of the most important developments of the late twentieth century was the emergence of democratic forms of government throughout most of the world. Indeed, the last quarter of the century has been heralded as the age of democracy, and the diffusion of these democracies has been labeled democracy's third wave. Democratization is a noteworthy global development primarily because of its beneficial effect on the lives of those who have embraced it. More than any other form of government, democracy provides the structure, stability, and dynamism needed to unleash human potential and to harness human and natural resources for the good of society. But democratization has also provided tangible benefits for other countries. Democracies tend to be "good neighbors." They trade more with one another and fight less; moreover, democracies are less likely to produce international terrorists than are more repressive forms of governments.

Looking ahead into the twenty-first century from the perspective of third wave developments, this chapter assesses democracy's prospects for the future. It asks a broad question: Can any country become a democracy? That is, can *every* country become a democracy? I first discuss what I mean by democracy. Then I briefly review the reach of democracy's third wave. This review provides important insights into the potential of democracy's reach in the coming decades. It also leads into the consideration of another issue that bears on democracy's prospects: the breadth of its appeal. In discussing the universality of democracy's appeal, I consider both economic and cultural factors. The fourth section considers the social, economic, and political forces that have driven democratization in the third wave. It then extends this discussion to two matters that will affect democracy's possibilities: Why have so few third wave democracies "died"? Why have some nations not democratized? I conclude by offering a set of recommendations that will foster the continued diffusion of democracy in the twenty-first century.

Conceptualizing Democracy

Democracy can be defined as a system of government in which the people choose their leaders at regular intervals through free, fair, and competitive elections. This notwithstanding, it is useful to distinguish between two types of democracies: electoral democracies and liberal democracies. *Electoral democracies* are democratic in only the most minimal sense: the principal positions of political power are filled through regular, free, fair, and competitive (i.e., multiparty) elections. *Liberal democracies* share all the attributes of electoral democracies, but they are also characterized by: vigorous adherence to the rule of law, extensive individual freedoms, strong protections for the rights of minority groups, a pluralistic and vibrant civil society, and civilian control over the military.[1] Few will quibble with the categorization of liberal democracies as truly democratic political orders. But many object to the inclusion of electoral democracies, which can exist in countries with significant violations of human rights, massive corruption, and a weak rule of law.[2] However, for a country to qualify as an electoral democracy, these defects must be sufficiently contained so that the will of the voters can be reflected in electoral outcomes. That is, the potential must exist for unpopular incumbents to be removed from office. This requires an open electoral arena, with substantial freedom for parties and candidates to campaign and solicit votes, and thus to speak, publish, assemble, organize, and move about the country peacefully for that purpose. It also requires neutral and fair administration of elections, a secret ballot, reasonable access to the mass media, and established legal procedures for resolving electoral disputes.[3]

Reservations about the use of "free, fair, and competitive elections" as the litmus test for electoral democracy are rooted in the assertion that such elections, by themselves, are not very meaningful. Some critics, for example, question the value of an "electoral" democracy in which the rights of women, minorities, and the poor are ignored, and where elected officials merely take turns plundering the national treasury and abusing power. To these critics, elections in such a political system merely crown temporary monarchs who can use and abuse power without constraint during their terms of office. In essence, these critics contend that electoral democracies do not provide for political accountability.

This can be seen in the work of Guillermo O'Donnell, who argues that a truly accountable political system requires three components. One is a *democratic* component, which enables citizens to choose their rulers in free and fair elections and to participate and express themselves in other political processes. The second is a *liberal* component, which limits the power of the state to encroach on the basic rights of individual, thus affirming civil liberties and minority rights. The third is a *republican* component, which provides for the rule of law and good government through institutions of horizontal accountability that check and balance governmental power, while holding all political actors, public and private, equal before the law.[4]

O'Donnell's analysis makes it clear that electoral democracies do not *necessarily* provide for horizontal accountability. It can be argued, however, that electoral democracies can be a useful transition stage for societies that are evolving toward a liberal democracy. Hence, they are useful to categorize as minimalist democracies. In *The Future of Freedom*, however, Fareed Zakaria challenges this notion. Within O'Donnell's framework Zakaria is arguing that democracy advocates concerned with the transformation of authoritarian states into liberal democracies should put less emphasis on the democratic component of political accountability. Rather, as a transitional strategy, they should place more emphasis on first developing the republican component. His point is that we might do better with less democracy and more rule of law.[5] Thus, to Zakaria, minimalist, electoral democracies do not have much to offer even as a transitional strategy.

Zakaria's analysis may have some utility for nations such as China and those in the Middle East. But it can only take us so far because, in reality, democracy and freedom are closely related throughout the world. This is true even if we set aside the wealthy countries of the West, all of which are liberal democracies. Examining only the developing and post communist countries, we find a strong correlation between democracy (using the minimalist definition offered above), the enjoyment of civil liberties, and the rule of law. This can be seen in the evaluations made by Freedom House, an independent think tank and democracy organization based in New York. Each year Freedom House rates each country from 1 to 7 along two scales—political rights and civil liberties—with 1 being most free and 7 most repressive. In recent years, there have only been two countries in the world that are not democracies and yet have a civil-liberties score below the mid-point on the seven-point scale: Tonga, and Antigua and Barbuda. And few will propose a theory of political development based on the example of two microstates (each with a population of about 100,000). Even Singapore, the much-vaunted example of a "liberal autocracy," is in fact not very liberal in the scope it gives its citizens to dissent and organize.

To be sure, there are some pretty illiberal governments in the world that would qualify as electoral democracies, governments that do not fare well in the areas of human rights and the rule of law.[6] What is undeniable, however, is that virtually the only countries that adhere to the rule of law and provide their citizens with extensive civic freedoms are democracies, including those minimalist democracies labeled here as electoral democracies. Thus, I find it useful to include electoral democracies as a type of democratic regime, and I include them in the analyses that follow.

Democracy's Third Wave

The 1974 triumph of democracy in Portugal marked the beginning of a long wave of democratic expansion, as Samuel Huntington has documented in his seminal work, *The Third Wave: Democratization in the Late Twentieth Century.*[7] When this third wave of democratization began, there were only about forty democracies in the world, and these were mainly in the advanced industrial countries. But after Portugal, Greece and then Spain followed shortly, and in the late 1970s, military rule began to unravel in Latin America. Between 1979 and 1985, the military withdrew in favor of elected civilian governments in Ecuador, Bolivia, Peru, Argentina, Uruguay, Brazil, and several Central American countries. Where military rule was more economically successful, in Chile, the transition was delayed, but it came in 1989 by means of a referendum. Table 2.1 documents the dramatic trend of the past three decades.

By the late 1980s, the third wave of democratization had spread to Asia, first toppling the dictatorship of Ferdinand Marcos in February 1986, and then forcing the complete withdrawal of the military in South Korea in 1987. That same year, martial law was lifted in Taiwan, and a more gradual transition to democracy began there, though it was not completed until 1996. But by 1991, Pakistan, Bangladesh, and Nepal had all become democracies, and democratic rule returned to Thailand. Thus, by 1987, the third wave had spread to the point where about two of every five states in the world were democracies (see Table 2.1). All of Western Europe, much of Asia, and most of Latin America were democratic. The gaping holes in Eastern Europe began to fill with the fall of the Berlin wall in 1989 and then the collapse of

Table 2.1 The growth of electoral democracy, 1973–2006

Year	Number of democracies	Number of countries	Democracies as a percent of all countries	Annual rate of increase in democracies
1973	40	150	26.7	
1980	54	163	33.1	
1984	60	166	36.1	
1987	65	166	39.2	
1988	67	166	40.4	3.1
1990	76	165	46.1	
1991	91	183	49.7	19.7
1992	99	186	53.2	8.1
1993	108	190	56.8	8.3
1994	114	191	59.7	5.3
1995	117	191	61.3	2.6
1996	118	191	61.8	0.9
1997	117	191	61.3	–0.9
1998	117	191	61.3	0
1999	120	192	62.5	2.6
2000	119	192	62.0	–0.8
2001	120	192	62.5	0.8
2002	120	192	62.5	0
2003	115	192	59.8	–4.2
2004	117	192	60.9	1.7
2005	120	192	62.5	2.6

Sources: Data from Freedom House, *Freedom in the World: The Annual Survey of Political Rights and Civil Liberties,* annual volumes. Figures reflect the counts at the end of each calendar year. Figures for 1973 through 1988 reflect my own scoring and for 1990–2006 are from the Freedom House survey for that year (published in the subsequent year), with the exception of the following reclassifications of countries that Freedom House considered democracies in these years but that I classify as non-democracies: Russia 2000–2003, Nigeria 2003–5, Venezuela 2004–6, and the Central African Republic in 2005–6. Closer inspection of a few smaller countries classified as democracies by Freedom House in recent years might also lead to reclassification.

the Soviet Union in 1991. By 1990, most of the states of Eastern Europe held competitive elections and began to institutionalize democracy.

The collapse of communism, and thus the end of the cold war, brought profound changes to Africa as well. Freed from the prism of the two superpowers' struggle for geopolitical dominance, and reeling from desperate fiscal crises, African countries began to democratize. In February 1990, just a few months after the fall of the Berlin wall, two seminal events launched a new wave of democratic transitions in Africa. In Benin, a coalition of forces in civil society seized governing power from the military Marxist regime that had ruled for nearly two decades and launched a transition to democracy. In South Africa, the apartheid regime seized upon the less threatening international climate to release Nelson Mandela from almost three decades of imprisonment. That initiated a process of political dialogue and normalization that led to the creation of a democratic regime in 1994.

At the time of these two events, there were only three democracies in Africa—Gambia, Botswana, and Mauritius (an island hundreds of miles from the African coast). Earlier in the third wave, Ghana, Nigeria, and Sudan had attempted democracy but failed. Beginning in 1990, however, Africa experienced a rolling tide of democratic change that came to be known as the "second liberation." Under heavy pressure from international donors as well as their own peoples, most African states began to legalize opposition parties and open space in civil society. A continent that had been composed mainly of military and one-party regimes suddenly witnessed a florescence of democratic politics. Many of these openings were largely a façade, marred by continued repression and blatant vote rigging. Nevertheless, by 1997, only four of sub-Saharan Africa's forty-eight states had not held a post-1990 competitive multiparty election at the national level.[8] And the number of democracies had grown to well over a dozen.

As a result of these third-wave developments, about three-fifths of all the world's states are democracies, a level that has remained stable for the past half-decade (see Table 2.1). To appreciate the global reach of democracy's third wave, consider the fact that at the end of 1973 there were forty democracies among the existing 150 states. Of the remaining 109 states, fifty-six subsequently made a transition to democracy; of those, only Pakistan, Sudan, and Russia are not democracies today. Twenty-six states since 1974 have become independent of European, American, or Australian colonial rule. Of these, fourteen became democracies upon independence and have remained so; another seven became democratic after a period of authoritarian rule. In all, *four of every five states that gained independence from Europe, the United States, or Australia since 1974 are democracies today.* Of the nineteen new postcommunist states, born mainly from the old Soviet Union or Yugoslavia, eleven (58 percent) are democracies (see Table 2.2). Overall, of the forty-six new states created since the third wave began, 70 percent are democracies, though the democratic credentials of some of the former Soviet Union states (such as Georgia and Moldova) are suspect.

As a result of the third wave, democracy has become, for the first time in history, the predominant form of government in the world. More important, by the dawn of the twenty-first century democracy had established itself as the only broadly legitimate form of government. Currently, there are no rivals to democratic governance as a model of government. Communism is dead. Military rule everywhere lacks appeal and normative justification.

Table 2.2 Transitions to and from democracy during the third wave (1974 to 2002)

Type of state	Number of states making democratic transitions	Total number of states	Percent of states making democratic transition
All states in April 1974[a]	63	150	42
Nondemocracies in April 1974	63	110	57[b]
New states post-April 1974			
Post-colonial states	14		52 (continuous)
	7	27	26 (later)[c]
	(21)		78 (total)
New post-communist states[d]	11	19	58
Total new states since April 1974	32	46[5]	70
Total states	95[e]	196[f]	48

[a]The total number of states in 1974 includes two states each for Germany, Yemen, and Vietnam, while the Soviet Union and Yugoslavia were then single states. India and Turkey were the only 2 of the 40 democracies at the start of 1974 then suffered breakdowns and then experienced transitions back to democracy.

[a]Percentage of the 110 authoritarian states in April 1974 that experienced a transition to democracy at some point before January of 2007.

[c]Countries that became authoritarian upon independence (or, in the case of Seychelles and Suriname, very soon thereafter) but later made transitions to democracy.

[d]Does not include Russia and Serbia, which are considered the core successor states. Slovakia is counted as new, not the Czech Republic.

[e]Six of the countries that experienced democratic transitions during the third wave subsequently suffered breakdowns and renewed transitions. In all, there were 100 transitions during this period.

[f]Includes the existing 193 plus the halves of Germany, Yemen, and Vietnam that disappeared with reunification.

One-party states have largely disappeared. None of these contemporary competitors can credibly claim the legitimacy to rule indefinitely. Only the vague model of an Islamic state has any moral or ideological appeal as an alternative to democracy— and then only for a small portion of the world's societies. Moreover, there is only one real example of an Islamic state—the increasingly corrupt, discredited, and illegitimate Islamic Republic in Iran, where its own people overwhelmingly desire to see it replaced by a truly democratic form of government.

The Breadth of Democracy's Appeal

Despite the global reach and status of democracy in the current era, some continue to argue that democracy is largely a Western, Judeo-Christian phenomenon with limited appeal outside the boundaries of its cultural origins. Others contend that it is an extravagance that impoverished people cannot afford. This section examines both of these contentions because, if either is true, it could have important implications for the spread of democracy beyond the current reach of the third wave.

ISLAM AND THE CULTURAL LIMITATIONS OF DEMOCRACY'S APPEAL

Data presented earlier shed some light on the breadth of democracy's appeal. But an examination of the regional distribution of democracies reveals a troubling void. Table 2.3 shows that at least a third of the states in every region of the world are democracies except for one area, the Middle East. In Latin America and the Caribbean, thirty of thirty-three states are democracies; and about half of them are now fairly liberal in terms of their levels of freedom, as reflected in the Freedom House index. Two-thirds of the former communist countries are now democracies, as well as half of the Asian states, and even about two-fifths of all African states. Only in the Middle East is democracy virtually absent. In fact, among the sixteen Arab countries, there is not a single democracy, and with the exception of Lebanon, there never has been.

The exception of the Middle East becomes even more striking when we examine trends in Freedom House's freedom index. Again, every region of the world except for the Middle East has seen a rather striking improvement in the level of freedom (a lower score in the Freedom House index means more political and civil freedoms). Most of the regions that had been strongholds of authoritarianism have seen their average freedom score on the seven-point scale improve by at least a point; in Asia it was only half a point. But in the Middle East the average level of freedom *declined* by almost half a point.

Skeptics have a ready answer for the freedom void depicted in Table 2.3: Islam. But a closer examination of the data demonstrates that this is an invalid inference. There are forty-three countries in the world that have a clear Muslim majority. The twenty-seven of these outside the Arab world had in 2002 an average freedom score (5.04), appreciably better than the score for the Arab states (5.81), and this gap has persisted. Almost a quarter of these non-Arab Muslim-majority states (seven of twenty-seven) are democracies. Moreover, as Alfred Stepan shows, when one examines the level of democracy in the non-Arab Muslim world in relation to level of economic development,

Table 2.3 Democracy and freedom by region, 2002

Region	Number of countries	Number of democracies (percent of total)*	Number (percent) of liberal democracies FH score < 2.5	Average freedom score for region 1974	2002
W. Europe and Anglophone states	28	28 (100%)	28 (100%)	1.58	1.04
Latin America and Caribbean	33	30 (91%)	17 (52%)	3.81	2.49
Eastern Europe and former Soviet Union	27	18 (67%)	11 (41%)	6.50	3.39
Asia (E, SE, and S)	25	12 (48%)	4 (16%)	4.84	4.38
Pacific Island	12	11 (91%)	8 (67%)	2.75	2.00
Africa (Sub-Sahara)	48	19 (40%)	5 (10%)	5.51	4.33
Middle East-North Africa	19	2 (11%)	1 (5%)	5.15	5.53
Total	192	120 (63%)	73 (38%)	4.39	3.38
Arab countries	16	0	0	5.59	5.81
Predominantly Muslim countries	43	7**	0	5.29	5.33

* The current number of democracies as classified by Freedom House, with the exception that Russia is classified as a nondemocracy.

** Bangladesh, Mali, Niger, Senegal, Indonesia, Turkey, and Albania.

Source: Adrian Karatnycky, "The 2002 Freedom House Survey," *Journal of Democracy* 14, 1 (January 2003).

one finds an unusual number of "electoral over-achievers." That is, given their level of economic development, these countries are more likely to have some form of democratic government than other nations. Further, Stepan shows, non-Arab Muslim countries have had a commendable experience with political freedom over the last thirty years.[9]

ECONOMIC PROSPERITY AND DEMOCRACY

It has long been argued that an advanced level of economic development is a precondition for the consolidation and persistence of democratic regimes. Forty years ago, in one of the seminal works in the field of democratization, Seymour Martin Lipset argued that the richer the country, the greater the chance it would sustain democracy.[10] In a more recent and methodologically sophisticated study, Adam Przeworski and his colleagues report that there was in fact a striking monotonic relationship between a nation's level of economic development and its probability of sustaining democracy. During the period 1950–1990, democracy in the poorest countries had a 12 percent chance of dying in any particular year, or an average life expectancy of eight years.

The experiences of at least some third-wave democracies raise questions about the continued validity of these findings. Third-wave democracies such as Benin, Mali, Malawi, Mozambique, and Nepal have already outlived their expected life span.[11] Even among the poorest countries, there have been few breakdowns of democracy. More time will be needed to determine whether the findings of Przeworski and colleagues apply to the contemporary era, but there is reason to be optimistic. This optimism derives from the fact that the contemporary world is so different from that of the cold war era, which dominated the period of their study (1950–1990). Consider the experience of Mali, which is an extremely poor, landlocked, and overwhelmingly Muslim country. A majority of Mali adults are illiterate and live in absolute poverty; the life expectancy there is forty-four years. If democracy can emerge and persist in Mali, as it has for a decade, then there is reason to believe that it can develop and prosper in most other very poor countries.

There is some empirical support for this assertion derived from contemporary data sources. If we examine the thirty-six countries that the United Nations Development Program (UNDP) classifies as having "low human development," thirteen were democracies (as classified by Freedom House) at the end of 2006. If we widen our scope to look at the bottom third of states classified by the UNDP, the percentage of democracies rises from 36 to 42 percent (twenty-five of fifty-nine). About a dozen of these have been democracies for a decade or longer. That there should be so many democracies among the world's least developed countries is a development at least as noteworthy as the overall predominance of democracy in the world. This finding is profoundly in defiance of established social science theories. Indeed, in examining data such as these in light of the contemporary global order, some scholars have turned conventional wisdom on its head. They argue that democracy is not an extravagance for the poor, but very nearly a necessity.

Amartya Sen won the Nobel Prize for Economics in 1998, in part, for showing that democracies do not have famines. "People in economic need," he argues, "also need a political voice. Democracy is not a luxury that can await the arrival of general prosperity." Moreover, he observes, "There is very little evidence that poor people, given the choice, prefer to reject democracy."[12] He notes the vigor with which Indians defended their freedom and democracy in the 1977 election, which tossed Indira Gandhi from office after she had suspended political and civil rights. There have been countless other instances—from Burma and Bangladesh to Senegal and South Africa-where poor people have mobilized passionately in support of democracy. The fact that democracy advocates have sometimes been crushed by sheer force while a timid world watched and protested ineffectually does not negate the overwhelming expression of their sentiment.

PUBLIC OPINION

The data on the distribution of democratic regimes in the wake of the third wave have established that democracy now exists in virtually all types of states in the world and in almost every region of the world. It is present in countries evincing every major religious or philosophical tradition: Christian, Jewish, Hindu, Buddhist, Confucian, and Muslim. It is much more common in developed countries but is now increasingly common among underdeveloped countries as well. It is much more common, and liberal, in small states, due largely to the legacy of British rule in the Caribbean and American rule in the Pacific. But most of the most populous countries in the world are also democracies (seven of eleven countries with populations over 100 million).[13] By virtually any category that is meaningful in the world today, there is only one set of countries that is completely undemocratic: the Arab world.

There is a possible retort to the inference from these data that democracy has a broad appeal, one that spans all cultures, societies, and regions of the world. The retort is that democratization is a fad or a contemporary concession to international pressure or diffusion. Underlying this contention is the notion that democracy and freedom are not truly valued by large portions of the world's inhabitants. Thus, because democracy and its ideals are not truly valued, the accomplishments of the third wave will have little staying power. Fortunately, we now have public opinion survey data from a wide array of nations to examine the validity of this assertion. These data indicate that democracy is widely valued across cultures.

The Afrobarometer, a research project based at Michigan State University and the Ghana Center for Democratic Development, has examined how Africans view democracy. Two-thirds of Africans surveyed in twelve (mainly poor) African countries around 2001 (in the first round of the Barometer) associated democracy with civil liberties, popular sovereignty, or electoral choice. About two-thirds of Africans surveyed (69 percent) also said democracy is "always preferable" to authoritarian rule. The same proportion rejected one-party rule, and four in five rejected military or one-person rule. Most Africans who live in democracies recognized there are serious institutional problems that must be addressed, but even those who are not satisfied with democracy believed for the most part that it is the best form of government.[14] Latin Americans—who have had more time than Africans to become disillusioned with how democracy actually performs—are more ambivalent. But overall, between 53 and 58 percent each year say that democracy is always preferable, while only about 15 to 17 percent "might" prefer an authoritarian regime. Public opinion in East Asia is also strongly supportive of democratic governance. Only a quarter surveyed during 2001–02 in Taiwan and Korea, about a fifth in Hong Kong and the Philippines, and less than a tenth in Thailand believe that democracy is not really suitable for their country. In all five of these systems, consistently strong majorities (usually upwards of two-thirds) reject authoritarian alternatives to democracy.[15] So do strong majorities (about seven in ten, overall) in the ten postcommunist countries that have recently entered the European Union.[16]

Although much has been made of the "clash of civilizations," especially since September 11, 2001, the Afrobarometer survey evidence indicates that Muslims are as supportive of democracy as non-Muslims. In four African countries with substantial Muslim populations (Mali, Nigeria, Tanzania, and Uganda), the Afrobarometer has found that large majorities of Muslims as well as non-Muslims support democracy. Moreover, any hesitancy in supporting democracy among African Muslims "is due more to deficits of formal education and other attributes of modernization than to religious attachments."[17] Data from central Asia and the Middle East point in a similar direction.[18] The Middle Eastern data are somewhat dated (from the 1990s) and severely limited by what could be asked. But they indicate that in two of the four countries studied (Egypt and Palestine), a majority attached at least some importance to the value of democracy. Weighing the evidence, Mark Tessler concludes, "Islam appears to have less influence on political attitudes than is frequently suggested." Indeed, he notes that "support for democracy is not necessarily lower among those individuals with the strongest Islamic attachments."[19] In Kazakhstan and Kyrgyzstan, Richard Rose finds that there is little difference among religious groups in support for democracy: "The most observant Muslims are almost as democratic as those who are nonobservant." Also, in each country, majorities of all religious groups—Muslim and Orthodox, observant and non-observant, as well as those with no religion—believe "democracy is better than any other form of government."[20]

These popular orientations among Muslims correspond with the thinking of increasingly outspoken moderate Muslim intellectuals. These intellectuals are making the case for a more liberal interpretation of Islam. They would de-emphasize the literal meaning of sacred Islamic texts while stressing the compatibility between the moral teachings of Islam and democratic principles such as accountability, freedom of expression, and the rule of law.[21] Islam is undergoing a kind of reformation now, and there is growing momentum among Muslim religious thinkers for a separation of mosque and state. Perhaps as a result of these intellectual developments some Arab elites have begun to challenge the democracy and freedom deficit that currently pervades the Arab world.

The Arab authors of the *Arab Human Development Report*—an extraordinary document published by the UNDP in 2002—recognize that the global wave of democratization "has barely reached the Arab states. This freedom deficit undermines human development and is one of the most painful manifestations of lagging political development."[22] These authors noted: "There can be no real prospects for reforming the system of governance, or for truly liberating human capabilities, in the absence of comprehensive political representation in effective legislatures based on free, honest, efficient and regular elections. If the people's preferences are to be properly expressed and their interests properly protected, governance must become truly representative and fully accountable."[23]

Amartya Sen argues that the mark of a universal value is not that it has the consent of everyone, but that "people anywhere may have reason to see it as valuable."[24] By this standard, there is growing evidence that democracy is becoming a model of government with truly universal appeal.

Contemporary Drivers of Democratization: The Third Wave and Beyond

To assess democracy's prospects for future expansion it is important to understand the forces that have fostered democracy in the third wave. The first subsection outlines the factors commonly believed to drive democratization in the last quarter of the twentieth century. I then extend this discussion to two matters that bear on the immediate future: What explains the remarkable persistence of third-wave democracies? Why have some states so tenaciously resisted democratization? This discussion will shed valuable light on the prospects for democracy in the twenty-first century.

UNDERSTANDING THE THIRD WAVE

ECONOMIC DEVELOPMENT IN THE THIRD WAVE Huntington argues that economic development was one of the most important factors driving democratization. In sharp contrast, Przeworski and his colleagues find no evidence that transitions to democracy are more likely to occur at higher levels of economic development. Their view is that democracies in economically more developed societies simply persist longer. But their findings are distorted by the inclusion of the oil-rich countries such as those in the Persian Gulf. The inclusion of the

Persian Gulf states is important because the real effects of economic development are indirect. Increases in national wealth facilitate democratization only to the extent that they generate such developments as higher levels of education, the creation of a diverse and independent middle class that transforms state-society relations, and the emergence of a pluralistic, active, and resourceful civil society. As Eckstein notes, these changes jointly generate a culture and social structure that is more broadly congruent with democracy.[25]

These broad societal transformations have accompanied economic development in a number of countries in recent decades. South Korea and Taiwan stand as the classic examples of economic growth bringing about diffuse social, economic, and cultural change that then generates diffuse societal pressure for democracy. At a somewhat lower level of economic development, this has also been the story of Thailand, Brazil, Mexico, and South Africa. However, where states have managed successfully to control and co-opt civil society, and to manipulate cultural symbols and belief systems in a way that at least partially legitimizes semi-authoritarian rule, the internal pressure for democratization has been preempted or deflected. This has been the case with Malaysia and especially Singapore, the richest authoritarian state in the history of the world. Another exception to the indirect effects of economic development can be seen in the oil-rich states, where its liberalizing forces are thwarted by the state's centralized control of the oil sector. As Huntington asserts, "Oil revenues [and other forms of mineral wealth] accrue to the state: they therefore increase the power of the state bureaucracy and, because they reduce or eliminate the need for taxation, they also reduce the need for the government to solicit the acquiescence of its subjects to taxation. The lower the level of taxation, the less reason for publics to demand representation."[26] Thus, with the exception of nations such as Malaysia and Singapore, as well as the oil-rich oligarchies, economic development has had important indirect effects during democracy's third wave. These effects are manifested in the liberalization of society and the generation of powerful pressures for democratization.

GOVERNMENTAL PERFORMANCE The second factor that has driven democratic change during the third wave is the record of authoritarian regimes. Many conventional authoritarian regimes justify their rule on the basis of performance imperatives—in stark contrast to those that appeal to higher ideological or theological principles. Essentially, they claim that their rule is necessary to clean up corruption, fight subversion, unify the country, and/or generate economic growth.

This claim to legitimacy puts these authoritarian regimes in a dilemma. Unlike democracy, which can be legitimized on ideological grounds, conventional dictatorships have only performance imperatives by which to justify their rule. If they fail to perform, these rulers forfeit their moral entitlement to rule. However, if authoritarian rulers succeed in overcoming the performance crises that brought them to power, then many citizens will eventually feel the rulers have served their purpose—and outlived their usefulness, as authoritarian performance often comes at a great cost to other values. Thus, if authoritarian rulers deliver rapid economic development, as in Taiwan and South Korea, they are likely to become victims of their own success. Even if authoritarian rulers deliver rapid development that then implodes, citizens may set aside the government's earlier accomplishments and punish the regime for its immediate failure. A recent example of this is the collapse of the Indonesian government in 1997, which was precipitated by the East Asian financial crisis. Thus, performance-based legitimacy is a delicate and perilous strategy for sustaining authoritarian rule. This tenuousness contributed to third-wave transitions to democracy.[27]

THE REORIENTATION OF THE ROMAN CATHOLIC CHURCH Another factor in facilitating third-wave democracies, according to Huntington, was the reorientation in the doctrine, political alignment, and leadership of the Roman Catholic Church. It was a particularly important factor within Latin America and the Philippines. The Church, which historically had been closely associated with and even supportive of ruling establishments, swung into active opposition against authoritarian rule, social oppression, and injustice. Particularly with the accession of John Paul II to the papacy in 1979, the Vatican became a moral and institutional advocate of social justice, human rights, and, by implication, democracy. As a result, today most of the predominantly Catholic countries in the world are democracies.

INTERNATIONAL ACTIONS AND PRESSURES Another influential factor in third-wave transitions was change in the policies, actions, and expectations of the established democracies, particularly the United States and a variety of international organizations. U.S. presidential administrations, beginning with Carter and continuing through Reagan, became active in pressing for democratic change. New U.S. institutions, such as the National Endowment for Democracy, were created to foster democratic movements, civic organizations, interest groups, parties, and institutions. By the late 1990s, the United States was spending over half a billion dollars annually to foster and support democratic development abroad. Direct and indirect diplomatic pressure toward democratic change was exerted on the Latin American military dictatorships, the Marcos dictatorship in the Philippines, the South Korean military, the KMT regime in Taiwan, and the apartheid regime in South Africa. With the end of the cold war, these pressures widened and increased.

The effects of the United States re-emphasis on democratic values and principles were particularly noteworthy in Africa. A number of African states that had been pawns on a superpower chessboard were suddenly viewed on their own terms. American pressure for democratic reform dramatically increased, and many African governments that had been lavishly financed and repeatedly bailed out from their misrule suddenly found themselves in acute fiscal crisis. Out of cash and global political support, most of these African dictatorships felt compelled to legalize political opposition and hold competitive elections. In a number of instances, the old rulers lost and a new democracy ensued.

The United States was not alone in pressing for democracy during the third wave. The European Union also became increasingly active and outspoken advocates for democracy. Its efforts were particularly visible in its financial and organizational efforts to promote political change in post communist Europe. The driving wedge of Western Europe's democratizing impact, first on the south and then on the east of Europe, was a simple and unyielding condition that all states seeking to join their union had to manifest "truly democratic practices and respect for fundamental rights and freedoms." This conditionality provided an important boost for democratic reforms in the Iberian Peninsula and Greece.[28]

Much European Union technical and political assistance over the past seventeen years has gone into helping the candidate states meet its political and economic conditions for entry.[29] The European Union's efforts have been effectual because they have affected the incentive structures of national leaders in transitional states, which is of profound importance in developing and sustaining democracy. In the case of nations such as Spain, Portugal, and Greece in the late 1970s and 1980s, a regression away from democracy became unthinkable—largely because of the economic and political costs that isolation from the community of European states would impose. The same is now true of central and eastern Europe as well as Turkey. Few political leaders can ignore such costs in strategizing about the future, and this has contributed to the consolidation of fledgling democracies.

More recently, regional pressure for democracy has begun to take hold in the Americas. In June 1991 the Organization of American States (OAS) adopted the "Santiago Commitment to Democracy," which required immediate consultation if a democracy was overthrown. While Latin American efforts to support democratic regimes began slowly in Haiti and Peru, they have begun to be more effective, as seen in its interventions in Guatemala and

Paraguay.[30] Moreover, the OAS, along with other international actors such as the United Nations, has begun to monitor transitional or controversial elections in a number of its emerging or transitional democratic states. In fact, international election observation, concluding with explicit judgments about the freeness and fairness of elections, has become one of the most common means of international intervention. These international actors intrude without apology, and typically by invitation, into the internal politics of sovereign countries. These intrusions are reshaping the very idea of Westphalian sovereignty, thereby negating the longstanding presumption that states are free to do what they like within their own borders.

CHANGING INTERNATIONAL NORMS AND EXPECTATIONS One final factor that has driven political changes during the third wave is the normative value attached to human rights in international discourse, treaties, law, and collective actions. The old conception of sovereignty is creaking under the weight of international scrutiny of domestic governance. The world community is increasingly embracing a shared normative expectation that all states seeking international legitimacy should manifestly "govern with the consent of the governed." Thus, a "right to democratic governance" is increasingly seen as a legal entitlement.[31] The Universal Declaration of Human Rights and the International Covenant on Civil and Political Rights already effectively imply such a right. Moreover, a "right to democratic governance" has been articulated more and more explicitly in the documents of regional organizations like the Council of Europe, the Organization for Security and Cooperation in Europe (OSCE), and the OAS. In addition, the growing number of interventions by those organizations and by the UN has affirmed these democratic expectations and rights.

Also, during the 1990s, the UN Human Rights Committee (composed of experts) and then the Human Rights Commission (composed of member states) expanded interpretations of existing human rights conventions to incorporate democracy in various ways. In 2000, the commission acknowledged as a human right the right to vote "in a free and fair process open to multiple parties."[32] In June 2000, 106 states gathered in the conference "Toward a Community of Democracies" agreed to "respect and uphold" a detailed list of "core democratic principles and practices"—including individual liberties, the rule of law, and freedom of association and political party organization. Despite the fact that some of these states were not democracies, they provided perhaps the most explicit international endorsement of democracy ever made: "The will of the people shall be the basis of the authority of government, as expressed by the exercise of the right and civic duties of citizens to choose their representatives through regular, free and fair elections with universal and equal suffrage, open to multiple parties, conducted by secret ballot, and monitored by independent electoral authorities, and free of fraud and intimidation."[33]

For some observers, these various trends suggest the world is moving toward establishing a global guarantee of constitutional democracy to every nation. Such a guarantee would be similar to the clause in the U.S. Constitution that requires the federal government to "guarantee to every State . . . a Republican Form of Government" (art. 4, sec. 4).[34] A meaningful universal guarantee of democracy is doubtless years away. But significant erosion of the principle of nonintervention in the internal affairs of a country is already discernible. This erosion has both lowered the political threshold for international intervention and emboldened domestic advocates of democracy and human rights. Thus, the emergence and strengthening of an international consensus over the value of democracy has been a powerful force in driving and sustaining the third wave of democratization.

THE PERSISTENCE OF THIRD-WAVE DEMOCRACIES

Perhaps the most remarkable aspect of democracy's third wave is the durability of incipient democratic regimes, including those lacking virtually all of the supposed "conditions" for democracy. If we set aside the three military coups that occurred in Africa before the third wave actually reached the continent in 1990, then only four democracies have been overthrown by the military. Two of those (Turkey and Thailand) returned fairly quickly to democracy, and the other two (Pakistan and the Gambia) have felt compelled at least to institute civilian multiparty elections—though Thailand's democracy was again overthrown by the military in 2006. Several democracies have been suspended in *autogolpes* ("self-coups") by elected civilian leaders (from India's Indira Gandhi in 1975 to Peru's Alberto Fujimori in 1992), while other elected rulers strangled democracy more subtly.[35] The unusual nature of these reversions can be seen by the fact that from the beginning of the third wave in 1974 through the end of 2006, only nineteen of the 141 democracies that have existed have reverted to authoritarianism. In eight cases of breakdown democracy has been restored.[36]

Disturbingly, however, democracy has broken down in recent years in big and strategically important countries, such as Pakistan, Thailand, Russia, Venezuela, and Nigeria, though in the last three this has come through the more subtle means of executive strangulation or electoral fraud.

The remarkable durability of democracies in the contemporary era can best be understood in reference to the earlier discussion of forces driving the third wave. Three factors are particularly important here. First, some countries became democracies after they had become relatively rich. Przeworski and his colleagues found that between 1950 and 1990, no country with a per capita income higher than $8,773 (in 2000 purchasing power parity dollars) had ever suffered a breakdown of democracy.[37] Taiwan and Korea became democracies at levels of economic development richer than this and are now much richer than this. Several postcommunist democracies in Europe are also beyond this development level already; and their durability is further enhanced by the EU's unyielding democratic conditionality. In Latin America, Mexico and Uruguay approach this development level; Argentina and Chile have already moved beyond it. South Africa is the only African democracy that has surpassed this minimum level of development.

The second factor accounting for the remarkable durability of democracies in the contemporary era is rooted in the unique status of democracy vis à vis its competitors. In many newly democratized regimes, citizens are broadly dissatisfied with the performance of the political system and distrustful of its political institutions and actors. Yet they do not see an alternative to democracy. No finding in the new wave of public opinion research on democracy is more noteworthy than this. Even in Brazil, where active support for democracy stood at only 37 percent in 2002, people do not prefer authoritarian rule. Indeed, only 15 percent of Brazilians could imagine wanting it.[38] The alternative, rather, is apathy and withdrawal. While this is bad for democracy, it is not as bad as people actively clamoring for an authoritarian alternative.

Belief in the legitimacy of a political system is always a relative judgment, as Winston Churchill noted in his famous 1947 remarks in the House of Commons. But in the past several decades, almost every form of nondemocratic government imaginable has been tried: absolute monarchy, personal dictatorship, military rule, colonial rule, fascism, communism, Ba'athism, the socialist one-party state, other forms of one-party rule, the Islamic Republic, pseudo-democracy, semi-democracy, and numerous other permutations of these models. Despite this, people have opted for democracy—at an accelerating rate. "As democracy has spread, its adherents have grown, not shrunk," Amartya Sen observes.[39] Thus, the evidence is mounting that—whatever their naïve assumptions at the beginning—people are sticking with democracy without illusions. They remember in their lifetime one or more of these other forms of rule and they do not want to go back.[40] This, of course, has contributed to democracy's durability.

The third factor accounting for the resiliency of democratic regimes in the contemporary era is related to the second; it stems from the remarkable changes in the international climate noted earlier. Most of all in Europe, but to some considerable extent in Latin America as well, political and military leaders know that they will pay a high price in terms of economic and political standing within their regions if they reverse democracy. On specific occasions, some such leaders who have been tempted to reverse democracy—in Guatemala, in Paraguay, perhaps in Venezuela, and probably in Turkey—have been deterred from doing so by explicit interventions from neighboring countries or the United States.

THE HOLDOUT STATES

The seventy or so states that have resisted democratization during the third wave fall into several different categories. Various factors account for the resistance to democratic reform in each category. One of the smallest groups of holdout states includes those where continued authoritarianism can be explained by the regime's success. This category includes Singapore and Malaysia, and perhaps China, given its recent rapid economic growth. The tenuousness of performance-based authoritarian regimes has already been noted, and it would be remarkable if these nations were able to resist the global trends and international pressures for democracy indefinitely. An equally small group of holdout states includes those authoritarian nations that have persisted using the insular, repressive logic of communist control: Vietnam, Laos, North Korea, and Cuba. This category of holdout states have been able to resist democratization for decades, but their persistence is at least as tenuous as that of performance-based authoritarian regimes. As globalization—in the form of foreign trade, investment, study, and travel—penetrates these states, the force of the regime's insular, repressive logic will weaken. At some unpredictable point in the future a regime crisis is likely to ignite a transition to democracy in these countries.[41]

Another category of holdout states includes the oil-rich Arab states in the Middle East. These states, which have staggering revenues and relatively small populations, have been able to maintain authoritarian rule because they have had the wealth to buy off their peoples while lavishly financing structures of internal security and control. As a result, the formal political arena has been closed off to all but a relatively small circle of establishment parties and interest groups. An Arab underground exists, but it consists largely of Islamist parties and groups, many of them with an antidemocratic—even neo-totalitarian—orientation. More moderate and prodemocratic groups, both Islamist and secular, have been squeezed between the iron fist of the state and the subterranean pressure of radical Islam, effectively neutralizing them.

The success of authoritarian Arab regimes in resisting democratic reforms has been bolstered by another factor that is unique to the Middle East. Authoritarian rulers in this region have been able to evade responsibility for the deficiencies of their regimes by deflecting attention away from their stewardship and toward issues centered on the existence of Israel, the Israeli-Palestinian conflict, and, more recently, the conflict in Iraq. These issues have proved to be particularly useful to Arab leaders as the older forms of nationalism and pan-Arab nationalism have lost their appeal. These authoritarian leaders have used Israel-centric issues relentlessly in legitimatizing their regimes, and their efforts to cloak themselves in the symbolically powerful struggle over Arab identity and dignity have resonated well with their domestic audiences. These diversionary tactics have been particularly successful in channeling much of the energy of Arab intellectuals and political activists into the Israeli-Palestinian conflict and away from national political failings. Consequently, over the past several decades, these tactics have generated a heavy fog over Arab politics, diminishing political visibility, transparency, and accountability.

Despite these impediments to democracy, popular ferment has been brewing in such Arab nations as Kuwait, Qatar, Bahrain, and Lebanon, where a variety of groups have been pressing for more freedom and self-determination. But until the fog that has settled over Middle East politics is lifted, the prospects for widespread and meaningful democracy are dim. Only when this fog is lifted will the peoples of the Arab world be able to see and debate adequately the real nature of the obstacles to national progress. Only then will authoritarians and radical Islamists be deprived of their most emotive instruments for mobilizing political support. Even with the lifting of this fog, however, the more moderate elements of Arab society will need time to surface, organize, advocate, and campaign. Moreover, an institutional infrastructure necessary to the functioning of liberal democracy will have to be created.

The final category of holdout nations is, by far, the most common. It includes those states in which the resistance to third-wave democratic reforms is rooted in the existence of unchallenged power in the hands of government leaders, their desire to retain unchallenged power, and their ability to realize their desires. The unchallenged power of these autocrats has often enabled them to accumulate substantial personal wealth, which has enhanced their desire to retain unchallenged power and strengthened their resolve to resist reforms that would diminish their power. These observations are noteworthy because they suggest that the persistence of authoritarianism in the largest category of holdout nations has little to do with the circumstances or the beliefs and attitudes of their citizens. Rather, these observations support an argument that the most important impediments to the spread of democracy lie with the ruling elites who have commandeered the structures of state power and barricaded themselves inside.

This argument does not rest on the notion that the majority of people consciously desire a fully democratic system, or that they even understand what real democracy entails. It does, however, rest on the assertion that most people value freedom and desire a secure, prosperous, and predictable life. The realization of these fundamental political desires is inconsistent with the logic of authoritarian rule in most of these countries. That particular brand of authoritarian logic fosters the generation of private goods that buy the loyalty of the army, the secret police, and the cronies and ruling party hacks that sustain the regime.[42] The generation of public goods that can produce economic growth and improve human well-being ranks low among the priorities of most authoritarian regimes. Given this, most people would like to be able to constrain the arbitrary power of government and to replace poor and/or corrupt leaders. Some form of democratic rule is often the best and most efficient way for ordinary citizens to realize their most basic political preferences.

The hopeful message of this argument is that international actors, norms, and values can play an important and meaningful role in fostering democratic reforms. Most predatory authoritarian regimes are not adept at generating resources organically from their own societies. They inhibit domestic investment, innovation, entrepreneurship, and economic growth by violating property rights and other individual freedoms. They discourage foreign investment—except in the enclave economy of oil or other natural resource extraction—for the same reason. If they do not have natural resources, they become heavily in need of foreign loans and aid. This makes them vulnerable to international pressures.

Thus, international factors can play an important role in facilitating democratization in the future; perhaps their greatest effect lies in their potential contributions to the development of a democratic culture. They can help citizens understand democracy's rules, possibilities, obligations, and limits, as well as its norms of tolerance, civility, participation, and mutual respect. Some of this cultural change happens with economic development, increasing education, and exposure to the global environment. But much of it can and should happen through deliberate programs of civic education and civil society construction. Efforts of external democracy promotion programs efforts have made some progress toward these goals, but much more remains to be done.

Negotiating the Future: International Actors and Democratization

In thinking about the continued diffusion of democracy in the twenty-first century, it is useful to keep in mind one important lesson derived from third-wave democratic transitions. In the case of nations with little previous experience with popular rule, democratic reform follows no single path. There is no one formula for achieving democracy, or for structuring it so that it will work reasonably well. Different countries need different sequences, strategies, and structures for democratic change. In some cases, the transition to democracy could and should proceed fairly rapidly, as governance is poor, and viable democratic forces and groups already exist. In other cases the transition to democracy may need to proceed more slowly and incrementally. This is particularly true in many of the Arab states, where many groups have long been repressed. In these states an interim period of political liberalization may be needed to create and strengthen independent structures of horizontal accountability. The development of republican institutions that can ensure meaningful electoral competition and constrain electoral victors is vital to the attainment of truly liberal democracies in the Middle East.

With these observations and caveats in mind, the long-run future for democratization looks promising, despite recent setbacks in important countries such as Russia, Venezuela, Nigeria, and Thailand. This optimism stems from both democracy's demonstrated record and the fact that there are concrete actions that international actors can take to foster the spread and health of democracy in the twenty-first century. Three are particularly important, and they stem from the earlier discussion of holdout states. I address these three initiatives below, giving most attention to the reform of foreign aid policies.

The first initiative deals specifically with the Arab world. It is simply essential that the international community pursue—vigorously and relentlessly—a settlement of the Israeli-Palestinian conflict on the basis of the only broadly viable solution. The general contours of this solution involve the permanent coexistence and mutual recognition of two separate states. One is an Israel that relinquishes most of its settlements in the West Bank and Gaza; the other is a largely demilitarized Palestinian state. Only the settlement of this conflict can create a political climate in which Arab dictatorships have no more political cover for their deficiencies and Arab societies can focus on the real sources of their misery and frustration. In the same vein, it would help a great deal if Iraq could at least be stabilized, though it seems increasingly likely that the violence there will worsen, providing yet another excuse for Arab autocrats to defer real political reform.

The second initiative is a concerted international effort to open up the closed societies of the world, countries like Cuba, Vietnam, Burma, and North Korea. This initiative should be achieved by promoting trade, travel, and exchanges of all kinds rather than by inundating these countries with foreign aid. People in countries like North Korea are among the most physically and intellectually isolated, as well as the most brutalized, of any in the world today. Citizens in these insular countries are wholly unaware of how the rest of the world lives, and it is unlikely that their regimes would be able to endure once they find out.

The third initiative involves a reconceptualization of policies on foreign aid and debt relief. To maximize the realization of a democratic future for the world it is particularly important that U.S. policies on aid and debt relief be redesigned to reward political freedom and accountability.[43] Moreover, these policies should be coordinated with those of other nations and multilateral donors. Only through radically new unilateral and multilateral strategies on foreign aid and debt relief can the international community lock into place the institutions and practices of democracy and good governance. The end of the cold war gave rise to the hope that these aid policies could be reinvented. But inertia, the perverse incentives and logic of international aid organizations, humanitarian concerns about the fate of citizens in weak, oppressive states, and conflicting priorities of donor states have all impeded reform. Moreover, with the onset of the war on terrorism, the problem of compromising principles in order to nurture authoritarian clients has been reborn with a vengeance.

The Bush administration took an important step toward the reorientation of aid policies in 2002 when it announced the creation of a Millennium Challenge Account. This program promised to generate a $5 billion dollar increment in development assistance (about a 50 percent increase over the 2002 U.S. foreign aid budget) to a select number of low- and lower-middle-income countries, who were to compete for this aid on the basis of three criteria: ruling justly (i.e., democratically and accountably), investing in people, and promoting economic freedom. This was an important departure-indeed, a conceptual revolution—in U.S. foreign aid policy. But it has never been fully funded, the aid has been too slow to be disbursed, and conceptually, the innovation does not go nearly far enough. The United States also needs to re-examine how it allocates the remainder of its foreign aid budget, much of which goes to countries ruled by corrupt, authoritarian regimes. Too much of that aid is wasted and there is too little effort invested in leveraging it to achieve meaningful political change. Where the suspension of aid to corrupt states is unthinkable on humanitarian grounds, delivering it through civil society should be considered.

As important as a reorientation of U.S. aid policy is to the fostering of democratic reform, the United States cannot be content to act alone. Its aid and debt-relief policies must be coordinated with those of other major donors: the World Bank, the regional development banks, the Japanese, and many of the European aid agencies. Moreover, in the case of debt relief for highly indebted poor countries, future relief should be granted only to countries that have demonstrated a basic commitment to good governance by allowing a free press and civil society, an independent judiciary, and serious countercorruption efforts. Even in these cases, the debt should not be relieved in one fell swoop but should be suspended and retired incrementally, generating ongoing incentives for adhering to good governance.

Democratic change is possible in the remaining corrupt dictatorships of the world, but it will require a radical manipulation of the incentives their leaders confront. They must know that they can no longer play one powerful donor against another. If the United States and other major donors were to move together toward such a comprehensive strategy that made democracy and good governance as the basis for development aid and debt relief, it would generate very powerful new pressures for democratic reform. Not all nondemocratic states would be immediately affected, because not all of them depend on these flows of assistance. But the overall global climate would shift emphatically in favor of democratic change, generating potent demonstration effects even on more insulated regimes.

Notes

This chapter draws from my book *The Spirit of Democracy: The Struggle to Build Free Societies Throughout the World* (New York: Times Books, 2007).

1. Larry Diamond, *Developing Democracy: Toward Consolidation* (Baltimore: Johns Hopkins University Press, 1999): 10–12.

2. For a fuller consideration of these dimensions of electoral democracy, see Larry Diamond, "Elections without Democracy: Thinking about Hybrid Regimes," *Journal of Democracy* 13 (April 2002): 28–29.

3. To be sure, these requirements do not always easily permit an "either/or" judgment. India is clearly a democracy, but in some of its localities and states, violence and fraud mar the electoral process. Even in our supposedly "model" democracy in the United States, we could not choose a president in 2000 without bitter dispute

about who really won. In the world today, more than a dozen regimes are "ambiguous;" many people consider them democracies, but it is far from clear that elections are sufficiently free and fair, or that those elected to government office have the real power to rule in the country. For details, see Larry Diamond, The Spirit of Democracy: The Struggle to Build Free Societies throughout the World (New York: Times Books, 2007).

4. Guillermo O'Donnell, "Horizontal Accountability in New Democracies," in Andreas Schedler, Larry Diamond, and Marc F. Plattner, eds., *The Self-Restraining State: Power and Accountability in New Democracies* (Boulder, Colo.: Rienner, 1999): 29–51.

5. Fareed Zakaria, *The Future of Freedom: Illiberal Democracy at Home and Abroad* (New York: Norton, 2003).

6. However, once these abuses descend to the level of Chavez's contemporary regime in Venezuela, for example, it is legitimate to question whether we can call them democracies any longer. In these regimes it is questionable whether leadership positions can still be filled through truly free and fair electoral contestation.

7. Huntington defines a "wave of democratization" as "a group of transitions from nondemocratic to democratic regimes that occur within a specified period of time and that significantly outnumber transitions in the opposite direction during that period." He adds that in such waves, some other authoritarian regimes that do not democratize nevertheless become liberalized—more open and competitive, and less repressive. Samuel P. Huntington, *The Third Wave: Democratization in the Late Twentieth Century* (Norman, Okla.: University of Oklahoma Press, 1991), 15.

8. Michael Bratton, "Second Elections in Africa," in Larry Diamond and Marc F. Plattner, *Democratization in Africa* (Baltimore: Johns Hopkins University Press, 1999), 18–33.

9. Alfred Stepan and Graeme B. Robertson, "An 'Arab' More than a 'Muslim' Democracy Gap," *Journal of Democracy* 14 (July 2003): 30–44.

10. Seymour Martin Lipset, *Political Man* (Baltimore: Johns Hopkins University Press, 1981). The first edition of this book was published in 1960, and in fact Lipset's article on this theme, "Some Social Requisites of Democracy," was published in the *American Political Science Review* in 1959.

11. Their poorest category was under $1,000 in 1985 purchasing power parity dollars, which is equivalent to $1,449 in year 2000 dollars. See Adam Przeworski, Michael E. Alvarez, Jose Antonio Cheibub, and Fernando Limongi, *Democracy and Development: Political Institutions and Well-Being in the World, 1950–1990* (Cambridge: Cambridge University Press, 2000): 92–103.

12. Amartya Sen, "Democracy as a Universal Value," in Larry Diamond and Marc F. Plattner, eds., *The Global Divergence of Democracies* (Baltimore: Johns Hopkins University Press, 2001): 13.

13. The democracies in this set are Bangladesh, Brazil, India, Indonesia, Japan,

Mexico, Nigeria, and the United States. The nondemocracies are China, Pakistan, and Russia—and many observers judge Russia to be a democracy (of sorts).

14. "Key Findings about Public Opinion in Africa," Afrobarometer Briefing Paper No. 1 (April 2002), http://www.afrobarometer.org/papers/AfrobriefNo1.pdf. See also Michael Bratton and Robert Mattes, "How People View Democracy: Africans' Surprising Universalism," *Journal of Democracy* 12, no. 1 (January 2001): 107–21.

15. Data from the East Asia Barometer, collected in 2001. More abstract support for democracy—as indicated by agreement with the standard item "Democracy is always preferable to any other kind of government"—is weaker, however: 40 percent in Taiwan and also in Hong Kong, 47 percent in Korea, 64 percent in the Philippines, and 84 percent in Thailand (which evinces the strongest support for democracy on many measures).

16. "A Bottom-Up Evaluation of Enlargement Countries," *New Europe Barometer 1,* Studies in Public Policy 364, Centre for the Study of Public Policy, University of Strathclyde, 2002. The proportion rejecting the suspension of parties and parliament in favor of a strong leader ranges from 87 percent in the Czech Republic to 60 percent in Lithuania and Estonia. Overall, 71 percent reject a dictator, 94 percent reject army rule, and 82 percent reject a return to communist rule. In Russia, the percentage favoring a return to communism is much higher, 47 percent.

17. "Islam, Democracy, and Public Opinion in Africa," Afrobarometer Briefing Paper No. 3, September 2002, http://www.afrobarometer.org/papers/AfrobriefNo3.pdf.

18. Richard Rose, "How Muslims View Democracy: Evidence from Central Asia," *Journal of Democracy* 13 (October 2002): 102–11; Mark Tessler, "Islam and Democracy in the Middle East: The Impact of Religious Orientations on Attitudes toward Democracy in Four Arab Countries," *Comparative Politics* 34 (April 2002): 337–54.

19. Tessler, "Islam and Democracy," 348.

20. Rose, "How Muslims View Democracy," 107.

21. See the essays on Islam and democracy in Larry Diamond, Marc F. Plattner, and Daniel Brumberg, eds., *Islam and Democracy in the Middle East* (Baltimore: Johns Hopkins University Press, 2003).

22. *Arab Human Development Report* (New York: United Nations Development Program, 2002): 2.

23. Ibid, 114.

24. Sen, "Democracy as a Universal Value," 12.

25. Larry Diamond, "Economic Development and Democracy Reconsidered," in Gary Marks and Larry Diamond, eds., *Reexamining Democracy: Essays in Honor of Seymour Martin Lipset* (Newbury Park, Calif.: Sage, 1992): 93–139.

26. Huntington, *The Third Wave,* 65.

27. If it is mainly its own survival that a dictatorship cares about, its best strategy would seem to be to seal off the country, limit international influences, and divert the country's wealth to a narrow segment of military and ruling party loyalists who

ruthlessly uphold the regime. In other words, they should mimic nations such as North Korea, Burma, Iraq, and Cuba. This strategy runs the risk that the regime will simply run out of resources, bringing about overthrow or, as in the case of Zaire, Liberia, and many other African countries, state decay and collapse into violent conflict. But if they have oil, or even some more limited sources of export earnings (whether it is tropical timber, sugar, or weapons of mass destruction), such regimes may survive for quite some time.

28. Laurence Whitehead, "International Aspects of Democratization," in Guillermo O'Donnell, Philippe C. Schmitter, and Laurence Whitehead, eds., *Transitions from Authoritarian Rule: Comparative Perspectives* (Baltimore: Johns Hopkins University Press, 1986): 21–23; see also Huntington, *The Third Wave,* 87–89.

29. For an early summary of these and other international democratic assistance efforts, see Larry Diamond, *Promoting Democracy in the 1990s: Issues and Actors, Instruments and Imperatives,* A Report to the Carnegie Commission on Preventing Deadly Conflict (New York: Carnegie Corporation, December 1995), available at http://wwics.si.edu/subsites/ccpdc/pubs/di/fr.htm.

30. Arturo Valenzuela, "Paraguay: The Coup that Didn't Happen," *Journal of Democracy* 8 (January 1997): 43–55.

31. Thomas Franck, "The Emerging Right to Democratic Governance," *American Journal of International Law* 86, no. 46 (1992): 50.

32. Roland Rich, "Bringing Democracy into International Law," *Journal of Democracy* 12 (July 2001): 20–34.

33. For this and other excerpts of the "Warsaw Declaration," and a list of signatory countries, see *Journal of Democracy* 11 (October 2000): 184–87.

34. See Morton H. Halperin and Kristen Lomasney, "Toward a Global 'Guarantee Clause,'" *Journal of Democracy* 4, no. 3 (July 1993): 60–69; and Morton H. Halperin, "Guaranteeing Democracy," *Foreign Policy* (Summer 1993): 105–22.

35. These more subtle strangulations include actions by Frederick Chiluba in Zambia, Vladimir Putin in Russia, and Hugo Chavez in Venezuela.

36. It should be noted that, for a variety of reasons, three of the four large countries that have restored democracy—India, Turkey, and Thailand—seem unlikely to suspend it again. Unfortunately, the same cannot be said for the fourth, Nigeria. It is one of the most corrupt and ethnically fractious countries in the world. It is a state that remains on the precipice of collapse and its tenuous democracy faces a realistic possibility of collapsing.

37. This was the per capita income of Argentina in 1975, the richest country ever to have suffered a coup against democracy. Przeworski et al., *Democracy and Development,* 98.

38. See the extensive data in Marta Lagos, "Latin America's Lost Illusions: A Road with No Return?" *Journal of Democracy* 14 (April 2003): 163–73. In Latin America overall, support for democracy has declined by five percentage points since 1996, but the bigger drift has been toward apathy ("it doesn't matter," or no response)

rather than to authoritarianism. In the ten candidate states for EU accession within postcommunist Europe, 61 percent are dissatisfied with the way democracy works in their country, yet overall, 72 percent would not approve of its suspension (and no more than one in six even in the most skeptical country, Estonia, thinks it could happen). Even in the states where more people approve of the old communist regime over the new democratic one—Slovakia, Latvia, Lithuania, and Romania—substantial majorities disapprove of all imaginable authoritarian alternatives.

39. Sen, "Democracy as a Universal Value," 12.

40. It is, of course, possible that some new form of nondemocratic rule will emerge to capture the passions and imagination of some peoples. But at this point, almost two decades after the collapse of communism, there is no sign on the horizon of an antidemocratic ideology that could even begin to generate universal claims. Most likely, where authoritarian rule reasserts itself in the coming years, it will do so apologetically, wrapping itself in the moral purpose of democratic restoration and insisting that the suspension of democracy would be temporary.

41. A plausible alternative scenario for these insular nations would be continued international isolation that facilitates crisis and then collapse. But the United States has tried this strategy for nearly fifty years in Cuba, and all it has done is impoverish the people and entrench their repressive rulers.

42. Bruce Bueno de Mesquita, James Morrow, Randolph Siverson, and Alistair Smith, "Political Competition and Economic Growth," *Journal of Democracy* 12 (January 2001): 158–72.

43. The strategy briefly summarized here is consistent with a new report issued by the U.S. Agency for International Development. I was a consultant to the agency and helped develop a strategy for improving the allocation of foreign aid. The report, "Foreign Aid in the National Interest: Promoting Freedom, Security, and Opportunity," was released in January 2003; it is available at www.usaid.gov.

3

Is Democracy Contagious?

Diffusion and the Dynamics of Regime Transition

ZACHARY ELKINS

Transitions to democracy tend to cluster both temporally and spatially, leading many to employ a wave metaphor in describing democratization. Widespread use of the wave metaphor implies the intriguing possibility that a democratic transition in one country increases the probability of a transition in a neighboring country, a useful definition of diffusion. That democracy diffuses seems almost axiomatic. Nonetheless, democratization scholars are only now beginning to develop hypotheses and marshal the evidence needed to understand the causal processes underlying such interdependence.[1] Foot-dragging on the part of social scientists, however, does not seem to have affected foreign-policy makers, many of whom have pinned their hopes for democratic future in the twenty-first century on diffusion. Indeed, an implicit justification for the 2003 U.S.-led invasion of Iraq was the notion that a democratic beachhead in the Middle East would foster the spread of democracy throughout the region.

But does one transition to democracy increase the odds of another? If the wave metaphor is empirically well grounded, what mechanisms power these waves? What can diffusion theory add to our understanding of democratization and its wake? This chapter examines these questions. This is a timely inquiry because, if a fourth wave of democracy is imminent (as several contributors to this volume intimate), diffusion processes are likely to play an important role in how it unfolds. Before these questions can be addressed, however, it is important to clarify two key terms that will be used throughout this chapter: democracy and diffusion.

As Diamond (chapter 2) and Anderson (chapter 5) note, there are many competing conceptions of democracy. Like Diamond, I employ a minimalist conception, one that focuses on electoral processes and representative institutions. More specifically, I use a simple operationalization of democracy that hinges on whether the chief executive is elected in fair elections and whether an elected representative body has real power. Now that a majority of the world's countries have such institutions, there are compelling reasons to employ more refined conceptions of democracy that incorporate qualitative and substantive differences among polities. However, given the type of historical analyses employed here, the use of a more basic conception of democracy is justified. Moreover, significant electoral "holdouts" remain, particularly in Africa and the Middle East. In these locales democratization is still very much about convoking elections and establishing representative institutions as much as protecting liberties and building a healthy participatory culture.

The concept of diffusion also merits clarification. A principal source of confusion concerns its usage as both an outcome and a process (Simmons and Elkins 2004). For some (Eyestone 1977), the term suggests simply the dispersion or dissemination of a phenomenon across space, a phenomenon that goes under the term "wave" or "cluster" here. Others conceive of diffusion not as an outcome but as the flagship term for a large class of causal processes associated with the spread of phenomena (Simmons and Elkins 2004). The latter sense matches my use of the term here. Thus, in this chapter the term diffusion refers to the set of processes by which one actor's adoption of governance practices alters the probability that another will adopt them. Critical to this conception of diffusion is the notion of interdependence. In particular, the notion is one of uncoordinated interdependence, uncoordinated in the sense that a country's decision to democratize is not imposed by another. This idea distinguishes diffusion from other international explanations, such as those on which Russett (2004) focuses.

I begin by empirically scrutinizing the wave metaphor. The main body of the chapter outlines the types of explanations that have been used to explain these waves of democratization, focusing mainly on the potential utility of diffusion models. It identifies and discusses two diffusion mechanisms that are particularly useful for the study of democratization: adaptation and learning. The third section discusses the implications for societal welfare that flow from these two distinct mechanisms.

Wave or Rising Tide?

The notion that diffusion theory can help us understand democratization rests on the assumption that the spread of democracy conforms to the uneven, punctuated process that typifies diffusion. The current belief in the wave-like quality of democratization is so pervasive that its empirical foundations are rarely scrutinized. But if democratization can best be characterized as a rising tide (i.e., an even, secular trend) as opposed to uneven, wave-like processes that produce temporal and spatial clusters of new democracies, then the wave metaphor may not be justified. And diffusion theory may not be a fruitful source of insights for understanding democratization.

We begin by taking a longer view of democratic history. Figures 3.1 and 3.2 report data on the proportion of democracies and the incidence of democratic transitions, using only countries with populations over one million. In these figures the top line represents the percentage of governments in the sample that are democratic, and the bars represent the number of transitions in either direction. One can clearly see why scholars have described the eras immediately following World War I and World War II, as well as the period from the 1970s to the 1990s, as three waves of democracy. The incidence of

Figure 3.1 Transitions to electing executives

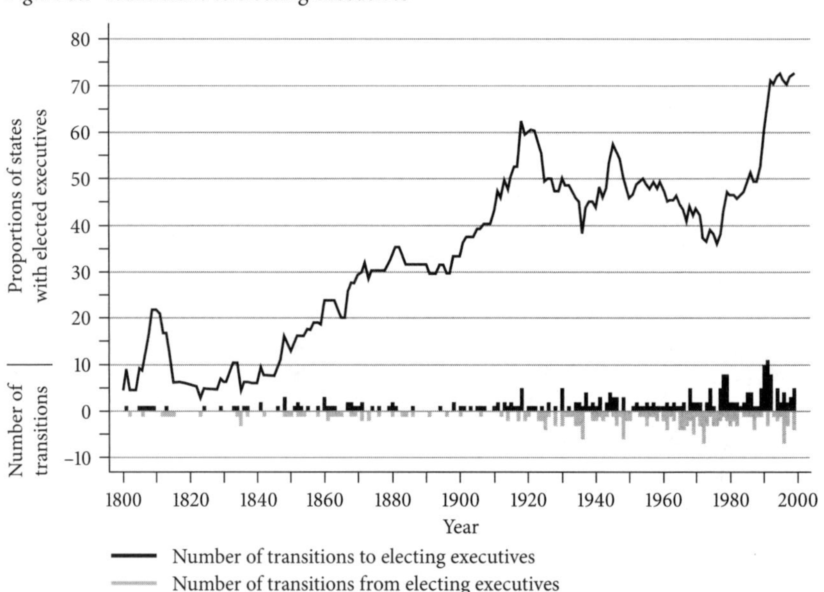

Figure 3.2 Transitions to legislative constraints on the executive

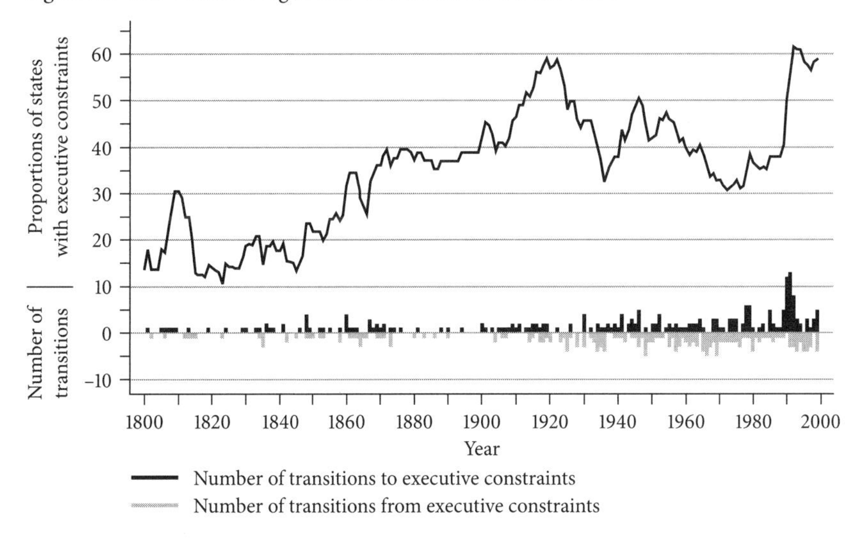

democratic institutions certainly spikes up during these eras, providing some empirical justification for the wave metaphor.[2]

Taking a longer view, however, one should recognize the second half of the nineteeenth century as an equally productive—if more gradual—period of democratic development. From 1840 to 1900 the proportion of democratic states increases almost fourfold. Table 3.1 reports transition rates for four eras: 1800–1900, 1900–1945, 1945–1966, and 1966–2000. Interestingly, despite the increase in democracies throughout the 1800s, the transition rates indicate that a transition to authoritarianism was more likely than a transition to democracy during this period. Also, the probability of a democratic transition increases during the next century, but authoritarian transitions remain almost as likely. Thus, while democratic transition activity increases (as represented by the bars on the lower part of Figures 3.1 and 3.2), the activity is not as intense as we might suppose from the wave rhetoric. Also, there appear to be almost as many authoritarian transitions as there are democratic ones during the three waves.

These observations about democratic transitions raise some questions about the utility of the wave metaphor. More important, they suggest a more refined conception of our understanding of democratization processes, one that emphasizes the distinction between democratic transitions and births. The steady increase in the number of states in the international system suggests that the birth of democracies may contribute as much to the observed

Table 3.1 Transitions to and from democratic policies

	States with populations over 1 million, 1800–2000					
	Transitions to Democratic Policies			Transitions to Authoritarian Policies		
	Elected Executive	Empowered Legislature	Competition	Elected Executive	Empowered Legislature	Competition
1800–1900						
Number of countries ever at risk	169	55	146	80	179	136
Years at risk	4,116	3669	2,404	983	3,147	2,033
Number of transitions	66	51	125	41	123	112
Markov Transition Rate (%)	**1.38**	**1.50**	**1.85**	**4.47**	**3.10**	**1.16**
1900–1945						
Number of countries ever at risk	105	58	97	60	110	95
Years at risk	2,713	2,058	2,007	781	2,500	1,627
Number of transitions	49	49	107	38	108	96
Markov Transition Rate (%)	**3.88**	**3.18**	**4.45**	**3.56**	**3.75**	**2.08**
1946–1970						
Number of countries ever at risk	64	100	49	20	69	41
Years at risk	1,403	1,548	397	202	647	406
Number of transitions	17	40	18	3	15	16
Markov Transition Rate (%)	**2.66**	**2.47**	**2.45**	**4.28**	**5.62**	**4.29**
1966–2000						
Number of countries ever at risk	64	2,494	49	20	69	41
Years at risk	1,403	126	397	202	647	406
Number of transitions	17	92	18	3	15	16
Markov Transition Rate (%)	**3.91**	**5.36**	**4.95**	**3.17**	**2.76**	**2.75**

Source: Center for International Development and Conflict Management, Polity IV Project; data available at http://www.cidcm.umd.edu/polity.

spread of democracy as does the transition of authoritarian states to democratic ones. If this were the case, we would have to conclude that some sort of generational effect, as opposed to a period effect, is at work: we are seeing increasing numbers of democracies because states are originating during democratic times.

Figure 3.3 plots the birth and mortality rates of states as well as their number over the last two hundred years. It certainly appears that the second and third waves—and even the first to some extent—are boom years for the formation of new states. During the last two hundred years, 193 states with over one million citizens have come into existence, while thirty-two states have disappeared. Of these, twenty-three disappeared without an elected executive, while only nine did so with one. Of the 127 born in the twentieth century, seventy have been born with an elected executive while only fifty-seven have been born without one. This ratio is constant throughout most of the century except for the 1980s, the beginning of the third wave. Since 1980, twenty-seven states have come into being, of which nineteen (roughly 70 percent) began with elected executives. Clearly, some of the growth in democracy is explained not by regime transition, but by the proliferation of states over the last century—states that are more likely to be born democratic than they are authoritarian.

Figure 3.3 Number of states, state births, and state deaths

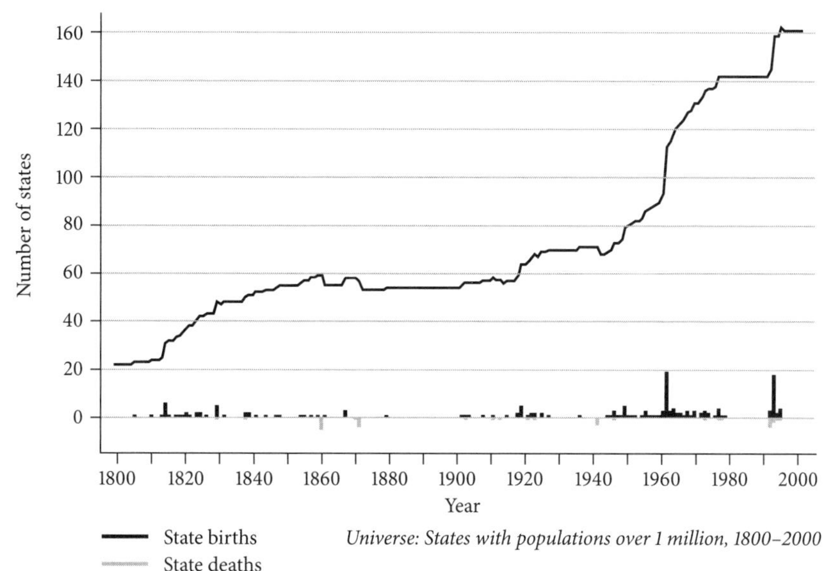

To put this differently, one sees clear generational patterns in the development of states. Those coming of age during the third wave are much more likely to have electoral and representative institutions mixed into their foundation—a foundation that might be fairly resistant to change. The result is a wave-like pattern, one generated not by transitions to democracy, but by a boom in democratic births. These symptoms may well indicate the presence of diffusion—albeit diffusion at the hands of founders and framers of new states.

Explaining Waves of Democratization: The Role and Utility of Diffusion Models

The existence of wave-like patterns of democratization is crucial to the application of diffusion models to the study of democratization. But the mere existence of temporal and spatial clusters does not mean that diffusion processes power these waves. Indeed, three general classes of explanations might account for the existence of democratic waves; I focus on diffusion models here because of their unique potential to enhance our understanding of democratization. The role of diffusion models in this enterprise can be seen in Figure 3.4.

The most conventional and longstanding explanation is that transitions to democracy are coincidental: countries respond similarly, but independently,

Figure 3.4 Explanations for clusters of democracy

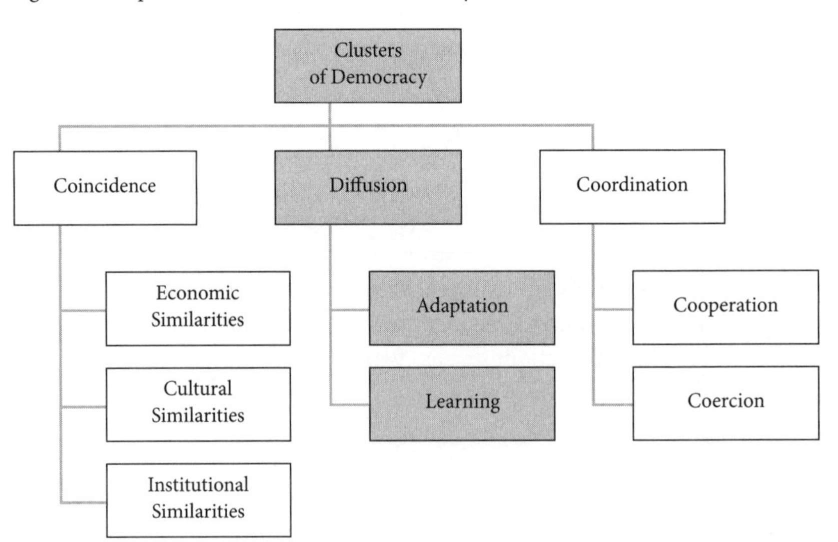

to similar domestic conditions. For example, a long tradition of scholarship suggests that certain internal structural attributes encourage democracy. These include the level of wealth (Lipset 1959), a particular combination of class alignments (Moore 1966), and the right mix of cultural ingredients (Almond and Verba 1963). The confluence of these sets of conditions at certain times and in certain areas would generate clusters of democratic transitions/births. The assumption underlying such explanations is that decision makers operate without regard to the behavior (perceived or predicted) of other states. We might think of such an explanation as the baseline answer, one predominant in comparative politics and, undoubtedly, one with some causal power.

A second class of explanations includes those in which clustered democratic reform is coordinated by external actors, such as hegemonic powers or international organizations. The mechanisms that power waves of democratization within this class of explanations include the "horizontal" processes of international collaboration and cooperation described by scholars of "epistemic communities" (Haas 1992), or the "vertical" processes such as coercion by important donor countries and international financial institutions (Russett 2004).

The third class of explanations, diffusion, combines an element from each of these first two classes. Diffusion models are characterized by interdependent, but uncoordinated, decision making. Under this conception, governments are independent in the sense that they make their own decisions without cooperation or coercion (as in coincidental explanations), but they are interdependent in the sense that they factor in the choices of other governments. In other words, diffusion models involve uncoordinated interdependence.

To be sure, diffusion models constitute a decidedly general class of processes. These include learning, imitation, bandwagoning, emulation, and mimicry. Even economic competition, to the extent that it affects policy choice, can be thought of as a diffusion mechanism (Elkins, Guzman, and Simmons 2007; Simmons and Elkins 2004). Indeed, the value of diffusion models to the study of democratization derives from the rich body of mechanisms that can used to enhance our understanding of how democracy spreads. The following sections discuss two mechanisms with distinct causal logics that are particularly valuable to the study of democratization: adaptation and learning. Adaptation involves situations in which one country's transition alters the benefits of democracy for another country. Learning involves situations in which one country's transition alters the information set regarding democracy for another country.

DIFFUSION VIA ADAPTATION

In this class of mechanisms, the policy decisions of one government alter the conditions under which other governments base their decisions. Typically, the decisions alter the value of democracy for others. In this sense, one can think of these decisions as producing network externalities, to extend the language used to describe the effect of the number of users of a product on that product's value (Katz and Shapiro 1985). One can imagine any number of mechanisms that might fit under this class. I identify three critical ones below: cultural norms, support groups, and competition.

CULTURAL NORMS Many have observed that democracy's third wave has altered global norms of acceptable governance. Norms are common practices whose value to an actor stems from their prevalence in a population. We can think of them as network externalities, then, since the benefits of adopting them increase with adoptions by others. But what kinds of benefits accompany increases in prevalence? In terms of norms, the predominant benefit is reputational. Joining a growing majority of other actors confers a degree of legitimacy or, in the case of a negatively valenced practice, protection from criticism. Governments risk rebuke and international derision for not having democratic institutions and will be comfortable with such derision only if a critical mass of others also bear it.

The logic behind norms follows very closely the "tipping," or "threshold," models that Schelling (1978) and Granovetter (1978) have described. The basic intuition is that most actors are highly sensitive to the number, or proportion, of other actors who have adopted a practice. The idea of "thresholds," or "critical mass points," is a useful (although not necessary) device with which to understand the process. Consider an example from Granovetter (1978). An individual faces the decision of whether or not to participate in a riot. Arguably, the probability that one would participate in a riot increases as the number of participants increases; the logic here is that the greater the number of participants, the greater the immunity from apprehension.[3] There is a certain level of participation, a threshold at which an individual will decide to participate in the riot. Presumably, these thresholds will be different for different individuals. For example, Schelling suggests that it is usually the case that 5–10 percent of the population is committed to one choice or the other, regardless of what others decide to do; the rest are highly dependent, but to different degrees, on the choices of others.

Schelling (1978) provides a number of examples of threshold behavior.

These examples demonstrate that an increase in adoptions confers a certain degree of legitimacy (or immunity, in cases of illicit practices) on potential adopters. I suggest that this dynamic describes the way social norms function with respect to democratization. Consider the case of political rights policies. There one sees that a country's propensity to maintain a policy that is viewed negatively in the international community—say, the death penalty—decreases as the proportion of countries with that policy decreases. It is only a small number of countries (e.g., the United States) whose threshold for world approbation is so high that they have, at least to date, resisted the wave of changes. The death penalty is but one example. Other political and civil rights should work the same way.

Of course, the tipping effect can go in the opposite direction as well. That is, actors may be tempted to opt out of a practice once a certain number of others have adopted it. This will occur if there is some fear of crowding or a desire for uniqueness. One may imagine that this dynamic occurs with "isolate" nations such as Libya or Cuba. However, while isolate nations may be more comfortable with their uniqueness, it is not the case that they seek it. Cuba under Fidel Castro, for example, found itself alone only after the cold war. Until then, Castro sought a much more central position in the international community and actively promoted a "tip" in the opposite direction than that which occurred in 1989.

SUPPORT GROUPS The availability of external support is another diffusion mechanism that produces behavior-altering benefits to nations considering political reform. As economists who study industry standards have found, users derive practical benefits from a strong network of other users (Katz and Shapiro 1985; Katz and Shapiro 1986). The simplest case is that in which the number of users directly increases the value of the product. Consider, for example, the case of a telephone network: the greater the number of individuals who subscribe, the more people there are with whom one may communicate. Another well-known example of this mechanism is the QWERTY keyboard. Because of the positive network externalities associated with the QWERTY standard (that is, access to the growing number of QWERTY typists), typewriter manufacturers failed to adopt more efficient keyboards (David 1985).

One can also imagine a set of more indirect benefits arising from a strong network of users, benefits that are critical to the choice political practices. One of these is an increase in technical support. It is well known that consumers of everything from automobiles to computer software are drawn to the technical support benefits accompanying a large network of users. For example, in the social sciences, the statistical software Stata, and more recently R, have become predominant in part because of the enormous advantages of add-on program code developed and shared by their large communities of users.

Forces of this kind are equally strong in the development of democratic practices and institutions. Rules to regulate the powers of the legislature and the president are not especially easy for a government to design and maintain on its own. For many new democracies torn by ethnic division, the design of fair and workable democratic institutions is challenging. It is extremely helpful to have a community of users, preferably one with skills and knowledge, who are committed to refining and improving the practice. Adopting countries desire pools of expertise that they can draw on for policy enhancements and ancillary policies.

Elkins (2003) shows that these sorts of services are important to constitutional delegates faced with the choice of electoral system and that of presidentialism versus parliamentarism. Pragmatic policy makers considering political reform are cognizant that they are joining a network of other users from which they can derive advice, support, and service. As with cultural norms, the technical support mechanism rests on the dynamic that Schelling (1978) and Granovetter (1978) describe in their tipping models. That is, thresholds exist that have a marked impact on the benefits that can be derived from adopting democratic reforms.

COMPETITION Competition over scarce resources is another diffusion mechanism that alters the payoffs of democracy for governments. Essentially, one country's transition to democracy can have a very strong effect on its competitiveness, whether for foreign capital, direct loans, a contract to host the Olympics, or any other type of benefit. Simmons and Elkins (2004) make this argument with respect to transitions to liberalization in the capital account, current account, and exchange rates. The logic is straightforward and works well for democratic reform. If we assume that governments are interested in attracting capital investments in their country, and that political restrictions and authoritarian uncertainty increase the risk associated with investing in a country, then one country's adoption of democracy will disrupt the competitive equilibrium across countries. By removing authoritarian restrictions, the price of a country's investment products dips and lures investors away from investments in other countries. Ceteris paribus, these external changes generate domestic pressures to adopt democratic reform. Of course, there are benefits to restrictive policies (namely, economic and political stability), which may predispose a government to restrict absent competition.

DIFFUSION VIA LEARNING

The second broad class of diffusion mechanisms concerns the exchange of information, or from the perspective of the transitioning government, learning. In a critical sense, these approaches are quite different from those discussed above. In learning processes, another actor's adoption does not alter the conditions of democracy. Rather, the action provides information about such conditions, including the benefits and drawbacks of democracy.

The operative force behind learning mechanisms is that the actions of others are more instructive to an actor than are internal drives or needs. The work of social psychologists has done much to substantiate this premise in the last fifty years. Among others, Festinger's (1950) theory of social comparison and Merton's (1968) work on reference groups are prominent statements of this doctrine. Bandura's (1977) social learning theory has been especially useful to diffusion scholars. In Bandura's model, individuals are not equipped with internal repertoires of behavior. Except for the most basic reflexes, actors are almost fully dependent upon external models for understanding the consequences of certain actions.

How does social learning operate in the context of democratization? Under the best of circumstances, policy makers in nation-states learn in the same way social scientists might. That is, they recognize a problem with the effectiveness of a policy, develop a theory about how to solve the problem, review the various solutions available, and attempt to ascertain the relative effectiveness of alternative solutions. Such is the "laboratory of democracy," where California can learn from Wisconsin's welfare experiment or from Oregon's health care trials. The same process occurs at the international level. Westney's (1987) account of policy borrowing in Japan during the nineteenth century demonstrates this sort of learning.

What is interesting about learning, from a diffusion perspective, are the numerous ways that it can go wrong. The worldwide policy environment turns out to be a sloppy laboratory, and inefficiencies develop as a result of some predictable biases and limitations in the learning process. The fundamental problem with social learning at this level is that national policy makers often have difficulty assessing the consequences of the various policies. Policy makers are "cognitive misers" (Fiske and Taylor 1991) as much as anyone else. As boundedly rational actors, they rely upon a set of cognitive heuristics to make sense of these sometimes complicated policy choices. I describe three important learning "methods" (or, rather, biases) that cognitively constrained policy engineers follow.

INFORMATION CASCADES In the situations involving great uncertainty, policy makers may have no other information than the knowledge of whether others have adopted the governmental reform. In this case, individuals may reason that they should take advantage of the accumulated wisdom of past actors' decisions. The logic is the same that one would use in choosing between two restaurants that are similar in obvious characteristics: a common decision rule is to choose the restaurant with more patrons. The trouble, of course, is that aggregated decisions can point to what appears to be a clearly optimal restaurant (or policy, as it were) even if these decisions are the result of a few and important choices by early adopters (who may or may not have had good information).

We can call this sort of problem an information cascade. Bikhchandani, Hirshleifer, and Welch (1998) develop a model of this process, which demonstrates that choices of an entire sequence of actors can depend exclusively on the decisions of the first two or three actors. This can be true not only if the actors are initially indifferent about the choice, but also if they are predisposed against the choice of the first three!

Thus, it is conceivable that information cascades will produce convergence toward one policy choice even in situations in which actors know nothing other than who has adopted what policy. Of course, in reality, actors may try to gather more information than simply who has adopted what practice. Specifically, they may hope to draw inferences about the effectiveness of the various policies. Again, however, policymakers are limited by the data available to them, their resources to undertake analysis, and their own cognitive faculties. These limitations encourage a process of learning characterized by a dependence on highly selective samples of policy models. Below, I describe two processes that have predictable diffusion effects: learning from available models, and learning from those in one's reference group.

LEARNING AND AVAILABILITY Individuals often have difficulty retrieving a full sample of information and tend to base their decisions on only the information that is readily available to them (Kahneman, Slovic, and Tversky 1982; Weyland 2004).[4] The result is that the choice set of policy makers is often limited to practices of states that are immediately accessible. These more accessible models bias the learning process in a number of ways. One way, of course, is that the more available the model, the more likely it will be included as a data point in the analysis of alternatives. As such, these models will also be amenable to less scientific methods of analysis by policy makers; some, seeking to legitimate predispositions or conclusions they already hold, may introduce these more accessible cases as representative examples.

Another way that a policy's availability can affect an actor's decision is through increased familiarity. Taste—whether for food, music, art, or political parties—is often acquired, and individuals have a tendency to prefer practices familiar to them. Such attraction might stem in part from a strategy of risk reduction: familiar choices may appear to be safe choices. However, it is also probable that familiarity breeds appreciation and shapes tastes. As such, being surrounded by democratic governments can lead to an appreciation, or at least tolerance, for their institutions and practices.

Thus, a governance model's availability can distort the learning process and increase its chances of adoption in another country in a number of ways. In the international arena, which governance models will be more available than others? One clear expectation is that experiences of those governments with which one communicates and interacts will be most available. Indeed, the idea that communication among actors transmits ideas is one of the prevailing assumptions in the broad diffusion literature (Rogers 1995). However, it is also likely that the policy of prominent nations will be highly available and, consequently, policy makers will tend to weight those cases disproportionately. For example, it is likely that for many democratizing countries the United States will be the most available case of presidentialism. So, while the performance, however measured, of presidential systems may be poor in the sample at large, it may appear high to those who have difficulty retrieving less-well-known (and less-well-performing) cases of presidentialism.

The most available governance models, perhaps, are those that are reputed to have been successful. Decision makers will understandably be drawn to such a model, sometimes letting its success bias their evaluation of its effectiveness. Consider an example from Kahneman, Slovic, and Tversky (1982: 10): "In a discussion of flight training, experienced instructors noted that praise for an especially smooth landing is typically followed by a poorer landing on the next try, while harsh criticism after a rough landing is usually followed by an improvement on the next try. The instructors concluded that verbal rewards are detrimental to learning."

These practiced analysts made this judgment while ignoring the phenomenon of regression to the mean. Political actors often do the same thing. For example, they observe a short period of tremendous success or failure and make projections for the governance model based on those early high or low marks. Enthusiasm over the initial success of a model—for example, the fiscal program Domingo Cavallo designed for Argentina in the early 1990s—can fuel fad-like adoptions. Similarly, a year or so of abject failure can lead analysts to soundly reject any program of its kind. Long-term trends or low-profile cases—both of which are less "available"—will have less effect.

LEARNING AND REFERENCE GROUPS Actors may pay more attention to some governance models than others because information about them is more accessible. But they may also be attracted to successful models from countries that are similar to theirs. In fact, a reliable finding in the voluminous literature on diffusion and social influence is that entities that share similar cultural attributes tend to adopt the same practices.[5] This is true not only of individual behavior like teen smoking (Coleman, Katz, and Menzel 1966) and voting (Huckfeldt and Sprague 1995) but also of collective behavior with respect to corporations (Davis and Greve 1997), nonprofit organizations (Mizruchi 1989), subnational states (Walker 1969), and, indeed, nations (Deutsch 1953). Why is this so? The primary reason is that imitating similar individuals is one of the simplest and most effective cognitive heuristics in the calculation of utilities. Actors negotiating a complex set of political choices regard the actions of actors with perceived common interests as a useful guide to their own behavior. A growing number of political scientists suspect that such shortcuts allow the mass public to negotiate a complicated political world (Brady and Sniderman 1985; Lupia and McCubbins 1998), and it is likely that the same sort of process describes the reasoning of leaders making difficult policy decisions. Rosenau (1988: 359; 1990: 213) posits just such a process, suggesting that decision makers have a strong "cathectic" sense of what their nation should look like and model their government accordingly.

So which countries are likely to be relevant reference groups? For decision makers, the easiest way to identify appropriate reference groups is to compare their visible characteristics. Some of the more visible and defining national characteristics are geographic and cultural: the country's region, the language its citizens speak, the religion they practice, and the country's colonial origins. It follows, then, that policy makers will align their country's policies with those of geographically and culturally proximate nations.

Substantive Implications of Diffusion Mechanisms

Diffusion models can contribute much to the study of democratization; they lead to a focus on factors that other classes of explanations ignore, as illustrated in Figure 3.4 and the accompanying discussion. Diffusion models are particularly intriguing in that they imply that governments make choices that they would not make if left to their own devices. These "detours" in the developmental paths of nations are interesting for a variety of academic reasons. But they also portend important consequences for the quality of government policies. Two are particularly important here. Policy detours may mean that governments adopt suboptimal or inappropriate policies designed for the needs of others. Alternatively, detours may mean that governments adopt policies superior to those they have the resources or knowledge to engineer for themselves.

Stated differently, the prospect that diffusion effects drive democratization gives rise to the concern that nations are led to adopt ill-fitting but fashionable governmental practices. The alternative, of course, is that diffusion leads nations to adopt more functional and efficient practices. We might lean toward the second conclusion, if only for our cultural preference for creativity and originality over imitation and conformity. However, the first conclusion appears equally plausible, especially after a number of scholars have begun to burnish the image of imitation, emphasizing its utility as a cognitive shortcut for problems whose answers are not always obvious (e.g., Lupia and McCubbins 1998). Imitation, in this light, is not slavish. It is an efficient and effective mode of behavior for policy makers. Below, I argue that these outcomes depend crucially on the particular mechanism of diffusion.

Recall the distinction between adaptation and learning. This categorization divides two classes of mechanisms with wholly different theoretical foundations—theoretical, that is, in the sense of the individual behavioral motivations and processes at work. The intrinsic difference rests on whether individuals are motivated by changes in the payoffs associated with different practices, or if they are motivated by changes in their "scientific" evaluation of the practices. As a practical matter, this distinction is useful in that it stakes out the theoretical space well: the simple binary division is exhaustive, while still parsimonious. In the interest of knowledge accumulation, the hope is that this division organizes mechanisms into useful "schema," which will be useful to future researchers. While such organization can be useful in the interest of improving scholarly discussion, the theoretical distinction that I suggest divides two sets of mechanisms with potentially opposite implications for social welfare. That is, the distinction between classes of diffusion has real consequences for the quality of democratic reform. Specifically, I suggest that mechanisms of diffusion in the adaptation class are likely to lead to the adoption of suboptimal institutions—institutions inferior even to those that actors could engineer themselves. On the other hand, those mechanisms in the learning class are likely to result in optimal institutions,

institutions that actors would not necessarily have the means or motivation to design themselves.

This difference in outcome results from two unrelated factors. First, actors driven by a shift in payoffs (adaptation) may or may not develop practices that are suited to their needs. By definition, the actors' focus is not on the merits and outputs of the institutions themselves but on the ancillary benefits associated with the adoption of the institution. In the case of learning, however, actors are focused squarely on the merits of the institution. In fact, the desire for a more efficient set of institutions is the very motive for their search through the foreign database of policy alternatives. Admittedly, some of what I call learning is hardly scientific. Indeed, some scholars may prefer a more general label for such mechanisms—say, "information motives"—that does not imply a studied, deliberate decision process. Nonetheless, even through cognitively constrained methods of research, actors can be successful in approximating the results of a more sophisticated methodology. Also, their motive to improve their institutions suggests that they will more often than not do better for themselves by searching internationally than they would if left to their own devices.

A second factor that distinguishes the welfare effects of these two sets of processes is the level of commitment and internalization associated with the adopted institution. Here, I suggest that institutions really work only when there is a firm commitment to their installation. Part of this commitment involves what we might call the "internalization" of the principles undergirding the reform. Actors internalize the principles and rationale of the reform when they accept and understand the need for reform, as well as the logic of the reform. Accepting the rationale and the logic of the reform leads to a certain degree of commitment to implementing the reform and seeing it through.

Therefore, we can expect diffusion to have very different implications for social welfare according to the particular mechanism at work. Identifying the mechanisms of diffusion, in this sense, takes on more importance than a simple accounting of historical sources. Indeed, understanding the path to democracy tells us much about the quality of democracy. With the widespread adoption of democracy and market reforms, albeit with very different degrees of success, such distinctions become increasingly important.

Conclusion

Is it right to speak of waves of democracy? Yes, but a closer look at the historical record reveals that the source of the large-scale shift has more to do with generational turnover than an about-face in a country's political direction. States "born" after World War II are simply more likely to be born democratic. Nonetheless, that the initial constitutions of such countries are largely democratic has much to do with the momentum implicit in a wave of democracy: the experiences of geographically, culturally, or economically proximate states are likely to be influential for a number of compelling reasons. A principal goal of this chapter is to identify a useful set of concepts and mechanisms for the empirical investigation of such democratic diffusion. Given the recent acceleration in empirical work on the subject, however, I also hope to stimulate a more active and focused research program examining the language and causal processes of diffusion. Understandably, the empirical methods and data needed to test the presence of various mechanism will likely lag behind their specification. Nonetheless, it is essential to map out potential causal paths, whether or not they can be subjected to empirical validation. Most important, it is critical that researchers develop expectations for the substantive implications of their theorized causal paths. Investigation of these implications represents a logical extension and payoff for democratization scholars.

Notes

I appreciate helpful comments from Peter Nardulli, Beth Simmons, and Susan Stokes. A more general version of these ideas appears in Elkins (2002).

1. This is not to say that democratization scholars have ignored diffusion. Amidst the more widely cited findings of the O'Donnell, Schmitter, Whitehead volumes is a chapter by Whitehead (1986) entitled "International Explanations of Democratization." There, Whitehead brainstorms a list of plausible "international" hypotheses for democratization, many of them cases of what we would call diffusion in this study. Years later, Whitehead (2001) would include that chapter, together with a fascinating set of case studies exposing a set of international connections underlying the pattern of transitions in the third wave. Huntington's (1991) book takes a longer view, identifying three waves of democratization and clearly linking the clustered pattern of democratizations with some interdependent mechanism. To cite another prominent example, Ruth Collier (1993), also appealing to case-study insights, takes the bold analytic step of assessing the strength of international explanations of democracy against a set of domestic factors. The recent production of a series of high-quality empirical studies on the geographic diffusion of democracy (Starr 1991; Markoff 1996; O'Loughlin et al. 1998; Coppedge and Brinks 1999; Kopstein and Reilly 2000; Gleditsch and Ward 2004) constitutes a critical mass of large-N studies of democratic diffusion. On the basis of this work, we have good reason to believe that transitions are highly correlated spatially.

2. This observation does not derive from simply "eyeballing" the data. Count models provide valuable techniques to test for clustering. One conventional test is to compare the distribution of adoptions across time with that predicted by a Poisson distribution (Siverson and Starr 1991). The Poisson is a rare-events distribution that assumes events occur independently and that the susceptibility of a particular event is homogenous across countries. A count of transitions to democracy does not fit the Poisson very well. A chi-square test of equivalence of distributions suggests that, for each of the two features of democracy, we can reject the null hypothesis that they follow a Poisson pattern ($X = 79.42$, $p < .01$). It is unlikely, therefore, that democratization is an independent choice taken across a set of governments that are equally susceptible to it.

3. Corroborating experimental research from social psychology substantiates the principles of the tipping model. For example, Asch's (1951) work on conformity showed that individuals were much more likely to trust their own information when they had just one or two confederates siding with them. Some "safety in numbers" is also evident in the Milgram (1975) experiments on obedience.

4. Kurt Weyland (2004) links this and other cognitive heuristics to diffusion in a very useful framework.

5. As Rogers (1995: 274) states, "The transfer of ideas occurs most frequently between individuals . . . who are similar in certain attributes such as beliefs, education, social status, and the like."

References

Almond, Gabriel Abraham, and Sidney Verba. 1963. *The Civic Culture: Political Attitudes and Democracy in Five Nations.* Princeton, N.J.: Princeton University Press.

Asch, Solomon E. 1951. "Effects of Group Pressure Upon the Modification and Distortion of Judgement." In *Groups, Leadership, and Men: Research in Human Relations,* ed. H. Guetzkow. Pittsburgh: Carnegie Press.

Bandura, Albert. 1977. *Social Learning Theory.* Englewood Cliffs, N.J.: Prentice Hall.

Bikhchandani, Sushil, David Hirshleifer, and Ivo Welch. 1998. "Learning from the Behavior of Others: Conformity, Fads, and Informational Cascades." *Journal of Economic Perspectives* 12 (3): 151–70.

Brady, Henry, and Paul Sniderman. 1985. "Attitude Attribution: A Group Basis for Political Reasoning." *American Political Science Review* 60:880–98.

Coleman, James S., Elihu Katz, and Herbert Menzel. 1966. *Medical Innovation: A Diffusion Study*. Indianapolis: Bobbs-Merrill.

Collier, R. B. 1993. "Combining Alternative Perspectives: Internal Trajectories versus External Influences as Explanations of Latin-American Politics in the 1940s." *Comparative Politics* 26 (1): 1–29.

Coppedge, Michael, and Daniel Brinks. 2006. "Diffusion is No Illusion: Neighbor

Emulation in the Third Wave of Democracy." *Comparative Political Studies* 39 (4): 463–89.

David, Paul. 1985. "Clio and the Economics of Qwerty." *American Economic Review* 75:322–37.

Davis, Gerald F., and Henrich R. Greve. 1997. "Corporate Elite Networks and Governance Changes in the 1980s." *American Journal of Sociology* 103:1–37.

Deutsch, Karl Wolfgang. 1953. *Nationalism and Social Communication: An Inquiry into the Foundations of Nationality.* Cambridge: Technology Press of MIT; New York: Wiley.

Elkins, Zachary. 2003. "Designed by Diffusion: International Networks and the Spread of Democracy." PhD diss., University of California, Berkeley.

Elkins, Zachary, Andrew Guzman, and Beth A. Simmons. 2006. "Competing for Capital: The Diffusion of Bilateral Investment Treaties, 1960–2000." *International Organization* 60:811–46.

Eyestone, Robert. 1977. "Confusion, Diffusion, and Innovation." *American Political Science Review* 71:441–47.

Festinger, Leon. 1950. *Social Pressures in Informal Groups: A Study of Human Factors in Housing.* Stanford, Calif.: Stanford University Press.

Fiske, Susan T., and Shelley E. Taylor. 1991. *Social Cognition.* 2nd ed. New York: McGraw-Hill.

Gleditsch, Kristian Skrede, and Michael D. Ward. 2004. "Diffusion and the International Context of Democratization." *International Organization* 60 (4): 911–33.

Granovetter, Mark S. 1978. "Threshold Models of Collective Behavior." *American Journal of Sociology* 83:1420–43.

Haas, Peter. 1992. "Knowledge, Power, and International Policy Coordination." *International Organization* 46:1–390.

Huckfeldt, R. Robert, and John D. Sprague. 1995. *Citizens, Politics, and Social Communication: Information and Influence in an Election Campaign.* Cambridge: Cambridge University Press.

Huntington, Samuel. 1991. *The Third Wave: Democratization in the Late Twentieth Century.* Norman: University of Oklahoma Press.

Kahneman, Daniel, Paul Slovic, and Amos Tversky. 1982. *Judgment under Uncertainty: Heuristics and Biases.* Cambridge: Cambridge University Press.

Katz, Michael, and Carl Shapiro. 1985. "Network Externalities: Competition and Compatibility." *American Economic Review Papers and Proceedings* 75:424–40.

———. 1986. "Technology Adoption in the Presence of Network Externalities." *International Social Science Journal* 51 (1).

Kopstein, Jeffrey, and David Reilly. 2000. "Geographic Diffusion and the Transformation of the Postcommunist World." *World Politics* 53:1–37.

Lipset, Seymour Martin. 1959. "Some Social Requisites of Democracy: Economic Development and Political Legitimacy." *American Political Science Review* 53:69–104.

Lupia, Arthur, and Mathew D. McCubbins. 1998. *The Democratic Dilemma: Can Citizens Learn What They Need to Know?* Cambridge: Cambridge University Press.

Markoff, John. 1996. *Waves of Democracy: Social Movements and Political Change.* Thousand Oaks, Calif.: Pine Forge.

Merton, Robert K. 1968. *Social Theory and Social Structure.* New York: Free Press.

Milgram, Stanley. 1975. *Obedience to Authority : An Experimental View.* New York: Harper.

Mizruchi, Mark S. 1989. "Similarity of Political Behavior among Large American Corporations." *American Journal of Sociology* 95 (2): 401–24.

Moore, Barrington. 1966. *Social Origins of Dictatorship and Democracy: Lord and Peasant in the Making of the Modern World.* Boston: Beacon.

O'Loughlin, John, Michael D. Ward, Corey L. Lofdahl, Jordin S. Cohen, David S. Brown, David Reilly, Kristian S. Gleditsch, and Michael Shin. 1998. "The Diffusion of Democracy, 1946–1994." *Annals of the Association of American Geographers* 88 (4): 545–574.

Rogers, Everett M. 1995. *The Diffusion of Innovations.* New York: Free Press.

Rosenau, James N. 1988. "Patterned Chaos in Global Life: Structure and Process in the Two Worlds of World Politics." *International Political Science Review* 9 (4): 327–64.

———. 1990. *Turbulence in World Politics: A Theory of Change and Continuity.* Princeton, N.J.: Princeton University Press.

Russett, Bruce. 2004. "A Fourth Wave? The Role of International Actors in Democratization." Paper presented at the University of Illinois Centennial, Urbana.

Schelling, Thomas C. 1978. *Micromotives and Macrobehavior.* New York: Norton.

Simmons, Beth. A., and Zachary Elkins. 2004. "The Globalization of Liberalization: Policy Diffusion in the International Political Economy." *American Political Science Review* 98 (1): 171–89.

Siverson, Randall, and Harvey Starr. 1991. *The Diffusion of War: A Study of Opportunity and Willingness.* Ann Arbor: University of Michigan Press.

Starr, Harvey. 1991. "Democratic Dominoes: Diffusion Approaches to the Spread of Democracy in the International System." *Journal of Conflict Resolution* 35 (2): 356–81.

Walker, Jack L. 1969. "The Diffusion of Innovation among American States." *American Political Science Review* 63:880–99.

Westney, D. Eleanor. 1987. *Imitation and Innovation: The Transfer of Western Organizational Patterns to Meiji Japan.* Cambridge, Mass.: Harvard University Press.

Weyland, Kurt Gerhard. 2004. *Learning from Foreign Models in Latin American Policy Reform.* Washington, D.C.: Woodrow Wilson Center.

Whitehead, Laurence. 1986. "International Aspects of Democratization." In *Transitions from Authoritarian Rule: Comparative Perspectives,* ed. G. O'Donnell, P. Schmitter, and L. Whitehead. Baltimore: Johns Hopkins University Press.

———. 2001. *The International Dimensions of Democratization.* Oxford: Oxford University Press

4

A Fourth Wave?

The Role of International Actors in Democratization

BRUCE RUSSETT

The "third wave" of democratization (Huntington 1991) may have begun to crest in the mid 1990s, but it certainly has not ebbed. In 1995, Freedom House rated the world's countries as 40 percent free, 32 percent partly free, and 28 percent not free on political and civil liberties. In 2005, the respective groupings were 46 percent free, 30 percent partly free, and 24 percent not free. The proportionate increase in free countries thus came from both the partly free and not free categories. Similarly, using Freedom House's somewhat generous definition of "electoral democracy" (free elections, though perhaps with some irregularities and substantial deficiencies in civil liberties), the percentage of the world's countries that met that definition went from 61 percent to 64 percent.[1]

By the more reliable but slightly less current Polity IV ratings, the proportion of democracies showed a clear uptick from 1995 to 2006, while that of autocracies fell markedly and the middle category of anocracies remained about constant. This is shown in Figure 4.1, which depicts the number of governments in each category. Going back to 1946, the number of democracies and autocracies was twenty for each; by 2006 the number of democracies had risen to more than ninety, while that for autocracies dropped to about twenty-five. The number of anocracies went from thirty to just over forty. Almost all the new democracies are low- or middle-income countries.

The upward slope at the right edge of Figure 4.1 may mark the start of a fourth wave, though we cannot yet know. Some countries have recently gone down (e.g., Russia) or essentially sideways (Nigeria) but nevertheless are less autocratic than they had been earlier. More states have improved

Figure 4.1 Global trends in governance, 1946–2006

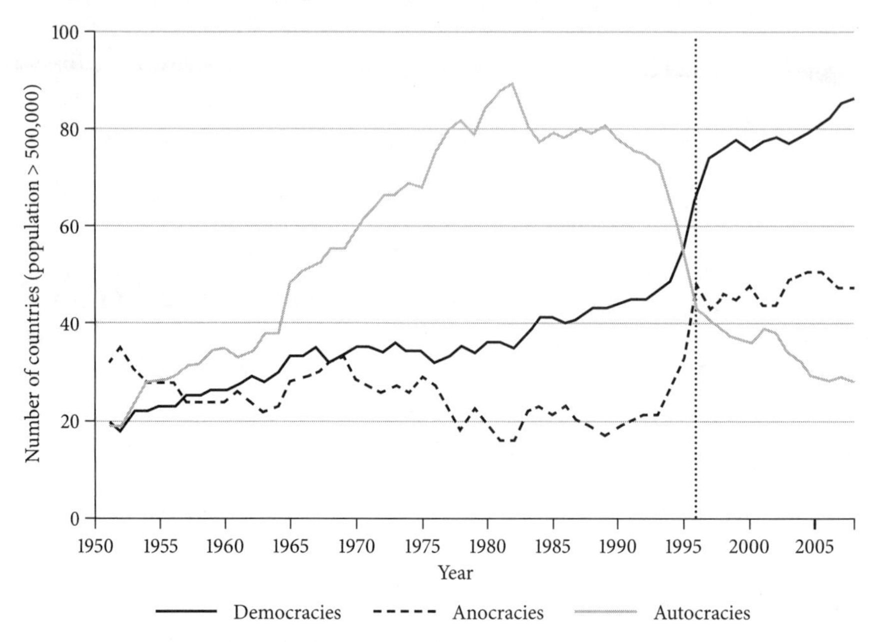

Source: University of Maryland, Center for International Development and Conflict Management

their rankings, sometimes dramatically though maybe not permanently, as in the case of Ukraine. Developments in Indonesia, a very populous country, are especially encouraging, as most of its population is Islamic. So the base for a fourth wave exists and may ripple upward. Thus, I explore two broad questions pertinent to democratization and its possible fourth wave: To what degree can international influences be credited with the success of the past decades? If international influences have been effectual, what are they and how might they be strengthened in the coming decades?

My emphasis on international influences is somewhat unusual because it has long been common in comparative politics writing (e.g., O'Donnell, Schmitter, and Whitehead 1986; Diamond, Linz, and Lipset 1989; Huntington 1991) to give greater credit to domestic than international influences for the success of democracy. While the former probably do predominate overall, a strong case can be made that in particular instances international influences are important, and sometimes critical. But broad generalizations about the relative influence of domestic and international influences on democratization and its consolidation are dangerous and should be made cautiously. Transition and consolidation are, of course, two separate phenomena, and they do not necessarily respond to the same influences. Generalization is further complicated by the complexity of external influences, which range from those attributable primarily to the actions of states, to intergovernmental organizations (IGOs), and to international nongovernmental organizations (INGOs). Moreover, the success of international support and intervention depends on the goals, skill, and resources applied by the external actor, as well as conditions internal to the transitional state. Domestic politics in the intervening power also are relevant, both for the initial intervention decision and for the stamina often required for ultimate success.

In this chapter I first discuss the role of international military interventions in seeding new democracies, differentiating between military actions initiated by states' actions and those initiated by IGOs. I then discuss nonmilitary actions by IGOs.[2] I first review the types of activities that IGOs have engaged in to support democratization and its consolidation. Then I introduce a principal-agent framework to help us understand the ways in which IGOs can affect the democratization process. I conclude that successful democratization results more from peaceful example and incentives than from external force, and that IGOs often play a key role in the fourth wave.

Figure 4.2 reports the growth in memberships within international organizations (IGOs) since 1885.[3] This information gives some historical perspective to the discussions that follow. The numbers in Figure 4.2 are based on memberships in organizations whose members are recognized states in the international system; included here are global and regional organizations as well as general purpose and functional organizations. Note that these data are not for the simple number of IGO memberships. Rather, they reflect the number of dyadic IGO memberships (i.e., the number of IGO memberships held in common by all pairs of states in the international system). These data demonstrate that there has been an approximate doubling of these dyadic memberships since 1945. This reflects both a large increase in the absolute number of IGOs and the fact that individual states are increasingly enmeshed into a dense multi-organizational network of institutions. Many of these institutions have expanded greatly—not only in number of members, but also in the scope and efficacy of their powers. The European Union is the exemplar organization here. While other international organizations (like the UN, the WTO, and many regional organizations) have also expanded their powers, these expansions have not matched those of the EU.

Figure 4.2 Shared intergovernmental organization memberships, 1885–2000

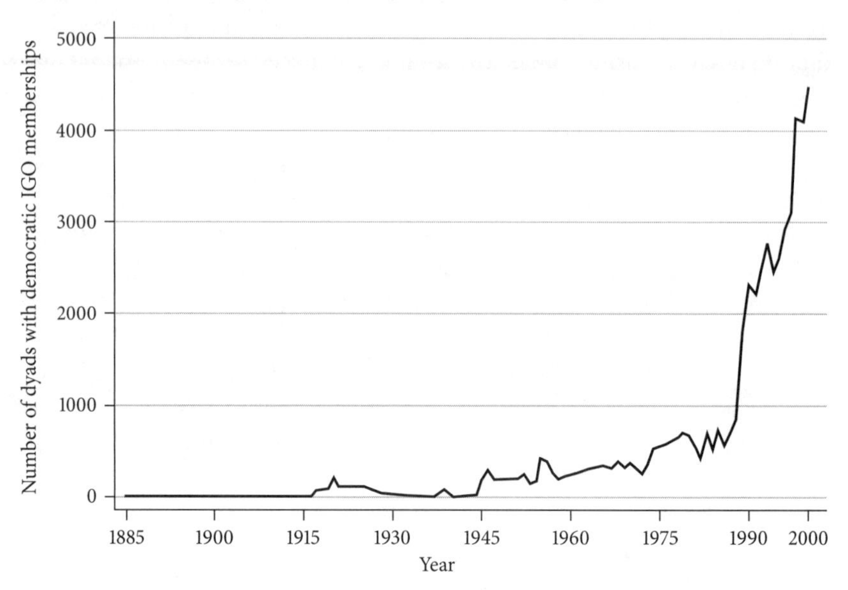

Democracy Imposed by External Military Force: National Intervention

The most controversial model for external intervention is that of regime change by "fight them, beat them, and make them democratic." It is controversial not only in theory, but because certain very prominent examples are invoked on both sides of the argument. One side cites the post –World War II experience of the Allied forces in Germany, and of the United States in Japan. Their goal at the beginning of the war was one of avoiding defeat, not regime change per se. But as early as the Atlantic Charter in August 1941, and before the United States was actually at war, Churchill and Roosevelt declared that their vision of peace in a postwar world included self-government for all peoples (Dallek 1979: 285). Certainly their postwar policy was built on the principle that the former German and Japanese governments could never have been peaceful, and that democratization of their systems was essential. To this end they devoted enormous material and intellectual resources. Their success served as an exemplar to those in the Bush administration who hoped to achieve a similar result in Iraq.

The difficulty, as is so often the case when making policy by analogy, was that Germany and Japan were poor analogues. Not only had the Allies been willing and able to carry on a long occupation and provide massive economic assistance, Germany and Japan met most of the conditions for successful transitions and consolidation that political analysis has since identified.[4] In Iraq, the negative influences included many of those most prominent in the literature of comparative politics, including low per capita income (at least after years of wars and sanctions), no previous history of democracy, the "resource curse" of a society dependent on petroleum exports (which allow dictators to keep themselves wealthy and in power), and the alleged authoritarian character of Islamic and especially Arab culture (Fish 2002).[5] This is a simple, short list, but Iraq also falls short on many other domestic factors commonly cited in the comparative politics literature on democratic transitions. Also working against democratization in Iraq: its geographic situation at the center of a neighborhood populated largely by dictatorships who do not wish democracy well, and its history of militarization and violent international conflict (Donno and Russett 2004). So it was a hard case from the start, even had the postinvasion occupation and reconstruction not been bungled—executed on the cheap and with stunning incompetence (Diamond 2004). Carothers's (1999: 351) earlier warning should have been heeded: "The limitations of democracy promotion . . . are still there in best-case situations where a peaceful, stable country is attempting democratization and is open to influence from the outside. Even military intervention—a tool useful only in a narrow range of circumstances—is no guarantee of democratic results. Interventions only sometimes get rid of the dictators they are directed against. Even when a full-scale invasion is mounted to ensure that the strongman is ousted, the underlying political pathologies are difficult to heal."

Sometimes there may be little choice—a need to remove a government that is a threat to international peace, or for humanitarian interests when a government is viciously oppressing many or most of its own people. Democratization should be a key piece in the consequent responsibility to put the defeated country back together again, with a decent government. But that is quite different from imposing democracy when truly vital national or humanitarian interests are not at stake. As a general principle it is full of practical and moral dangers, depending on many conditions, including highly unpredictable contingencies, and not to be undertaken as the purpose in a war of choice (Russett 1993: 134; Russett and Oneal 2001: 303). Immanuel Kant ([1797] 1970: 168–70) would agree.

I will not address the overall ethical question of whether or when regime change in a sovereign state should be engineered by force, but instead I concentrate on the empirical question of when it may have a good chance of success. To think about the utility of war in establishing democracy in the twenty-first century, the history of the previous century—carefully analyzed with appropriate theory—provides the best evidence available. If the odds of success are bad from the start, much of the empirical part that needs to go into a moral calculus is already available. The following survey is necessarily done in a broad sweep, and the research cited is illustrative but neither conclusive nor exhaustive.

One important study (Dobbins et al. 2003) was published only after the U.S. occupation of Iraq had begun, but because the work started at RAND in 1993, people in the American government must have known about it prior to the invasion. It looks at seven previous U.S. efforts of nation building and democratization, of which Germany and Japan were the only clear successes. The authors state that while political culture and level of development helped, the keys to success were substantial, sustained financial assistance and military presence. They credit Bosnia and Kosovo as moderate successes, with more modest economic and military capacity that nonetheless continued for more than five years. Efforts in Somalia and Haiti failed, with weak and fleeting commitments. While the Afghanistan effort was still much too recent to judge the outcome, the authors found both the financial and military commitments to be the lowest of all, and hardly promising. By their criteria Iraq falls far closer to the failures than to the successes.

A study of ninety United States interventions from 1898 to 1992 found that in only two instances did a democratic government become nondemocratic, whereas fourteen became democratic in the year after the intervention—and almost all remained democratic ten years later (Peceny 1999: 195). This implies some success, but in the vast majority (85 percent) of interventions, democracy building was not part of the agenda. More relevant is what happened following those interventions wherein political liberalization was one of the explicit goals of the intervention. Of the fourteen countries that did become democratic, thirteen were ones in which the United States "actively supported pro-liberalization policies." Democratization failed in six other cases where it started as an American goal but was abandoned by the end of the intervention (South Vietnam is an example), and in ten instances even a sustained liberalization project failed. So the count is thirteen successes for a policy of democratization, and sixteen failures. When democratization was not an explicit goal, it virtually never happened.[6]

A more recent study (Peceny and Pickering 2006) distinguishes among United States, British, and French interventions between 1946 and 1996, with a further distinction between friendly interventions intended to prop up a favored local government, and hostile interventions to produce regime change. British intervention, whether supportive or hostile, never produced political liberalization, and indeed often resulted in less democratic governments. French interventions were usually in support of endangered and undemocratic clients, though some of the later actions produced more liberal governments, notably in Comoros, when in 1989 French troops ousted a French mercenary who had led a coup, and democratic elections followed shortly. As with the other powers, U.S. supportive interventions had no systematic effect, but unlike the others, three U.S. hostile interventions in this period produced some liberalization. Of those three, however, only the 1989 intervention in Panama had long-term effects. United Nations peacekeeping interventions had the best record of success in democratization.

Selection effects are probably at work here as in other studies. That is, democratization may have been tried largely in cases that were more promising in terms of the comparative politics criteria, or the success of intervention may have been affected by U.S. domestic politics. Nevertheless, two relevant influences are that: (1) states with no previous experience of democracy were less likely to become democratic after intervention, and (2) states that experienced a civil war, either before or after the intervention, were much less likely to democratize. Moreover, and related to the civil war problem, when the United States made a major push to strengthen the country's military establishment, democratization often failed (Peceny 1999: 212–16). Democracy and militarization make bad barracks-mates.

Another study (Tures 2005) confirms no systematic effect on the likelihood that a more democratic state will emerge. This study reports on 228 U.S. "military operations," including a wide range of actions covering war, peacekeeping, humanitarian missions, interdiction, border control, and military training. In 42 percent of the cases there was no change in the target country's political regime; in 30 percent it became less democratic, in 28 percent more democratic.

An even more recent analysis (Bueno de Mesquita and Downs 2006) starts with the premise that democratic leaders will, in committing resources to transforming other countries' governing structures, be influenced more by the policy interests of their own domestic constituents than by possible democratic aspirations abroad. Thus they will be unlikely to sustain a long and expensive commitment, especially in instances where a truly democratic government in another state would be likely to pursue foreign policy goals that conflict with those of the intervening state. In looking at the impact of military interventions during the period 1946–2001, the authors find that by ten years after an intervention by a democratic state, the average effect was actually a lower level of democracy in the target country, except for a modest average increase where the initial form of government was extremely authoritarian.

Two other analyses (Enterline and Grieg 2006; Enterline, Grieg, and Miller 2006) deserve attention. They ask whether and why externally imposed political regimes are likely to be stable (i.e., free from large-scale violent or other major illegal challenges directed toward the government). They examine sixty imposed polities—some of democratic systems, others autocratic—over the period 1815–1994. They find that imposed democratic systems are more likely to be stable than autocratic ones, but with many important qualifications. The chances of a democracy being unstable are greater with recent experience of an armed internal challenge; a high degree of militarization (which diverts resources from satisfying civilian needs and may degrade the system's legitimacy); the country's degree of ethnic diversity; only a short-term presence by the imposing state; the experience of war with another state; and when neighboring regimes are not democratic. They then apply their results to predict the likelihood that the imposed regimes in Afghanistan and Iraq will be stable. The results are not encouraging. On the basis of reasonable assumptions, even including a continuing supportive foreign military presence, they forecast a 60–70 percent chance that democratic Afghan and Iraqi governments will still face major political challenge in 2008 and 2009. The likelihood they will last more than a total of six years is under 30 percent. Perhaps surprisingly, democratic governments are less likely to be stable than autocratic ones.[7]

One more study by these authors (Enterline and Grieg 2005) asks whether externally imposed democratic regimes serve as effective "beacons" to create politically desirable outcomes in neighboring countries. They look at twenty-seven cases from the twentieth century, distinguishing between "bright and "dim" democratic beacons. The former are states that score in the clearly democratic end (+7 or higher) of Polity's −10 to +10 scale, and the latter are those from +1 to +6. The bright beacons do not seem to increase regional democratization, but they do seem to contribute to regional prosperity. Dim beacons undermine both democracy and prosperity in their neighborhoods. Iraq has a long way to go to be a bright beacon.

All this does not mean that democratization by forcible intervention cannot work. It sometimes does, but no systematic analysis of the costs and benefits—or even just the costs—has ever been done. By these and other evaluations the prospects of success in Iraq are miserable, and at best we will not know for at least another decade whether a stable and/or democratic regime can emerge. The probabilities and costs of failure, as in a protracted civil war and incubator of terrorism in Iraq, are huge. This review suggests why the American effort was at best unpromising even before its flawed execution.

Military Intervention by IGOs

Military intervention by the United States was more likely to target democratization as a goal, and achieve its objective, since World War II than before. UN military intervention in civil wars and failed states has been largely a phenomenon of the post –cold-war years and has coincided with an explicit commitment to promoting democracy (Boutros-Ghali 1992, 1996). Democracies have contributed personnel to UN operations in disproportionate numbers (Lebovic 2004).

Simplistic views of UN peacekeeping efforts emphasize the failures and ignore many of the successes. Traditional UN peacekeeping, largely evolved to mitigate international conflicts (as between India and Pakistan in Kashmir, or between Israel and its neighbors), was almost exclusively an impartial operation designed chiefly to separate warring parties. These interventions were contingent on the mutual consent of the warring parties and limited to lightly armed forces authorized to shoot only in self-defense. But the end of the cold war lifted the lid on many civil conflicts. This led UN practice, and then its doctrine, to evolve into more muscular forms of peacekeeping. Sometimes termed peace enforcement, these efforts were designed to vigorously resist efforts to interfere with the UN's humanitarian mission (Boutros-Ghali 1992) while still not taking a partisan position between the parties. These more muscular efforts, in turn, led to a greater willingness to intervene in an overtly partisan fashion to prevent one side from conducting massive ethnic cleansing and/or committing other major human rights violations.

Such vigorous interventions inevitably led to major efforts to build a peace by helping to actively disarm the participants and put together the pieces of the warring country. Then peacekeeping expands into peace building: setting up multidimensional operations, with programs for the reconstruction and development of the economy; disarming and resettling former fighters from both sides; constructing or reconstructing civil administration and a legal system; instituting an open and reasonably honest electoral process; building new political parties capable of competing in elections; securing the conditions for free political expression; and making an effort to bring some reconciliation to hostile factions. If there is some peace enforcement, it should not favor a particular party in principle, but it should prevent violent efforts by any party to break the peace agreements. Nearly all of these activities in reasonably successful UN peace-building initiatives have included democratization as a goal (Russett and Oneal 2001: 200–211; also Kumar 2002). This is true whether the UN has acted alone or with other IGOs and INGOs.

All UN peace-building operations require a clear and appropriate mandate (authority to act) from the UN Security Council, and sufficient human and material capabilities. Achieving a sustainable peace requires matching the right level and kind of international capacities to the degree of destruction and political hostility resulting from the war. The weaker the economic capacity of the war-torn state, the greater the international economic assistance must be. Promoting economic development is necessary for successful democratization as well as peacebuilding. An international organization like the UN is often regarded as more legitimate than a single outside country whose intentions and real interests may be mistrusted by large parts of the population.

Some peace-building efforts try to achieve too much, with rapid liberalization of state, society, and economy. One view (Barnett 2006; Paris 2004) is that it is better to concentrate on building state institutions regarded as legitimate and therefore stable and equipped to govern effectively. By this view, early elections and establishment of free markets can be undesirable because they limit state power. Yet this recommendation can become a rather vague appeal for respecting local views and accepting a coercive state authority. Certainly there are examples in which democratization failed, but the balance of evidence from many examples does not support the claim that democratization generally works against stable peace. It is essential to look behind the generalizations to specific examples to see the often very different initial conditions in various countries and the very different strategies and capabilities of the peace builders.

Some of the best examples of multidimensional peace building by the United Nations have been in Namibia, Cambodia, El Salvador, and Mozambique. Namibia was the first, following a deeply internationalized civil war. The experience of Khmer Rouge genocide has been lifted from Cambodia, and while its government is not very democratic (only +2 on the Polity scale), it has been stable and generally regarded as legitimate. But peace building for Cambodia in the early 1990s was not cheap: it cost nearly two billion dollars. El Salvador and Mozambique had two of the peace-building efforts that ranged most broadly across the spectrum of political and economic reform. Rwanda exemplifies perhaps the greatest failure of all the UN efforts in the 1990s: it was a poor, failed state, riven by ethnic hatreds, and the UN's response, abetted by the great powers' unwillingness to do more, was much too little and much too late as a peace-enforcing enterprise and never developed into a real peace-building mission (Barnett 2002).

Generally the UN has developed a record of substantial achievement, especially as it and associated IGOs and INGOs learned over time from their mistakes as well as their successes. Doyle and Sambanis (2006; also see Fortna 2004) offer a sophisticated and exhaustive analysis particularly sensitive to selection effects. They find that multidimensional operations by the UN usually are successful in keeping the peace and establishing reasonably democratic regimes for about two to five years from initiation of the operation. After that, there remains some residual beneficial effect. But unexpected shocks, like aggression by a neighboring country, collapse of an international commodity market, or a severe natural disaster may disrupt the established order. International assistance may be insufficient, or may not last long enough.[8] But the UN's record would seem to be pretty good, and it is superior to similar efforts mounted solely by single countries or regional organizations or coalitions. And in joint operations, UN involvement strengthens the effect of the non-UN actors. This too provides an interesting reflection on the U.S. experience in Iraq, where neither NATO nor the UN has been eager to risk soldiers or civilians in a unilateralist peace-building operation controlled by the United States.

Nonmilitary Interventions by IGOs in Support of Democratization

As the mention of multidimensional interventions by the UN suggests, an emphasis on military actions cannot do justice to all the ways in which international organizations foster democratization. The concern among many IGOs with democracy is a reflection of the desires of their member states. Democracies have vested interests in having stable democratic neighbors. Fellow democracies are likely to provide larger and more reliable markets, to be more politically stable and less likely to fight their democratic neighbors, and to avoid human rights abuses and civil wars with consequent cross-border spillovers of refugees. Democratic neighbors are also more apt to form a mutual protection society against unconstitutional usurpation of powers at home, as well as join in collective security endeavors against common external foes. Many regional international organizations are formed among neighbors largely for these purposes. Those IGOs composed mostly or exclusively of democratic governments are especially likely to pursue these goals, and to do so successfully. Since the demise of the Soviet Union, even the United Nations, which still includes many dictatorships, has been able and willing to take on tasks of democracy promotion.

The distinction between democratic transition and consolidation is relevant here. In addition to their multidimensional efforts, the UN, the EU, and the OAS all have substantial experience in monitoring, supervising, and legitimizing free elections. Because the end of the cold war made it possible for the UN to support democracy in its member states, its Electoral Assistance Division has done so in ninety-three countries.[9] Many of those, though not a majority, have followed civil conflicts. The history of OAS election monitoring goes back to a small mission requested by Costa Rica in 1962 (Santa-Cruz 2005). In 1990 the OAS formed its Unit for the Promotion of Democracy to serve that purpose on a regular basis. IGOs go in, with substantial assistance from INGOs (Sikkink 1993), to help those who want to contest democratic elections rather than fight. If the IGOs determine the election is reasonably fair, they give legitimacy to the winner, whether that winner is the government or the opposition.

Conversely, an international organization's refusal to monitor an election—because they do not think the election really will be fair or because they cannot gain proper access to know what is actually occurring—can deprive a dictator of a seal of approval that he seeks by permitting some kind of election. In addition, if external groups monitor the election and conclude it was unfair, their judgment can deny legitimacy to a government seeking international acceptance. Thus, IGO election activities become highly important in facilitating democratic transitions under circumstances where many domestic groups desire it, or in situations where the government decides, perhaps reluctantly, that it needs external validation for an election it feels compelled to hold. Sometimes governments are unpleasantly surprised at the outcome of these elections, as happened to the Sandinista regime in Nicaragua. The need for international certification is why UN monitoring of the recent election in Iraq was so important, and why its difficulty in doing so convincingly, because of concern about the ability of Iraqi and U.S. forces to assure basic physical security to civilian observers, was costly.

International organizations' activities are not limited to post–civil war situations. The UN and other IGOs can also help to isolate and eventually remove a dictator who seizes power from a democratically elected government. This eventually happened in Haiti, and the OAS played a major role in preventing or promptly reversing military coups against the elected governments of Paraguay (1996), Ecuador (2000), and Venezuela (2002). Both the OAS and other regional organizations like the EU have the ability to levy severe economic and political sanctions (such as suspension of membership or the approval of military intervention by member states) after such a seizure of power.[10] The June 1991 Santiago Commitment to "defense and promotion of representative democracy and human rights . . . and respect for the principles of self-determination and non-intervention" made the OAS an important signaler of legitimacy for new governments. For many Latin American governments the greatest military threat has been from within rather than from neighboring states. Thus, the major subregional organization in Latin America—MERCOSUR, initially consisting of Argentina, Brazil, Uruguay, and Paraguay—was formed in large part to provide means for new democratically elected presidents to control their militaries more effectively. They were able to open up each other's markets and reduce the size of their military establishments under conditions of peaceful international relations. MERCOSUR's charter has a clause that requires its member countries to be democratic.

Not surprisingly, the OAS has trouble reconciling its commitment to democracy with its respect for its members' national sovereignty and a reluctance to intervene when antidemocratic acts are committed by a leader who first gained power in a free election. Legitimizing or strengthening democracies, or resisting a military coup, is easier than restraining accretion of power by a leader who, though more or less democratically elected, later seeks to consolidate his power as a dictator. In 1992, for example, the popularly elected president of Peru, Alberto Fujimori, conducted an autogolpe (self-coup) by suspending the constitution with a state of emergency and dissolving Peru's congress and many of the nation's courts. The OAS issued a declaration "deploring" his action. But because Fujimori was a popular president of a country under severe stress (with runaway inflation and a major civil insurgency), other leaders had considerable sympathy for him and did not sanction his government. Fujimori compromised by promising a plebiscite on a new constitution and new elections. The OAS agreed to monitor the elections, effectively granting legitimacy to the change in Peru's political order. In Venezuela, the attempted 2002 military coup against president Hugo Chavez failed quickly, but regional efforts to restrain his unconstitutional consolidation of executive power proved far more difficult to mount. Coups against democratic leaders constitute a threat by example to the leaders of other OAS states; autogolpes do not. In another case, the attempted 1993 autogolpe by democratically elected Guatemalan president Alberto Serrano was widely resisted within Guatemala and condemned by many Latin American governments. The OAS deplored the coup, but it did not play a central role in the coup's prompt collapse.

Understanding the Nonmilitary Effects of IGOs on Democratization

The manner in which international military interventions affect democratization is readily observable and relatively straightforward. The way in which nonmilitary interventions by IGOs influence democratization is not. And facts do not speak for themselves—they require theory to provide interpretation and explanation. Among the social science theories available for helping us understand the interactions among IGOs and nation-states, principal-agent models seem particularly appropriate. They can offer explanations of how IGOs constrain or empower domestic political actors who support democratization, and in turn how domestic actors can use IGOs for their purposes.

Good micromodels of domestic-international behavior have been developed for international relations only within the past fifteen years or so, and their applications to IGO activity are even less well developed. Thus, a substantial research program is needed to fully develop the potential of principal-agent models in helping us identify and understand the microlevel factors that drive the macrolevel effects such as democratization. Nevertheless, there is some work on IGO-domestic politics interactions to build upon. Micro-level theory and evidence are especially relevant to any effort to distinguish the causes of democracies clustering in particular geographic regions. As Zachary Elkins notes in chapter 3 of this book, causal mechanisms may include common internal conditions (as emphasized by comparative politics scholars); independent, uncoordinated actions that arise through processes such as emulation and learning; and actions coordinated externally by a group of countries, a globally or regionally hegemonic power, or international organizations—the subject of this chapter.

As Ikenberry (2001) reminds us (see also Beth Simmons, chapter 8), nearly all of the large global IGOs and many of the important regional ones were established by democracies. For about twenty-five years the OAS membership has consisted primarily of democratic states. Its experience illustrates some reasons democracies cluster geographically. Figure 4.3 modifies the information in Figure 4.2 to show the overall growth in the number of those IGOs whose members are mostly democracies. That growth took off only in 1990, increasing fivefold over the 1989 level. Joining and subsequent membership in regional international organizations composed largely of democratic countries reinforce both democratic transitions and the stability of democracies. The greater the proportion of stable democratic states in the IGO, the more credible its guarantees of assistance, the more interested it will be in promoting reforms, the more likely it will set constraining conditions, and the more likely it will enforce them. Thus these IGOs have the capacity to change the cost-benefit perceptions of domestic elites who may not be enthusiastic about democracy.

They can, for example, provide some guarantees of property rights for business and help socialize the military not to interfere in the democratic process. Particularly influential in changing the cost-benefit calculations of reluctant domestic elites are IGOs with serious economic assets to deploy as carrots for inducing attitudinal and behavioral changes. Consider the European Union and its effect on Turkey. Membership in the EU brings many economic benefits, and Turkey has sought to become a member of the EU

Figure 4.3 Shared memberships in densely democratic IGOs, 1885–2000

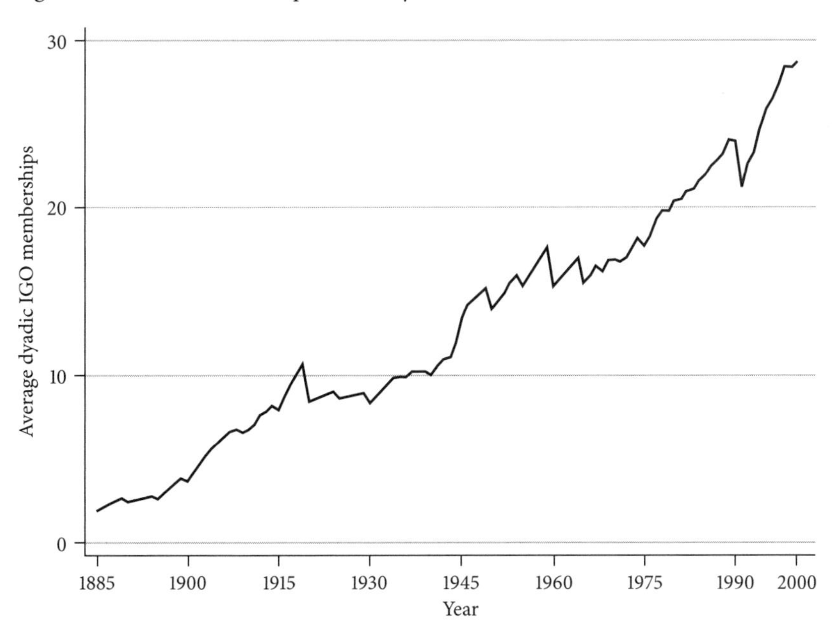

for decades. In order to comply with the stringent governance criteria the EU has established, the Turkish government has worked hard to improve its democratic structures and human rights record (Phillips 2004). Democratic IGOs can also make continued membership conditional on continued democracy. NATO now has such a condition. Though in the past NATO did not eject Greece or Turkey when their governments turned autocratic, its threat is more credible with the end of cold-war rivalries that dictators could use to their advantage.

If the threat to punish backsliders is credible, it induces regime leaders to keep their commitments to govern democratically. Moreover, IGOs can become as much an instrument of domestic democracy advocates as those advocates are instruments of IGOs. And this can be extremely important for domestic elites who require credible external support to continue their advocacy of democracy.[11] Thus, newly democratizing states are especially likely to join IGOs composed largely of democratic states, and largely democratic IGOs support democratic transitions and consolidations in their members.[12] The commitment of regime leaders to comply with costly IGO conditionalities on governance structures sends a useful signal of their wish for stable cooperative relations (Lipson 2003).

International organizations that make economic integration among their members a primary goal can be particularly effective as external agents for empowering domestic democracy advocates and stabilizing newly democratic regimes. International trade, as well as external investment and the free movement of persons, carries two kinds of influences (Russett and Oneal 2001: ch. 4). First, a nation's goods and services, and the processes by which they are exported, serve as a carrier of ideas, and basic ideas about desirable forms of political and economic institutions may be deeply embedded in the interactions among trading partners. The role of global commerce in spreading Western values, in ways not necessarily intended by sender or recipient, is well-recognized, whether by applause or by derision as "coca-colonization." Second, commercial exchanges create continuing economic interests in access to buyers and sellers of desired goods and services. To the degree that trade benefits consumers and producers broadly throughout a society, its beneficiaries have a stake in the continuation of commerce and in the reliability of institutions that provide continuity.[13]

Most human rights agreements have proved very difficult to enforce, and regimes with little regard for human rights may sign them because the agreements lack institutional "teeth" (Hathaway 2002). But outside the well-known human rights conventions and other agreements is a class of treaties devoted primarily to fostering economic integration. Preferential trade agreements often have human rights provisions. These agreements have been most effective in reducing violent repression when they incorporate "hard" rather than "soft" enforcement mechanisms (i.e., the ability to terminate trade agreements and impose sanctions on repressive member states, rather than mere verbal standards that do not affect membership or market access). Hard enforcement mechanisms empower human rights advocates and coerce elites who would otherwise practice repression. The Lomé treaties between the EU and states in Africa and Latin America usually have such provisions. Indeed, the Lomé Commission halted benefits after the 1994 Rwanda genocide, forcing the Rwandan army to prosecute some war criminals (Hafner-Burton 2005).

The EU has always had a commitment to democracy and, unlike NATO, it has never had a nondemocratic member. Democracy was a condition for membership in article 237 of the Treaty of Rome that began the integration process in 1950; that commitment was strengthened by the European Parliament in 1962, declaring that to join, states must guarantee "truly democratic practices and respect for fundamental rights and freedoms." After the Greek military coup in 1967 the European Commission suspended its association treaty with Greece and threatened to cancel the agreement entirely. As nearly half of Greece's total trade was with the EU, the damage to the Greek economy was widespread and its effects were felt across the political spectrum. Even the junta's conservative supporters began to desert it, contributing to the restoration of democracy in 1974. Rapid defeat of a 1981 coup attempt in newly democratic Spain was assisted by concern in the business community that backsliding would jeopardize their goal of entry into the EU. The democratization process in the Czech Republic, Hungary, and Poland was far advanced by the time their applications to join the EU were considered, but for later entrants the EU's democracy condition probably had a larger effect. Internal forces producing the reversal in 1998 of Vladimir Meciar's movement toward consolidating a one-party dictatorship in Slovakia were strengthened by the European Commission's highly critical report on the situation.

If being densely democratic gives an IGO a willingness to promote democratization, wealth gives it the capability to do so. The EU, populated exclusively by democracies, has enormous resources available for the economic development of its less prosperous members. Its combination of carrots and sticks can deeply affect many constituencies in candidate states. It is surely the most powerful international institution in this respect. Free-trade agreements among non-European states lack such strong incentives and resources, but many now typically require a commitment to democracy by their members.

MERCOSUR, mentioned above, is probably the most effective. Other trading groups in the Western hemisphere (CARICOM in Central America, and the Andean Pact) and Africa also require a commitment to democracy, but their lesser economic resources and members' less established commitment to democracy raise questions about their impact on domestic politics.[14]

One of the principal functions of an IGO is to provide greater flows of information to its members. This means fostering transparency and the conditions to enable credible commitments between members and with the IGO itself, thereby facilitating agreements (Martin 2000). For example, participation in NATO established strong ties among member states' defense and foreign policy bureaucracies, to the degree that they often cooperated with one another against elements of their own governments (Risse-Kappen 1995). This may be especially important to newly democratized countries. Countries receiving greater levels of information flows from IGOs, and increases in those information flows, are more likely to adopt laws supporting domestic government transparency.[15] It is likely that IGOs comprised largely of democratic states have a stronger effect than others.

A Fourth Wave? Go with the Flow

Since 1815, democracies have won nearly 80 percent of their wars. The reasons for their success may include superior organizational effectiveness and leadership (Reiter and Stam 2002), good civil-military relations (Biddle and Long 2004), and an ability to mobilize resources with their citizens' consent (Bueno de Mesquita, Smith, Morrow, and Siverson 2003). Also, because democratic leaders are easier to remove from office in the wake of military defeat, democratic nations seem to choose their wars more wisely than do dictatorships (though exceptions readily come to mind). Whatever the cause of democracies' success in wars, some analysts view their military success against dictatorships as a major factor in spreading democracy (Mitchell, Gates, and Hegre 1999). If this is a valid inference from the data on military conflicts, it must be noted that military actions have also produced many failed democracies. And the successes have been immensely expensive in lives and treasure. Moreover, military interventions are hardly the only international factor driving the democratic waves of the past sixty years.

Democracy has more than that going for it, especially the relative economic success of democracies. That success surely fed heavily into the loss of legitimacy of communism that produced the end of the cold war. On average, democracies may not show higher economic growth rates than dictatorships, but there is less variance. As well, the long-term experience of democracy does seem to produce better growth (Gerring, Bond, Barndt, and Moreno 2005). For every dictatorship like China and Singapore that succeeded in producing rapid growth, there are more like Mobutu's Congo or Hussein's Iraq. Most dictators have concluded that their interest is best served by a reliable system to skim off the rents for their personal enrichment and for rewarding the narrow coterie of cronies and security forces they need to stay in power. The people can eat grass so long as they can be repressed. But democratic states promote growth by being more politically stable, educating their population better, providing more stable social spending, and having more equally distributed incomes (Feng 2003; Brown and Hunter 1999; Ghobarah, Huth, and Russett 2004; Siegle, Weinstein, and Halperin 2004). The ability of most democracies to produce relatively steady and widely spread growth over time allows those democratic states that have reached a reasonable level of economic development to remain democratic (Przeworski, Alvarez, Cheibub, and Limongi 2000), and to serve as strong examples in an increasingly globalized and transparent world.

Furthermore, democracy thrives best in countries where peoples and governments do not see themselves as under a major external security threat: war and threats of war strain democratic liberties. Democracy is contagious. There appears to be an evolutionary process whereby the percentage of democracies in the system grows, often by regional clusters (Cederman 2001, Cederman and Rao 2001). Democracies are at peace with one another and are helped to remain so by membership in IGOs comprised mostly of democracies. Those institutions mediate disputes, help members to make credible commitments, and socialize members to peaceful settlement (Pevehouse and Russett 2006). Democracies tend to spend less of their GDP on the military (Fordham and Walker 2005). Democratic states with democratic neighbors are more stable and feel less threatened than do those with dictatorships on their borders. Democratization is more likely to succeed in a democratic neighborhood, partly through policies of collective security (Maoz 1996; Gleditsch 2002; Kadera, Crescenzi, and Shannon 2003; Starr and Lindborg 2003; Cederman and Gleditsch 2004; Gleditsch and Ward 2005).[16] We need to know more about how and when neighbors not embedded in IGOs affect democratization in their neighborhood.

The better alternative to regime change by force is democracy by example and democracy through peaceful incentives, which propelled the fourth wave. In those peaceful processes international organizations, and particularly those intergovernmental organizations composed primarily of democracies, have learned to play a major role. Those organizations have grown in number, functions, and experience. As John Freeman's chapter in this volume points out, the bureaucracies of even densely democratic IGOs may create democratic deficits of citizen power. The current EU is not nirvana, and politics is always about correcting existing flaws in our polities. Yet Europe is far better off with the EU's democratic deficit than it was with no EU and some very undemocratic governments. Areas of the world where IGOs are few and weak are likely to lag in democracy without new and stronger organizations. Continued forward movement of the democratic wave in the twenty-first century requires understanding and continued support by international organizations' member governments and peoples.

Notes

Portions of this chapter previously appeared as part of the 2005 article "Bushwhacking the Democratic Peace" in International Studies Perspectives 6 and are reprinted here with the permission of Blackwell Publishing.

I thank Daniela Donno, Peter Nardulli, Robert Pahre, and Susan Stokes for comments.

1. Since Huntington, McFaul (2002) and others characterize the subsequent period as a fourth wave. The criteria for "electoral democracy" are that candidates can campaign free from intimidation and voters can choose freely among competing groups and individuals not designated by the government, have access to information about candidates and platforms, and vote without undue pressure from the authorities. Some irregularities during the electoral process do not automatically disqualify a country from being an electoral democracy. A "liberal democracy" also requires substantial civil liberties. Definitions and data from: http://www.freedomhouse.org/, accessed July 14, 2006.

2. Despite many good case studies, systematic analytical and empirical work on INGOs is sparse. While INGOs can be invaluable as part of an operation that includes national governments and IGOs, without such wider participation INGOs often have little effect (Mendelson 2001; Pastor 1999; also see Larry Diamond, chapter 2 in this book).

3. The Polity data also extend back through most of the nineteenth century and show the first and second waves of democratization as well.

4. On the less demanding criterion of an occupation designed to produce a reasonably stable and friendly government, not necessarily a democracy, Iraq still was far less promising than Germany, Japan, and many other cases (Edelstein 2004).

5. I am skeptical about this cultural argument, for reasons cited in both the Anderson (ch. 5) and Diamond (ch. 2) contributions to this volume.

6. Also see Meernik 1996, and Hermann and Kegley 1998.

7. Also from previous examples, another model (Bennett and Stam 2006) predicts that the United States, following its attrition strategy against the punishment strategy of the insurgents, would have to stay in Iraq for at least seven years to produce a fairly stable regime.

8. Bueno de Mesquita and Downs (2006) report a negative impact of UN interventions on democracy after ten years, but do not seem to distinguish between peacekeeping and peacebuilding efforts.

9. Source: http://www.un.org/Depts/dpa/ead. Accessed July 14, 2006.

10. The discussion of the OAS draws on Parish and Peceny (2002) and Donno (forthcoming); see the latter for a more developed analytical typology of various IGO action options.

11. Conditionality as an enforcement capacity is common to many functional IGOs, both regional and global. The best-known examples of domestic elites using an external commitment to strengthen their hands for policies they want to choose anyway are from study of the International Monetary Fund. Many such conditionalities from the IMF, of course, are at best irrelevant to democracy promotion. See Vreeland (2003).

12. This paragraph and the one immediately preceding draw especially on Pevehouse (2003, 2005) and Mansfield and Pevehouse (2006); also see Reiter (2000).

13. There is good evidence that democracies trade more heavily with one another than with nondemocratic states, but of all the putatively causal linkages in Russett and Oneal's (2001) Kantian construct, the one from mutual trade to strengthening democracy has been the least systematically studied.

14. This paragraph and the one immediately preceding draw heavily on Marinov (2004).

15. Grigorescu (2003) reports this effect of transparency from an examination of seventeen IGOs, of which eight were regional IGOs composed largely of democratic states. A systematic comparison of the relative effects of the different kinds of IGOs remains to be undertaken.

16. Gibler and Sewell (2006) claim that cooperation with NATO, and the prospect of full membership, helped the Baltic states to consolidate their new democracies by decreasing their sense of threat from Russia.

References

Barnett, Michael. 2002. *Eyewitness to a Genocide.* Ithaca, N.Y.: Cornell University Press.

———. 2006. "Building a Republican Peace: Stabilizing States after War." *International Security* 30 (4): 87–112.

Bennett, D. Scott, and Allan C. Stam. 2006. "Predicting the Length of the 2003 U.S.-Iraq War." *Foreign Policy Analysis* 2 (2): 101–15.

Biddle, Stephen, and Stephen Long. 2004. "Democracy and Military Effectiveness: A Deeper Look." *Journal of Conflict Resolution* 48 (4): 506–24.

Boutros-Ghali, Boutros. 1992. *An Agenda for Peace.* New York: United Nations.
———. 1996. *An Agenda for Democratization.* New York: United Nations.
Brown, David S., and Wendy Hunter. 1999. "Democracy and Social Spending in Latin America, 1980–92." *American Political Science Review* 93 (4): 779–90.
Bueno de Mesquita, Bruce, and George Downs. 2006. "Intervention and Democracy." *International Organization* 60 (3): 627–49.
Bueno de Mesquita, Bruce, Alastair Smith, James Morrow, and Randolph Siverson. 2003. *The Logic of Political Survival.* Cambridge, Mass.: MIT Press.
Carothers, Thomas. 1999. *Aiding Democracy Abroad: The Learning Curve.* Washington, D.C.: Carnegie Endowment for International Peace.
Cederman, Lars-Erik. 2001. "Back to Kant: Reinterpreting the Democratic Peace as a Macrohistorical Learning Process." *American Political Science Review* 95 (1): 15–31.
Cederman, Lars-Erik, and Kristian Skrede Gleditsch. 2004. "Conquest and Regime Change: An Evolutionary Model of the Spread of Democracy and Peace." *International Studies Quarterly* 48 (3): 603–29.
Cederman, Lars-Erik, and Mohan Penubarti Rao. 2001. "Exploring the Dynamics of the Democratic Peace." *Journal of Conflict Resolution* 45 (6): 818–33.
Dallek, Robert. 1979. *Franklin D. Roosevelt and American Foreign Policy 1932–1945.* New York: Oxford University Press.
Diamond, Larry. 2004. "What Went Wrong in Iraq." *Foreign Affairs* 83 (5): 34–56.
Diamond, Larry, Juan Linz, and Seymour Martin Lipset. 1989. *Democracy in Developing Countries: Persistence, Failure, and Renewal.* Boulder, Colo.: Reinner.
Dobbins, James, John McGinn, Keith Crane, Seth Jones, Rollie Lai, Andrew Rathnell, Rachel Swanger, and Anga Timilsina. 2003. *America's Role in Nation-Building: From Germany to Iraq.* Santa Monica, Calif.: RAND.
Donno, Daniela. (forthcoming). *Regional Intergovernmental Organizations and the Collective Defense of Democracy.* PhD diss. prospectus, Yale University.
Donno, Daniela, and Bruce Russett. 2004. "Islam, Authoritarianism, and Female Empowerment: What Are the Linkages?" *World Politics* 47 (4): 582–607.
Doyle, Michael, and Nicholas Sambanis. 2006. *Making War and Building Peace: The United Nations after the Cold War.* Princeton, N.J.: Princeton University Press.
Edelstein, David M. 2004. "Occupational Hazards: Why Military Occupations Succeed or Fail." *International Security* 29 (1): 49–91.
Enterline, Andrew, and J. Michael Greig. 2005. "Beacons of Hope? The Impact of Imposed Democracy on Regional Peace, Democracy and Prosperity." *Journal of Politics* 67 (4): 175–98. http://www.psci.unt.edu/enterline.htm.
———. 2006. "Domestic Political Challenges in Imposed Polities: The Future of Iraq and Afghanistan." Manuscript, University of North Texas, Denton.
Enterline, Andrew, J. Michael Grieg, and Dawn Miller. 2006 "The Birth of Nations? The Durability of Imposed Polities and the Future of Iraq and Afghanistan." Manuscript, University of North Texas, Denton. http://www.psci.unt.edu/enterline.htm.

Feng, Yi. 2003. *Democracy, Governance, and Economic Performance: Theory and Evidence.* Cambridge, Mass.: MIT Press.

Fish, M. Steven. 2002. "Islam and Authoritarianism," *World Politics* 55 (1): 4–37.

Fordham, Benjamin, and Thomas Walker. 2005. "Kantian Liberalism, Regime Type, and Military Resource Allocation." *International Studies Quarterly* 49 (1): 141–57.

Fortna, Virginia Page. 2004. "Does Peacekeeping Keep Peace? International Intervention and the Duration of Peace after Civil War." *International Studies Quarterly* 48 (2): 269–92.

Gerring, John, Philip Bond, William Barndt, and Carol Moreno. 2005. "Democracy and Economic Growth: A Historical Perspective." World Politics 57 (3): 323–64.

Ghobarah, Hazem Adam, Paul Huth, and Bruce Russett. 2004. "Comparative Public Health: The Political Economy of Human Misery and Well-Being." *International Studies Quarterly* 48 (1): 73–94.

Gibler, Douglas, and Jamil Sewell. 2006. "External Threat and Democracy: The Role of NATO Revisited." *Journal of Peace Research* 43 (4): 413–31.

Gleditsch, Kristian. 2002. *All International Politics Is Local: The Diffusion of Conflict, Integration, and Democratization.* Ann Arbor: University of Michigan Press.

Gleditsch, Kristian Skrede, and Michael Don Ward. 2005. "Visualization in International Relations." In Alex Mintz and Bruce Russett, eds., *New Directions for International Relations: Confronting the Method of Analysis Problem,* 65–91. Lanham, Md.: Lexington.

Grigorescu, Alexandru. 2003. "International Organizations and Government Transparency: Linking the International and Domestic Realms." *International Studies Quarterly* 47 (4): 643–68.

Hafner-Burton, Emilie. 2005. "Trading Human Rights: How Preferential Trade Agreements Influence Government Repression." *International Organization* 59 (3): 593–629.

Hathaway, Oona A. 2002. "Do Human Rights Treaties Make a Difference?" *Yale Law Journal* 111(8): 1935–2042.

Hermann, Margaret, and Charles Kegley. 1998. "Ballots: A Barrier against the Use of Bullets and Bombs." *International Interactions* 24 (2): 436–60.

Huntington, Samuel. 1991. *The Third Wave: Democratization in the Late Twentieth Century.* Norman: University of Oklahoma Press.

Ikenberry, G. John. 2001. *After Victory: Institutions, Strategic Restraint, and the Rebuilding of Order after Major Wars.* Princeton, N.J.: Princeton University Press.

Kadera, Kelly, Mark Crescenzi, and Megan Shannon. 2003. "Democratic Survival, Peace, and War in the International System." *American Journal of Political Science* 47 (2): 234–47.

Kant, Immanuel. [1797.] 1970. *The Metaphysics of Morals.* Reprinted in Hans Reiss, ed., *Kant's Political Writings.* Cambridge: Cambridge University Press.

Kumar, Krishna, ed. 2002. *Post-conflict Elections, Democratization, and International Assistance.* Boulder, Colo.: Rienner.

Lebovic, James. 2004. "Uniting for Peace? Democracies and UN Peace Operations after the Cold War." *Journal of Conflict Resolution* 48 (6): 910–36.

Lipson, Charles. 2003. *Reliable Partners: How Democracies Have Made a Separate Peace.* Princeton, N.J.: Princeton University Press.

Mansfield, Edward, and Jon Pevehouse. 2006. "Democratization and International Organizations." *International Organization* 60 (1): 137–67.

Maoz, Zeev. 1996. *Domestic Sources of Global Change.* Ann Arbor: University of Michigan Press.

Marinov, Nikolay. 2004. "Does Integration Spread Democracy through Ideas or Conditionality?" Manuscript, Yale University.

Martin, Lisa. 2000. *Democratic Commitments.* Princeton, N.J.: Princeton University Press.

McFaul, Michael. 2002. "The Fourth Wave of Democracy and Dictatorship: Noncooperative Transitions in the Postcommunist World." *World Politics* 54 (22): 212–44.

Meernik, James. 1996. "United States Military Intervention and the Promotion of Democracy." *Journal of Peace Research* 33 (4): 391–402.

Mendelson, Sarah. 2001. "Democracy Assistance and Political Transition in Russia." *International Security* 25 (4): 68–106.

Mitchell, Sara McLaughlin, Scott Gates, and Havard Hegre. 1999. "Evolution in Democracy-War Dynamics." *Journal of Conflict Resolution* 43 (6): 771–92.

O'Donnell, Guillermo, Philippe Schmitter, and Laurence Whitehead. 1986. *Transitions from Authoritarian Rule: Comparative Perspectives.* Washington, D.C.: Woodrow Wilson International Center.

Paris, Roland. 2004. *At War's End: Building Peace after Civil Conflict.* Cambridge: Cambridge University Press.

Parish, Randall, and Mark Peceny. 2002. "Kantian Liberalism and the Collective Defense of Democracy in Latin America." *Journal of Peace Research* 39 (2): 229–50.

Pastor, Robert. 1999. "The Third Dimension of Accountability: The International Community in National Elections." In Andreas Schedler, Larry Diamond, and Marc Plattner, eds., *The Self-Restraining State: Power and Accountability in New Democracies,* 124–44. Boulder, Colo.: Lynne Rienner.

Peceny, Mark. 1999. *Democracy at the Point of Bayonets.* University Park: Pennsylvania State University Press.

Peceny, Mark, and Jeffrey Pickering. 2006. "Forging Democracy at Gunpoint." *International Studies Quarterly* 50 (3): 539–59.

Pevehouse, Jon. 2003. "Democratization, Credible Commitments, and IGOs." In Daniel Drezner, ed., *Locating the Proper Authorities: The Interaction of Domestic and International Institutions,* 25–48. Ann Arbor: University of Michigan Press.

———. 2005. *Democracy from Above? Regional Organizations and Democratization.* New York: Cambridge University Press.

Pevehouse, Jon, and Bruce Russett. 2006. "Democratic Intergovernmental Organizations Promote Peace." *International Organization* 60 (4): 969–1000.

Phillips, David. 2004. "Turkey's Dreams of Accession." *Foreign Affairs* 83 (5): 86–97.
Przeworski, Adam, Michael Alvarez, Jose Cheibub, and Fernando Limongi. 2000. *Democracy and Development: Political Institutions and Well-Being in the World, 1050–1990*. New York: Cambridge University Press.
Reiter, Dan. 2000. "Why NATO Enlargement Does Not Spread Democracy." *International Security* 25 (4): 41–67.
Reiter, Dan, and Allan C. Stam III. 2002. *Democracies at War*. Princeton, N.J.: Princeton University Press.
Risse-Kappen, Thomas. 1995. *Cooperation among Democracies: The European Influence on U.S. Foreign Policy*. Princeton, N.J.: Princeton University Press.
Russett, Bruce. 1993. *Grasping the Democratic Peace: Principles for a Post –Cold War World*. Princeton, N.J.: Princeton University Press.
Russett, Bruce, and John R. Oneal. 2001. *Triangulating Peace: Democracy, Interdependence, and International Organizations*. New York: Norton.
Santa-Cruz, Arturo. 2005. "Constitutional Structures, Sovereignty, and the Emergence of Norms: The Case of International Election Monitoring." *International Organization* 59 (3): 663–93.
Siegle, Joseph, Michael Weinstein, and Morton Halperin. 2004. "Why Democracies Excel." *Foreign Affairs* 83 (5): 57–71.
Sikkink, Kathryn. 1993. "Human Rights, Principled Issue-Networks, and Sovereignty in Latin America." *International Organization* 47 (3): 411–42.
Starr, Harvey, and Christina Lindborg. 2003. "Democratic Dominoes Revisited: The Hazards of Governmental Transitions, 1974–1996." *Journal of Conflict Resolution* 47 (4): 490–519.
Tures, John. A. 2005. "Operation Exporting Freedom: The Quest for Democratization via United States Military Operations." *Whitehead Journal of Diplomacy and International Relations* 6:97–111.
Vreeland, James Raymond. 2003. *The IMF and Economic Development*. New York: Cambridge University Press.

5

"Western Institutions" and "Universal Values"

Barriers to the Adoption of Democracy

LISA ANDERSON

[There are] essential principles common to every successful society, in every culture. Successful societies limit the power of the state and the power of the military—so that governments respond to the will of the people, and not the will of an elite. Successful societies protect freedom with the consistent and impartial rule of law instead of selectively applying the law to punish political opponents. Successful societies allow room for healthy civic institutions—for political parties and labor unions and independent newspapers and broadcast media. Successful societies guarantee religious liberty—the right to serve and honor God without fear of persecution. Successful societies privatize their economies, and secure the rights of property. They prohibit and punish official corruption, and invest in the health and education of their people. They recognize the rights of women.

—President George W. Bush, November 2003

To virtually all Americans and many Europeans[1], the failure of other societies to embrace liberal democratic political institutions is inexplicable. Democracy is not only self-evidently desirable, for many it is the natural or "default" political arrangement, its absence signaling some kind of social impediment or cultural defect. Much of the triumphalist rhetoric that attended the end of the cold war exhibited this perspective: Once communist ideas and agents no longer subvert the natural order of things, liberal democracy should flourish everywhere since it embodies universal values.[2] As President George W. Bush said in his November 2003 speech to the National Endowment for Democracy, "we believe that liberty is the design of nature; we believe that liberty is the direction of history."[3]

This conviction privileges the experience of a relatively small number of relatively recent political experiments, relegating the vast bulk of human experience to a residual category—"nondemocratic." It asks that we examine "nondemocratic," "democratizing" or "transitional" countries not for what they are but for what they might become, as if we expect to find what has sidetracked their natural evolution. Many politicians and policy advocates, both within the United States and around the world, share this disposition. Indeed, as an ideological or normative stance, such a preference for democracy is appealing to many. As an analytical perspective, however, the assumption that democracy is "natural" distorts our understanding of the empirical terrain and biases our hypotheses about the causes of democratic politics.

In this chapter I examine the impulse, and reception, of U.S. efforts to export democracy during the last three decades. I first treat the origins and consequences of the Western assumption that democracy is a "natural" expression of "universal values." The argument is that we know far less about how democracy arises, persists, or even how it works than we acknowledge. I then explore the consequences of that confusion for efforts to encourage the embrace of democratic institutions outside their Western birthplace, particularly in the Middle East. The contention is that efforts to assess where and when democracy has been adopted are hindered by conceptual confusion over what democracy is and where it comes from. This confusion has led scholars to define the problem by the availability of an apparent explanation and has undermined efforts at systematic explanation of patterns of acceptance and resistance. Examination of perspectives on democracy in authoritarian contexts reveals flaws in simple equations of Western institutions and universal values and suggests the value of an empirically and historically grounded perspective.

The current literature on democracy promotion and democratization extends a long tradition in American social science that examines the requisites, prerequisites, conditions, and circumstances of democratic transitions and democratic stability. This literature was born at the dawn of the cold war in the competition with communism for hearts and minds around the world. It draws on the still earlier European literature of modernization—Weber, Durkheim, and, ironically, Marx. But it is largely unmindful of the great debates about democracy in Europe itself, from Rousseau to Burke, or the United States, from the Federalists to the present. Indeed, the study of democratization borrows more from the now-discredited teleology of modernization theory than from the study of democracy that is embedded in the study of American politics.

Insofar as American politics is an orienting axis for this literature, it often inserts still more conceptual bias and theoretical selectivity. The debates about "what democracy is . . . and is not"[4] that pervade this literature are as often a reflection of ideological and normative commitments *within* the American political arena as they are about abstract definitional disputes or policy choices in distant lands. Preferences for accenting freedom over equality, or welfare instead of liberty, in the design and advocacy of democratic institutions often reveal far more about normative commitments within the American political arena than about abstract democratic principles or the circumstances of a particular democratizing country.

This context—the normative, ideological and political commitments of democracy advocates—shapes its reception around the world. Yet the burden of accounting for the failure of a particular country to embrace democracy is typically placed on the recalcitrant country itself. Thus we are told,

> A response heard in many "holdout" nations in the midst of democracy's third wave is that democracy is inconsistent with a nation's traditions and social structures. Local elites point to some mix of differences in values and beliefs, political institutions, or social structures and norms to argue that democracy could not be imported into their land.

And are asked,

> What is the basis for these assertions? What are the most incompatible aspects of democracy? How valid are culturally based arguments? How great an impediment are these cultural barriers to the diffusion of democratic forms of government? Can they be overcome? How?[5]

The argument proposed here is that there are two kinds of "cultural barriers" and two types of impediments to the diffusion of democracy. One is, of course, precisely the local traditions, values, and institutions in the receiving country presumed in these questions. As Abdelwahab El-Affendi recently and pungently observed, "the overriding political problem [in most Muslim countries] is not just the embarrassing absence of democracy, but the more basic failure to provide any form of stable, even minimally consensual governance at all. This problem is so glaring and of such long standing that it is difficult to dismiss out of hand the role of such 'prepolitical' factors as culture and, in particular, religion in explaining it."[6]

A second, and far less often noted, set of impediments to the spread of democracy derives from the very values, traditions, and institutions of democracies and democracy advocates. How democracy—its purposes, its values, and its evolution—is understood and practiced by its proponents influences the reception and effectiveness of democratic institutions around the world. "Prepolitical" normative and conceptual commitments (mixed, of course, with a bit of self-serving politics) on the part of the exporters of democracy have played important roles in confounding the export of democracy to many parts of the world.

This chapter begins by examining the second set of impediments first, reversing the conventional emphasis on defects in nondemocracies to focus on ambiguity and misapprehension of democratic institutions among their admirers and proponents. This accent on the confusion generated by the "exporters" of democracy is not to belittle the role of local factors in the "holdouts." As we shall see, many regimes have been far quicker to adapt and exploit the inconsistency, partiality, and confusion of the West than they have its democracy; and for that there are local as well as universal explanations. Moreover, this is not a problem of venal, dishonest, or harried politicians in the West or elsewhere. Although disingenuous uses of democratic rhetoric are widespread, even disciplined and well-intentioned scholars of democracy contribute to the ambiguity and complexity that hinder the diffusion of democracy.

"Western Values"? What Is Being Promoted?

> Democracy is the worst form of government, except for all those other forms that have been tried from time to time.
>
> —Winston Churchill, November 11, 1947

Winston Churchill's famous observation conveys the ambiguity and ambivalence that characterizes much of the discussion of democracy and democratization in established democracies. His wry frustration, expressed in the aftermath of his electoral defeat following World War II and before his return to power in 1951, is clearly mixed with profound attachment to the procedures and institutions of democracy. It is, however, of little help to the aspiring democrat trying to figure out exactly what this system is and why it evokes such regard. In that respect, it reflects the larger literature all too well.

We begin with the definitional problem. What, exactly, are we talking about or—as Jacques Barzun asks in his wonderful essay "Is Democracy for Export?"—"What is it exactly that we want others to copy? What is the theory of democracy that we mean to export? Not all democracies are alike."[7] Nor are all democratic theories. As Barzun continues,

> Some would point to the Declaration of Independence and the federal Constitution; others to Rousseau, Edmund Burke, Thomas Paine. Then there is Tocqueville's *Democracy in America* in two volumes and a wonderful little book by Walter Bagehot on the English Constitution, not to mention the *Federalist* papers and many eloquent pages from John Adams, Thomas Jefferson, and Abraham Lincoln. Taken loosely together, these writing would be regarded by many as making up the theory of democracy.
>
> Of course, they don't all agree; they don't form a system. The *Federalist* writers were afraid of democracy; John Adams disputes Thomas Paine and goes only part way with Jefferson. Burke and Rousseau sound like direct contraries. Tocqueville calls for so many of the special conditions he found here that his conclusions are not transferable.[8]

Not only are normative theories of democracy varied and sometimes contradictory, empirical democratic theorists often treat a variety of arrangements as if they were largely interchangeable: democracy, liberal democracy, republican government, free government, representative government, constitutional government, polyarchy, consensual popular rule, circulation of elites, indeed, even "Western institutions," as in the title of this chapter.

Each of these terms is intended to capture some essential element, usually one of the intrinsic dimensions of liberal democracy, liberty, and equality (although why these should be "Western" is rarely broached[9]). The Washington-based National Endowment for Democracy, for example, privileges "freedom," which it describes in its mission statement as "a universal human aspiration that can be realized through the development of democratic institutions, procedures and values." Many others emphasize popular sovereignty and accountability as the core values served by democratic institutions. As Ian Shapiro puts it, these theorists argue that "the goal of democratic decision procedures should be to discover something like a general will, referred to in the modern idiom as a social welfare function."[10]

Yet, many theorists argue that freedom and welfare are not necessarily equally and always well served by democratic institutions. Indeed, as El-Affendi reminds us, "liberalism—understood broadly as support for individual autonomy and the political and civil liberties that underpin it—has not always been democracy-friendly."[11] By the same token, democracy—understood as mass participation—has often been profoundly illiberal, as perennial worries about the tyranny of the majority suggest.[12]

Still, there are other rationales for advocating democracy, including its extrinsic benefits. Proponents of international perspectives draw on Michael Doyle's observation that democracies do not go to war with each other, for example, to argue that democracy should be promoted because it produces peace.[13] And some suggest that democracy cures whatever ails you. In 1995, for example, Larry Diamond wrote,

> On any list of the most important potential threats to world order and national security in the coming decade, these six should figure prominently: a hostile, expansionist Russia; a hostile, expansionist China; the spread of fundamentalist Islamic, anti-Western regimes; the spread of political terrorism from all sources; sharply increased immigration pressures; and ethnic conflict that escalates into large scale violence, civil war, refugee flows, state collapse, and general anarchy. Some of these potential threats interact in significant ways with each other but they all share a common underlying connection. In each instance, the development of democracy is an important prophylactic, and in some cases the only long-term protection, against disaster.[14]

This seems like an unreasonable burden to place on a regime—any type of regime—and it should be no surprise that observers in prospective democracies often exhibit some measure of skepticism about the claims democracy's proponents make for it.

The problems merely worsen as we move from the value of democracy to the institutional measures or indicators of democratic government. Here confusion is widespread. Periodic, free, fair elections seem to be necessary, though perhaps not sufficient, at least today. Many students of democracy and democratization adopt a "minimalist" standard like Joseph Schumpeter's: a political system in which the principal positions of power are filled "through a competitive struggle for the people's vote."[15] Samuel Huntington places a bit more emphasis on the liberal context of that struggle; for him, a democracy's "most powerful collective decision makers are selected through fair, honest and periodic elections in which candidates freely compete for votes."[16] Bernard Lewis's partly facetious definition, proffered in a discussion of the limitations of the regimes in the Muslim world—"a polity where the government can be changed by elections as opposed to one where elections are changed by the government"[17]—is probably not quite as amusing to American readers after the 2000 presidential election as it once was, but it does reflect the widespread emphasis on elections.

Why are elections so important? Seymour Martin Lipset argued decades ago that democracy is "a political system which supplies regular constitutional opportunities for changing the governing officials. It is a social institution for the resolution of the problem of societal decision-making among conflicting interest groups which permits the largest possible part of the population to influence these decisions through their ability to choose among alternative contenders for political office."[18] Elections are the mechanism that permits this choice. Michael Herb reminds us, however, that

> the success of representative institutions has been measured differently in different times. In the twentieth century, the mere emergence of representation has often been conceived as success—this equates to democratization. In the nineteenth century, elected parliaments with real constitutional powers often coexisted with monarchies that also had substantial powers. In this context, parliaments were seen as successful to the degree that they progressively constrained the authoritarian powers of the monarchy. . . . [M]edieval and early modern representative institutions [often, however,] existed precisely to buttress the power of rulers [against competitors].[19]

In other words, elections in and of themselves tell us little about the role of those elected, or about substantive political outcomes.[20]

Still, there is much debate about how to determine the freedom and fairness of elections; they must be administered by a neutral authority, for example, sufficiently "competent and resourceful to take specific precautions against fraud in the voting and vote counting."[21] In fact, however, it is often difficult to know if elections are really free and fair, if candidates have been able to campaign freely, and if the votes were counted fairly. It is even difficult to determine whether the most powerful collective decision makers ran for office, as opposed to sitting behind the scenes in back rooms or military barracks. To some extent this is why some democracy promoters are not always supportive of elections in transitional societies. Fareed Zakaria argues, for example, that "the West must recognize that its does not seek democracy in the Middle East—at least not yet. We seek first constitutional liberalism, which is very different. Clarifying our goals will actually make them more easily attainable. The regimes in the Middle East will be delighted to learn that we will not try to force them to hold elections tomorrow."[22]

Partly as a result of the focus on elections, a great many of the regimes in the world today are quite deliberately what Larry Diamond calls *pseudo-democratic,* "in that the existence of formally democratic political institutions, such as multiparty electoral competition, masks (often, in part, to legitimate) the reality of authoritarian domination."[23] Others have other names for these regimes: Guillermo O'Donnell and Philippe Schmitter call it liberalized authoritarianism; Fareed Zakaria worries about illiberal democracies; Richard Joseph talks about virtual democracies.[24]

Perhaps if democracy is hard to define and difficult to measure, we nonetheless "know it when we see it," as Justice Potter Stewart so famously said of pornography. Apparently not. As Larry Diamond asked recently,

> Is Russia a democracy? What about Ukraine, Nigeria, Indonesia, Turkey or Venezuela? There was a time when these were simple questions of regime classification. But the empirical reality in these countries is a lot messier than it was two decades ago, and so, in a way, is the never-ending dialogue on how to think about and classify regimes. . . . [T]he curious fact is that—a quarter century into the "third wave" of democratization and the renaissance it brought in comparative democratic studies—we are still far from consensus on what constitutes "democracy." And we still struggle to classify ambiguous regimes. More regimes than ever before are adopting the *form* of electoral democracy, with regular, competitive, multiparty elections. [And] many of these regimes—indeed, an unprecedented proportion of the world's countries—have the form of electoral democracy but fail to meet the substantive test, or do so ambiguously.[25]

And so we learn of a "substantive test" for this supremely procedural system.

And what is this substantive test? Diamond does not elaborate, and the criteria are not clear. As Barzun puts it, speaking of American democracy,

> To say "Here it is, come and observe, and then copy it" would be a cruel joke.
>
> If a detached observer turned to the American scene, he would note still other obstacles to the straightforward democratic process: gerrymandering, the filibuster, the distorting effect of opinion polls, the lobbying system, the maze of regulations governing registration for voting and nominating, the perversities of the primaries, and worst of all, the enormous expense of getting elected, which entails a scramble for money and the desperate shifts for abating its influence, including financial disclosure, codes of ethics, and the like.[26]

The legal maneuvering in Florida that attended the outcome of the 2000 presidential election did little to reassure observers around the world. As the head of a major election-monitoring organization remarked, "The image of U.S. congressmen calling into question the legitimacy of the entire election process on the floor of the House of Representatives was chillingly reminiscent of what often occurs in struggling democracies."[27]

Although American political scientists and policy makers cannot really define it, measure it, assess its success, or even practice it particularly well, the United States has supported democratization for decades. In discussions of the purposes of the United States' invasion of Iraq, the Rand Corporation evoked what it called the use of US military force to drive "a process of democratization" in Germany and Japan after World War II.[28] As leader of the "Free World" during the cold war, American resolve sometimes wavered: it has long indulged authoritarian regimes in the battle against totalitarianism, from Iran in the 1950s to Chile in the 1970s. But the American rhetorical commitment rarely flagged. Since the end of the cold war, and until the "War on Terror" intervened, the victorious West supported democracy and democratization with enthusiasm. The United States claims to have had a hand in expanding the number of electoral democracies in the world, said to have risen from thirty-nine in 1974 to 120 in 2000. The U.S. Agency for International Development provided election assistance in more than one hundred countries and millions of dollars in foreign aid to help build the capacity of national election commissions.[29]

For leaders in many developing countries, the occasional election is a small price to pay for the generous U.S. foreign aid available to ostensibly democratizing countries, access to the World Bank and International Monetary Fund, and other economic and political benefits. To some observers, the transparent cynicism of the pseudodemocrats undermines the process; others believe that existence of democratic institutions will create incentives for strategic behavior that will support democratic behavior even among nondemocrats. As Adam Przezworski famously argued, normative commitments are useful but not necessary to "generate compliance." His point is that strategic actors will calculate that it is in their interest to accept the prospect of defeat in the short run in order to be able to play another round.[30]

Unfortunately, few of the world's "pseudodemocracies" have exhibited either the predicted strategic calculation or emerging normative commitment. Indeed, it is not at all clear how durable democracies evolve. As Ian Shapiro notes, the current literature would suggest that "there is no single path to democracy and, therefore, no generalization to be had about which conditions give rise to democratic transitions. Democracy can result from decades of gradual evolution (Great Britain and the United States), imitation (India), cascades (much of Eastern Europe in 1989), collapses (Russia after 1991), imposition from above (Spain and Brazil), revolutions (Portugal and Argentina), negotiated settlements (Poland, Bolivia, Nicaragua, and South Africa), or external importation (Germany and Japan)."[31]

Thus, aspiring democrats around the world are justifiably confused and perplexed, while "holdout" rulers are justifiably confident that something both so vague and so complex as democracy could not possibly pose a threat to the stability of their regimes. It is a testament both to the normative power of liberty and equality and to the political power of the United States that democracy and democratization remain so much a part of global debate today.

"Western Institutions": Who Resists?

> The Middle East today stands in stark contrast to the rest of the world, where freedom and democracy have been gaining ground over the past two decades. . . . Why is this region the political basket case of the world? Why is it the great holdout, the straggler in the march of modern societies?
>
> —Fareed Zakaria, 2004[32]

While the failure of democracy to emerge in the third wave is not limited to the Middle East, this region does seem to have been especially resistant.[33] In its 2001 survey, for example, the influential Freedom House found that "[i]ndeed, the 'democracy gap' between the Islamic countries and the rest of the world is dramatic. In the 47 countries with an Islamic majority, only 11 (23 percent) have democratically elected governments, while 110 of the 145 non-Islamic states (76 percent) are electoral democracies. . . . Furthermore none of the 16 Arab states is an electoral democracy. . . . While the countries of Latin America, Africa, East Central Europe, and South and East Asia experienced significant gains for democracy and freedom over the last 20 years, the Islamic world experienced an equally significant increase in the number of repressive regimes."[34]

Fareed Zakaria concluded his survey of the Freedom House findings with the observation that "since September 11th, the political dysfunctions of the Arab world have suddenly presented themselves on the West's doorstep."[35]

Most observers have followed the lead of Freedom House in attributing these findings to "the weakness of democratic culture in many of the majority-Muslim states."[36] As Ghassan Salame suggests, in the aftermath of the failure of the third wave to break on the shores of the Middle East, "the idea of an Arab and/or Islamic 'exceptionalism' . . . re-emerged among both western proponents of universal democracy and established orientalists."[37] Sometimes, this exceptionalism is characterized as a sort of natural inclination towards despotism: "The seizure of power, particularly by assassination, inevitably creates a vicious circle that leaves no room for any other alternative, much less for alternation of power. The system is not angelic and it is not run by choirboys. Moreover, it is old—very old—in the Arab world. It is a tradition. In the history of the Arab-Muslim world, 'Oriental despotism' (the term is Montesquieu's) has always had its own ruthless and bloody logic."[38]

Many observers attributed this exception not to "tradition" in general but to Islam, and particularly to interpretations of Islam that merge rather than distinguish between the religious and the political. Bernard Lewis is one of the best-known advocates of this perspective. For example, he notes, "In Muslim theory, church and state are not separate or separable institutions. . . . Such familiar pairs of words as lay and ecclesiastical, sacred and profane, spiritual and temporal, and the like have no equivalent in classical Arabic or in other Islamic languages, since the dichotomy they express, deeply rooted in Christendom, was unknown in Islam until comparatively modern times."[39]

However compelling their logic, explanations for Middle Eastern exceptionalism based on Islamic culture are misguided since Muslim countries are not, in fact, less democratic than other countries. As Alfred Stepan has noted, "The 16 Arab countries form the largest singly readily identifiable group among all those states that 'underachieve' (relative to what one would expect from their levels of Gross Domestic Product per capital [GDPpc]) when it comes to the holding of competitive elections. In sharp contrast to this stands the scarcely less striking—yet undernoticed—situation among the world's 31 Muslim majority but non-Arab countries, which in fact form the single largest bloc of all those countries that 'greatly overachieve' relative to their GDPpc levels when competitive elections are in question."[40] Thus, whatever may account for the failure of democracy to take hold in the Arab world—or elsewhere—cannot be attributed to Islam.

Moreover, reliance on culture, tradition or other factors that are slow to change ignores the fact that, as Salame points out, "Until the 1980s the Middle East was not exceptional. Only with the gradual redemocratization of Latin America and Southern Europe at the beginning of the decade, and the tentative democratization of South Korea and Taiwan towards the end did the Middle East begin to appear behind the curve. The strong popular pressure for greater democracy in several sub-Saharan African nations coupled with the collapse of the eastern European communist regimes cast the Middle East in an even more unfavorable light."[41]

In fact, if the countries of the Arab world have been out of sync with a worldwide trend toward democracy, they have hardly been alone. As we are told in a recent volume on democratic reform in Africa,

> The current wave of democratization has bypassed some of the large and important countries in Africa, notably Sudan and the Democratic Republic

> of Congo, Libya, and Morocco. Second, many of the continent's democratic transitions have been protracted and stalemated, as in Burkina Faso, Cameroon, Cote d'Ivoire, Togo, and arguably Zimbabwe. Worse still, the prospects of consolidation remain weak in all but a handful of African countries (South Africa, Botswana, Mauritius, Senegal, and possibly Benin and Ghana). In some cases, elected incumbents are busily engaged in a process of denaturing or rendering hollow the democratic content of the newly installed political systems.[42]

Although in the early 1990s, many observers expected the "third wave" of democratization to swamp the remaining authoritarian regimes, by the end of the decade Thomas Carothers concluded

> that of the nearly 100 countries considered "transitional" in recent years, only a relatively small number—probably fewer than 20—are clearly en route to becoming successful, well-functioning democracies or at least have made some democratic progress and still enjoy a positive dynamic of democratization. ... By far the majority of third-wave countries have not achieved relatively well-functioning democracy or do not seem to be deepening or advancing whatever progress they have made."[43]

Thus, the erroneous assumption that democracy is the natural state of affairs led analysts to look for sources of resistance rather than explanations for adoption and consolidation of democratic institutions in the relatively rare instances where it has happened. Indeed, Eva Bellin has argued that "the exceptionalism of the Middle East and North Africa lies not so much in absent prerequisites of democracy as in present conditions that foster robust authoritarianism."[44] The availability of an apparently plausible explanation for "resistance"—Islam—distorted the collection of data on which countries actually have been "laggards," and we find democracy scholars accounting for a phenomenon that does not exist with an explanation that is not true.

This notwithstanding, viewing political change within Arab nations from the perspective of third-wave developments does yield useful and interesting insights. But generating these insights requires more of a nuanced analysis than is evidenced, for example, in the Freedom House's assertion that "since the early 1970s, when the 'third wave' of democratization began, the Islamic world—and its Arab core in particular—has seen little significant improvement in political openness, respect for human rights, or transparency."[45]

In fact, beneath the surface of stability, the societies and politics of the Arab world have changed considerably over the past several decades. Although autocratic rulers remain in power, both the ideological underpinnings and the institutional structures of their regimes have changed.[46] Lip service to liberal democracy is much more widespread, as an aspiration if not a fact. So too are some of the institutional trappings of democracy, including partially contested elections and growing, if still limited, press freedom.

As Aziz al-Azmeh notes,

> The ubiquity of Arab discourse on democracy in recent years requires little documentation or demonstration. The question of democracy, together with the allied concern with the notion of civil society, is addressed in the Arab world in a myriad of political, academic, journalistic and other writings, and is the subject of inveterate commentary in casual conversations, in politico-academic conventions and conferences. . . . With the exception of the radically primitivist Islamist discourse, the question of democracy has become a major constituent in the political vocabulary prevalent in the Arab world today virtually across the entire ideological and political spectrum; it is invading even the most archaic Arabian politics.[47]

"Universal Values": Why Resist?

> How is this fascinating democracy perceived? What is that *'afrita* [spirit], as it is called by my Aunt 'Aziza, who finishes listening to the eight-thirty news every night . . . by murmuring, 'But what is this *dimuqratiyya?* Is it a country or an *'afrita* or an animal or an island?'
>
> —Fatima Mernissi, 1992[48]

As is the case for some in the West, some Middle Easterners view democracy as a cure-all. For them democracy is, as al-Azmeh writes, "endowed with a virtually talismanic quality, as a protean force capable, when meaningfully put into practice, of solving all outstanding problems."[49] In fact, however, democracy in the Arab world, like democracy in the West, is a deeply ambiguous and highly contested notion, as it is for many in the West. Unlike in the West, however, democracy is not perceived as "natural" or even always desirable in the Arab world. Far from being the default political arrangement, democracy is often seen as a disguise for Western hegemonic designs on the region. Certainly, the tendency in both Western and Middle East discourse to associate democracy with the "West" has profoundly shaped its reception and understanding in the Middle East.

Although many observers have noted the role of external actors in shaping democracy's third wave, [50] the introduction into the Middle East of democratic institutions by the imperial European powers during the interwar period had a particularly powerful legacy in the region. For some analysts, the Arab experience with constitutions, parliaments, and contested elections between the 1920s and 1950s was constructive. Laith Kubba, for example, has suggested recently that "for more than three decades, Egypt, Syria, and Iraq had functioning democracies in which deputies were elected, government officials held accountable to laws and rules, the judiciary was independent, the press was free, and the people enjoyed equality before the law and basic civil and political rights. . . . Governments followed constitutional and legal procedures." Even he concedes, however, that these governments "did not address the needs of the people. Although the political process was open to all citizens, the high illiteracy rate and the slow pace of social and economic development excluded most people from the benefits of democracy. . . . The frustration of the majority was given expression by political activists who advocated radical alternatives."[51]

Malcolm Kerr's more astringent assessment of the Middle East's experience with Western constitutional democracy, written in the 1960s, is probably closer to the mark than Kubba's:

> The simplest explanation given for this new radicalism is that the brief experience of several Arab states since 1920 with western-style constitutional systems was an unhappy one, and therefore the experiment was abandoned on pragmatic grounds. A few years of rigged elections, musical-chair cabinets, suspended constitutions, arbitrary arrests, playboy monarchs, and absence of reform legislation should have been quite enough to convince the Arabs that they should give all this up and try something else—anything else. This was particularly the case after 1948, when it suddenly became clear that their governments were not only corrupt but, what was worse, that they were weak.[52]

The enthusiasm for socialism and nationalism that swept much of what was known as the third world in the 1950s and 1960s was well represented in the Arab world. While this enthusiasm represented a rejection of the institutions of Western democracy, it did not necessarily reflect a rejection of its underlying values, such as equality. As Kerr continues, "The Arab radical rejects the familiar western assumption that the division of power and initiative in society among competing groups is inherently desirable, and that too much concentration of power in the hands of the state is a natural threat to private right. For him, the essence of democracy is found not in the existence of a parliamentary opposition but in the creation of a socialist programme and the enlistment of mass support in implementing it."[53]

The conviction that the institutions associated with liberal democracy might betray the very values they are supposed to realize was widespread. In part this reflected the disproportionate influence of utopian, Rousseauian conceptions of democracy in the region in the interwar period.[54] Indeed, such influence was still apparent in the late 1970s, when Mu'ammar al-Qaddafi of Libya argued,

> Political struggle that results in the victory of a candidate with 51 percent of the votes leads to a dictatorial governing body disguised as a false democracy, since 49 percent of the electorate is ruled by an instrument of governing they did not vote for, but had imposed upon them. This is dictatorship. . . . Besides, this political conflict may produce a governing body that represents only a minority, for when votes are distributed among several candidates, one of them polls more than any other candidate. But if the votes polled by those who received less are added up, they can constitute an overwhelming majority. However, the candidate with fewer votes wins and his success is regarded as legitimate and democratic! This is the reality of the political systems prevailing in the world today. They are dictatorial systems and it seems clear that they falsify genuine democracy.[55]

There is no doubt that Qaddafi's "state of the masses" has been no better, and probably much worse, than parliamentary elections in realizing democratic values. But his critique would not be out of place in some strands of Western democratic theory.

For most Islamist activists, liberal democratic institutions are intimately associated with imperialism.[56] For some, Islam and democracy are intrinsically incompatible: sovereignty belongs to God and popular sovereignty is therefore a violation of Islamic doctrine. For others—indeed, for the vast majority—democratic values are embedded within Islam. As a prominent Jordanian Islamist leader put it, "We oppose the label 'democracy' because it reflects Western histories and particularities. We believe in the consultative system. However, if practiced properly by Muslims, this Godly system can perform many of the functions of democracy and even achieve more than it in terms of social justice and rights for the populace."[57]

As this activist suggests, the problem is not so much the values of democracy but the way it has been introduced to, and practiced in, the region. "Democracy's ideals are beautiful. But where is its humanist ethics? . . . The tragedy of the Arab world is that those Westerners who call themselves democrats have actively supported and imposed upon us their friends: Arab dictators!"[58]

Skeptics—Islamist and otherwise—argue that Western claims about popular sovereignty, human rights, and democratic institutions "are disingenuous, that it is the economically powerful groups who rule, and that elections are rituals that do not present genuine choices between substantively different policies."[59]

Whether or not this is true, in principle or in practice, elsewhere there is ample evidence to support these claims in the Middle East. As Fatima Mernissi points out,

> Some groups of people think [democracy] can promote their interests, especially those who know foreign languages, who have access to Western knowledge and culture. . . . This is generally the case with bourgeois city dwellers, both men and women, who operate in the fields of business and finance. It is also the case with university professors, artists and intellectuals. . . . Others may feel terribly threatened by that *dimuqratiyya*. . . . Can it be that the most dispossessed in our societies cling to Islam because they fear being forgotten by their own people, who have found another identity and are involved in other networks, especially those very strong ones that create profit on an international scale?[60]

The beneficiaries of this "*dimuqratiyya*" may not care whether the institutions and rituals in which they participate are actually democratic as long as they promote their access and serve their interests. As Mohammed Talbi suggests, in the Arab world, often "democracy in practice is no more than a theatrical production. We are actors in a democratic play, with all the stage settings and all the Western words that the play demands, including the suspense that surrounds the counting of the votes. . . . As matter of fact, elections in the Arab world are nothing but a bad joke, a farce, an immense masquerade.[61]

The rulers know this perfectly well, and occasionally they acknowledge it, if only inadvertently. Morocco's King Hassan II argued that democracy was a gift from him to his subjects: "Democracy is granted in Morocco because I am the first to demand it." He then complained that his munificence was not well appreciated: "Shouldn't my granting of democracy to my people be considered a noble deed?"[62] Algeria's rulers justified the military intervention that canceled parliamentary elections in 1992 by saying that "we must stop the electoral process in order to safeguard the democratization process."[63]

The willingness, even eagerness, with which Western powers have colluded with these regimes to take the appearance of democracy for its reality has profoundly handicapped local efforts to foster genuine democratization. The record of the superpowers in advancing the cause of democracy in the

Arab world during the cold war was little better than their interwar imperial predecessors. The post–cold-war performance of the United States, in its persistent support of authoritarianism in the Arab Middle East, continued this pattern. As Amy Hawthorne has argued,

> Despite numerous democracy aid programs and lofty pro-reform rhetoric, nowhere in the Arab world was democracy promotion, or the lack of it, a decisive force in U.S. policy. At no time did an Arab regime's restriction of civil liberties (such as in the Palestinian Authority or Egypt), cancellation of an electoral process (such as in Algeria), or the arbitrary detention of leading human rights figures (as in Egypt, Tunisia, or the Palestinian Authority) prompt the Clinton Administration to undertake punitive measures. In contrast, Clinton punished rulers in Latin America, Asia and Africa with sanctions in response to similar violations of liberty. . . . The gap between rhetoric and action was not lost on Arab leaders or Arab democracy activists, who tended to view the Clinton administration's democracy promotion efforts in their region with great skepticism.[64]

As a result, most regimes in the Arab world, and most of their opponents, take what might charitably be called an instrumental view of democracy.[65] The appearance of democracy serves to satisfy foreign donors while simultaneously humiliating domestic opponents. As Talbi points out, most elections in the region are won by vastly inflated vote totals. "These [high vote] percentages are not, as one might believe, the result of naiveté, and still less of political blunders. They are carefully calculated. As in all fascist states based on sham elections, they serve a specific purpose. . . . The regimes are able to discredit and dishonor the intelligentsia by making them swallow these sham results and even publicly affirm them. . . . They are neutralized, rendered servile."[66] Consequently, by the turn of the twenty-first century, there were very few advocates of liberal democracy in the Arab world still willing to engage in politics.

As Ghassan Salame wistfully concluded, "The fundamental political split . . . is not between opposing democratic forces but between forces which are often equally strangers to democracy (or equally uninterested in establishing democracy)."[67] Neither the governments nor their opponents exhibited any attachment to institutions designed to foster freedom, equality or even the circulation of elites. Lahouari Addi's observation about Algeria was but one illustration of this dilemma: "the democratic oppositionists are now at an impasse. On one side they face a regime that does not want to change and that wants to use them in order to perpetuate itself. On the other they face

Islamists who want to create their own version of a one-party state. The democrats cannot join forces with the regime, still less with the Islamists."[68]

Conclusions: "Universal Values" or "Western Institutions"?

> We are progressing step-by-step toward democracy; it is a difficult process. But Algeria is not some sort of boy wonder and democracy is not the natural outgrowth of human actions.
>
> —Anonymous Algerian official, quoted in *le Figaro,* January 11, 1992[69]

Democracy is not the default political arrangement in Algeria, the Middle East, or in most of the world. As a set of political institutions, it is associated with particular historical moments, particular international advocates, and certain subsets of domestic beneficiaries. Even its most fervent admirers in the West find it extremely difficult to define, measure, assess, implement, or practice. Its most enthusiastic advocates concede that it is a system of procedural rules with no clear substantive outcome, a system that might sometimes support the rulers and sometimes constrain them, a system apparently agnostic about the substance of policy all together.

Even its simplest elements are exceptionally complicated, as Jean Leca observes: "Voting is not a natural and self-evident process; it is an obscure rite whose practice requires some learning and, above all, a myth of some sort to transform 'crowds' into 'constituencies,' that is to say, a way of helping citizens find their way through the amazingly complex network of party lines claiming to connect grievances, demands, and forms of behavior into a single piece of paper to be dropped into a ballot box."[70]

Combine this complexity with the suspicion that these institutions may be little more than Trojan horses—seductive aspirations to equality and liberty that become malignant instruments of inequity and oppression outside their original home in the West—and it is not hard to understand why democracy meets resistance.

Thirty-five years ago, Dankwart Rustow argued that the "prerequisites" so often explored in the literature—the levels of GNP, literacy, or other economic, social, or cultural features that seem propitious—do not explain the choice of this risky and peculiar system. Indeed, as he suggested, plenty of prosperous, literate societies had resisted its temptations. Instead, he argued, there was only one important condition—"that the vast majority of citizens in a democracy-to-be must have no doubt or mental reservations as to which political community they belong to." After that, "the dynamic process of democratization itself is set off by a prolonged and inconclusive political struggle." This is not "a lukewarm struggle but a hot family feud," one that ends with "a deliberate decision on the part of political leaders to accept the existence of diversity in unity and, to that end, to institutionalize some crucial aspect of democratic procedure."[71] In other words, societies choose peaceful conflict resolution after—and perhaps only after—they have become attached to a political community and have learned the cost of violent conflict resolution to that community.

Rustow's hypothesis suggests that cultural attachments to liberty and equality, as such, are much less important prerequisites to democracy than membership in a recognized political community. Yet this sense of community is not nearly as common as might be expected. As Stepan suggests, "[M]any contemporary Arab states have relatively new and arbitrary boundaries because they were cut out of the Ottoman Empire, and were afterward occupied and reconfigured as European colonies. The weakness of their 'nation-state' or 'state-nation' political identities has been compounded by the widespread use throughout the Middle East and North Africa of Arabic as the dominant language, and especially by attempts to privilege pan-Arabism (and more recently pan-Islamism) as core elements of national identities."[72]

When there is "doubt or mental reservation as to which political community they belong," deep divisions between the beneficiaries of Western access and those deprived of such access are transformed from class distinctions into cultural divides: "Western institutions" become symbols of alienation rather than vessels of universal values.

Without consensus around a national identity and expression of that consensus in state institutions, as the United States learned in Iraq, "removing an oppressive coercive apparatus will lead, not to democracy, but rather authoritarianism of a different stripe, or worse, chaos."[73]

If, as President George W. Bush argues, democracy, or "liberty," "is the design of nature [and] the direction of history," it is also, as Tunisian President Habib Bourguiba said forty years ago, "a dangerous undertaking, an adventure filled with risks."[74]

Notes

The epigraph to this chapter is drawn from "George Bush Discusses Freedom in Iraq and the Middle East: Remarks by the President at the 20th Anniversary of the National Endowment for Democracy," the full text of which is available at http://www.ned.org/events/anniversary/20thAniv-Bush.html.

1. Although Europeans have been in the business of "democracy promotion" ever since the first Parliament was installed in an imperial possession, the United States

has taken up the cause most aggressively in recent years. I will therefore focus my attention largely on the American literature about what is known as the "third wave" of democratization, which is said to have began in the mid-1970s. For the original use of this term, see Samuel P. Huntington, *The Third Wave: Democratization in the Late Twentieth Century* (Norman: University of Oklahoma Press, 1993).

2. Francis Fukuyama's *The End of History and the Last Man* (New York: Avon Books, 1992) was among the best known of many examples of this sort of argument.

3. "Bush Discusses Freedom," http://www.ned.org/events/anniversary/20thAniv-Bush.html.

4. Terry Lynn Karl and Philippe C. Schmitter, "What Democracy Is . . . And Is Not," *Journal of Democracy* 2, no. 3 (Summer 1991): 87.

5. This is the charge provided for this chapter by the conference organizers of the 2005 centennial celebration for the Department of Political Science at the University of Illinois at Urbana-Champaign.

6. Abdelwahab El-Affendi, "The Elusive Reformation," *Journal of Democracy* 14, no. 2 (April 2003): 34.

7. Jacques Barzun, "Is Democratic Theory for Export?" in Joel Rosenthal, ed., *Ethics and International Affairs: A Reader* (Washington, D.C.: Georgetown University Press, 1999), 39.

8. Barzun, "Is Democratic Theory for Export?" 40.

9. Although I will not pause here to do so, there is much to be said about the connotations of "Western" in, say, colloquial Arabic. As Fatima Mernissi points out, the West "is the territory of the strange, the foreign . . . the place where the sun sets and where darkness awaits." Fatima Mernissi, *Islam and Democracy: Fear of the Modern World,* 2nd ed. (Cambridge, Mass.: Perseus, 2002), 13.

10. Ian Shapiro, "The State of Democratic Theory," in Ira Katznelson and Helen V. Milner, eds., *Political Science: The State of the Discipline* (New York: Norton, 2002), 237.

11. El-Affendi, "The Elusive Reformation," 35.

12. For a recent example, see Fareed Zakaria, *The Future of Freedom: Illiberal Democracy at Home and Abroad*, (New York: Norton, 2003).

13. See Michael Doyle, "Kant, Liberal Legacies and Foreign Affairs," in Michael E. Brown, Sean Lynn-Jones, and Steven E. Miller, eds., *Debating the Democratic Peace,* (Cambridge, Mass.: MIT Press, 1996). With regard to an effort to apply this in the Middle East, see Etel Solingen, "Toward a Democratic Peace in the Middle East," in Amin Saikal and Albrecht Schnabel, eds., *Democratization in the Middle East: Experiences, Struggles, Challenges* (Tokyo: United Nations University, 2003), 42–62.

14. Larry Diamond, *Promoting Democracy in the 1990s: Actors and Instruments, Issues and Imperatives,* A Report to the Carnegie Commission on Preventing Deadly Conflict (New York: Carnegie Corporation, 1995), 3. Several years earlier, Karl and Schmitter reminded everyone that "democratization will not bring in its wake economic growth, social peace, administrative efficiency, political harmony, free markets,

or 'the end of ideology.'" The best they could offer was that democracies "may not immediately produce all the goods mentioned above, but they stand a better chance of eventually doing so than do autocracies." ("What Democracy Is . . . And Is Not," 87.)

15. Joseph Schumpeter, *Capitalism, Socialism, and Democracy* (New York: Harper, 1947), 269.

16. Samuel P. Huntington, *The Third Wave: Democratization in the Late Twentieth Century* (Norman, Okla.: University of Oklahoma Press, 1993), 7.

17. Bernard Lewis, "Islam and Liberal Democracy: A Historical Overview," *Journal of Democracy* 7, no. 2 (April 1996), 53.

18. Seymour M. Lipset, "Some Social Requisites of Democracy: Economic Development and Political Legitimacy," *American Political Science Review* 53, no.1 (March 1959): 71

19. Michael Herb, "Taxation and Representation," *Studies in Comparative International Development* 38, no. 3 (Fall 2003): 7.

20. Jacques Barzun points out: "In different [democratic] countries the notions of freedom and equality have taken varying and sometimes contradictory meanings. Does a national health service increase freedom or reduce it? . . . Are the rules for zoning and landmark preservation a protection of property rights or an infringement [on] them? More generally, can the enormous increase in the bureaucracy needed to enforce endless regulations and the high taxes levied for all the new services be called an extension of freedom or a limitation? . . . Today the government machine is more like the circuitry of a mainframe computer, too complex for anybody but students of the science. Barzun, "Is Democratic Theory for Export?" 49.

21. Larry Diamond, "Elections without Democracy: Thinking about Hybrid Regimes," *Journal of Democracy* 13, no. 2 (April 2002): 29.

22. Fareed Zakaria, "Islam, Democracy and Constitutional Liberalism," in Demetrios James Caraley, ed., *American Hegemony: Preventive War, Iraq, and Imposing Democracy* (New York: American Academy of Political Science, 2004), 201.

23. Larry Diamond, "Introduction," in Larry Diamond, Juan J. Linz, and Seymour Martin Lipset, eds. *Democracy in Developing Countries* (Boulder, Colo.: Reinner, 1989), xviii.

24. Guillermo O'Donnell and Philippe Schmitter, *Transitions from Authoritarian Rule: Tentative Conclusions about Uncertain Democracies* (Baltimore: Johns Hopkins University Press, 1986); Fareed Zakaria, *The Future of Freedom;* Richard Joseph, "Democratization in Africa after 1989: Comparative and Theoretical Perspectives," in Lisa Anderson, ed., *Transitions to Democracy* (New York: Columbia University Press, 1999); Thomas Carothers lists "semi-democracy, formal democracy, electoral democracy, façade democracy, pseudo-democracy, weak democracy, partial democracy, illiberal democracy, and virtual democracy." See his "The End of the Transition Paradigm," *Journal of Democracy* 13, no. 1 (January 2002): 10.

25. Diamond, "Elections without Democracy," 21. Freedom House described all

these countries as democracies in 2001; Diamond and his collaborators dissented, saying "at best Ukraine, Nigeria and Venezuela are *ambiguous* cases."

26. Barzun, "Is Democratic Theory for Export?" 52–53.

27. Indeed, Russian parliamentarian Alexei Mitrofanov could not resist observing, "America has been lecturing us for eight years on democracy. Now it's our turn to lecture you." See Richard Soudriette, "Promoting Democracy at Home," *Journal of Democracy* 12, no. 2 (April 2001): 134.

28. James Dobbins et al., *America's Role in Nation-Building: From Germany to Iraq* (Santa Monica, CA: Rand, 2003), 1.

29. El-Affendi, "The Elusive Reformation," 35.

30. Adam Przeworski, *Democracy and the Market: Political and Economic Reforms in Eastern Europe and Latin America* (Cambridge: Cambridge University Press, 1991).

31. Shapiro, "State of Democratic Theory," 255.

32. Zakaria, "Islam, Democracy and Constitutional Liberalism," 189.

33. There is substantial literature on efforts at political liberalization and democratization in the Middle East. In addition to works cited elsewhere in the notes, of particular use are: Augustus Richard Norton, ed., *Civil Society in the Middle East* (Leiden: Brill, 1996); Iliya Harik and Denis J. Sullivan, eds., *Privatization and Liberalization in the Middle East* (Bloomington: Indiana University Press, 1992); *Arab Human Development Report, 2002, 2003* (New York: United Nations Development Programme, 2002, 2003).

34. Adrian Karatnycky, "The 2001 Freedom House Survey: Muslim Countries and the Democracy Gap," *Journal of Democracy* 13, no. 1 (January 2002): 104.

35. Zakaria, "Islam, Democracy and Constitutional Liberalism," 189.

36. Karatnycky, "2001 Freedom House Survey," 104.

37. Ghassan Salame, "Introduction: Where are the Democrats?" in Ghassan Salame, ed., *Democracy without Democrats? The Renewal of Politics in the Muslim World* (London: Tauris, 1994), 1.

38. Mohammed Talbi, "Arabs and Democracy: A Record of Failure," *Journal of Democracy* 11, no. 3 (July 2000), 59.

39. Cited in Adrian Karatnycky, "The 2001 Freedom House Survey," 105. See also his *What Went Wrong? Western Impact and Middle Eastern Response* (New York: Oxford University Press, 2002) and *The Crisis of Islam: Holy War and Unholy Terror* (New York: Modern Library, 2003).

40. Alfred Stepan with Graeme B. Robertson, "An 'Arab' More than 'Muslim' Electoral Gap," *Journal of Democracy* 14, no. 3 (July 2003): 30.

41. Salame, "Introduction: Where Are the Democrats?" 25. See also Lisa Anderson, "Democracy in the Arab World: A Critique of the Political Culture Approach," in Rex Brynen, Bahgat Korany, and Paul Noble, eds., *Political Liberalization and Democratization in the Arab World*, vol. 1, *Theoretical Perspectives* (Boulder, Colo.: Rienner, 1995).

42. E. Gyimah-Boadi, "Africa: The Quality of Political Reform," in E. Gyimah-Boadi, ed., *Democratic Reform in Africa: The Quality of Progress* (Boulder, Colo.: Rienner, 2004), 11.

43. Thomas Carothers, "The End of the Transition Paradigm," *Journal of Democracy* 13, no. 1 (January 2002): 9.

44. Eva Bellin, "The Robustness of Authoritarianism in the Middle East: Exceptionalism in Comparative Perspective," *Comparative Politics* 36, no. 2 (January 2004): 152.

45. Karatnycky, "2001 Freedom House Survey," 104.

46. Salame, "Introduction: Where are the Democrats?" 2.

47. Aziz al-Azmeh, "Populism Contra Democracy: Recent Democratist Discourse in the Arab World," in Salame, *Democracy Without Democrats?* 113.

48. Mernissi, *Islam and Democracy,* 52.

49. al-Azmeh, "Populism Contra Democracy," 115.

50. Nicolas van de Walle, "Elections without Democracy: Africa's Rage of Regimes," *Journal of Democracy* 13, no. 2 (April 2002): 74.

51. Laith Kubba, "Arabs and Democracy: The Awakening of Civil Society," *Journal of Democracy* 11, no. (July 2000): 85.

52. Malcolm Kerr, "Arab Radical Notions of Democracy," in Albert Hourani, ed., *Middle Eastern Affairs* 3, St, Antony's Papers (London: Chatto & Windus, 1963), 9.

53. Kerr, "Arab Radical Notions of Democracy," 11.

54. As Kerr put it, "To a great extent the liberalism in which many Arabs were schooled one or two generations ago [that is, in the interwar period], particularly in Egypt and Syria, was of a rather idyllic type. Arab liberals owed more to the universalism of the French enlightenment and to nineteenth century French Romanticism than to the English constitutionalists or utilitarians, and far more to the inspiration of the French Revolution than to the English Revolution of 1689." ("Arab Radical Notions of Democracy," 38).

55. Mu'ammar al-Qaddafi, *The Green Book, Vol. I: The Solution of the Problem of Democracy,* n.d. [1978], available at http://www.geocities.com/Athens/8744/readgb.htm.

56. Najib Ghadbian, *Democratization and the Islamist Challenge in the Arab World* (Boulder Colo.: Westview, 1997), 43.

57. Jordanian Islamist leader, quoted in Larbi Sadiki, *The Search for Arab Democracy: Discourses and Counter-Discourses* (London: Hurst, 2004), 369.

58. Jordanian Islamist leader, in Sadiki, *Search for Arab Democracy,* 136.

59. Ghadbian, *Democratization,* 43.

60. Mernissi, *Islam and Democracy,* 53.

61. Mohammed Talbi, "Arabs and Democracy," 60.

62. Quoted in Larbi Sadiki, *The Search for Arab Democracy: Discourses and Counter-Discourses* (London: Hurst, 2004), 237.

63. Anonymous Algerian official, quoted in *le Figaro,* January 11, 1992, cited in Jean

Leca, "Democratization in the Arab World: Uncertainty, Vulnerability and Legitimacy; A Tentative Conceptualization and Some Hypotheses," in Salame, *Democracy Without Democrats?* 48.

64. Amy Hawthorne, "Do We Want Democracy in the Middle East?" *Foreign Service Journal,* February 2001, available at http://www.afsa.org/fsj/feb01/hawthorne01.cfm.

65. As Donald K. Emmerson suggests of Indonesia, " Implicit in their lack of enthusiasm for the looming votes of 2004 was a results-dominated conception of free expression, competitive politics and accountable government. If such mainstays of democracy could deliver stability, legality and decent living standards, fine. If not, one might as well try something else." ("Indonesia's Approaching Elections: A Year of Voting Dangerously?" *Journal of Democracy* 15, no. 1 (January 2004): 99.

66. Talbi, "Arabs and Democracy," 60.

67. Salame, "Introduction: Where are the Democrats?" 16.

68. Lahouari Addi, "Algeria's Tragic Contradictions" *Journal of Democracy* 7, no. 3 (July 1996): 106.

69. Cited in Jean Leca, "Democratization in the Arab World," 48.

70. Jean Leca, "Democratization in the Arab World," 76.

71. Dankwart Rustow, "Transitions to Democracy," repr. in Anderson, *Transitions to Democracy,* 26–30.

72. Stepan, "An 'Arab' more than 'Muslim' Electoral Gap," 42.

73. Eva Bellin, "Robustness of Authoritarianism," 153.

74. Bizerte speech, 1964, cited in Dirk Vandewalle, "From the New State to the New Era: Toward a Second Republic in Tunisia," *Middle East Journal* 42, no. 3 (Autumn 1988): 602.

PART II

Globalization and Democracy

6

Issues, Information Flows, and Cognitive Capacities

Democratic Citizenship in a Global Era

JAMES H. KUKLINSKI,
PAUL J. QUIRK,
AND BUDDY PEYTON

Globalization's presence and importance grow daily. Proponents point to concrete manifestations such as improved standards of living, increasingly uniform standards of justice, and technological breakthroughs that no country alone could have achieved. By their accounts, people throughout the world live better lives than they would live in globalization's absence.

Globalization also poses problems, as various authors in this volume attest. Beth Simmons (chapter 8) notes, for example, that much of it occurs outside the public purview. She raises especially serious concerns about the generally unnoticed internationalization—what John Freeman (chapter 9) calls migration—of political authority. The growth of international political organizations, in Simmons's view, threatens to undermine the control and legitimacy of existing sovereign nations. "International organizations tend not to operate according to democratic principles. [The] serious challenges here include bureaucratic independence, the dominance of the powerful, and a general lack of transparency surrounding how decisions are made" (159). In a similar vein, Freeman observes that sovereign states increasingly lack control over their own economies.[1] They make fewer of the critical economic decisions and their domestic economies depend more than ever on other states' economic policies. Melissa Orlie's far-reaching analysis (chapter 10) leads her to conclude that globalization's potentially negative effects on environments, social communities, governing structures, and local and national economies demand a fundamental rethinking of the politics-economics relationship.

Underlying all of these concerns are two others: Can citizens, the ultimate targets of globalization-related decisions, meaningfully evaluate the economic and technical issues arising from globalization? By what process will they likely reach their judgments? If nation-states lose all their authority to nondemocratic international institutions, asking these questions would be pointless. So would it also be if nation-states failed to deliberate such issues publicly. We initially assume that neither condition fully pertains now, nor will it fully pertain in the foreseeable future, at least in many democratic countries.

Many observers see internationalization as generating unique decision-making challenges to democratic societies and their citizens. We first consider this proposition. Issues related to internationalization, we agree, possess unique features. However, these features do not increase or fundamentally change the challenges that citizens already face when trying to evaluate policies in other domains. For the most part, then, existing research findings on citizen decision making should apply to issues generated by globalization.

Political scientists do not speak with one voice about citizens and democratic governance, however. Two perspectives are of particular interest. The first currently dominates writing on the subject and emphasizes cognitive and informational differences among citizens. It distinguishes between more and less politically sophisticated citizens and says that the former will better perform when evaluating governmental policies. The second perspective, rooted in the seminal works of Anthony Downs (1957) and E. E. Schattschneider (1960), highlights the structures of modern political systems and the nature of information flows within them. It sees these features as severely limiting the capacities of all citizens.

On the surface, the perspective would seem to hold out more hope than the structural perspective for effective citizen evaluation of globalization and similar policies. This hope lies with the more politically sophisticated citizens. But, we argue in the third section, evidence showing that the more sophisticated make superior judgments is thin. A study revealing the biased mental processes they use to judge policy consequences raises additional questions about their presumed role in democratic governance.

In light of all the above, and by way of conclusion, we speculate about the likely nature and quality of democratic decision-making on globalization-related issues. Passage of the North Atlantic Free Trade Agreement (NAFTA) in the United States provides an opportunity to consider how one democratic country approached a unique globalization policy. Debate among politicians did not fall neatly along party lines. Available survey data indicate that ordinary citizens reached their judgments essentially by placing their faith with politicians whom they liked and trusted. This cue-taking, however, was not random: white collar workers aligned themselves with one set of politicians, blue collar workers with the other set.

More generally, how citizens and countries react to globalization-related issues will ultimately depend on the behavior of political elites. If policy decisions increasingly emerge from non-democratic bodies, as Simmons predicts and Freeman and Orlie lament, then public debates among elected politicians will most likely decline. More crucially, these politicans, like the citizens they represent, will find themselves functioning as outsiders. They will face all the constraints and limitations that have long afflicted citizens. Under these conditions, the challenges confronting sovereign democracies will be considerable. But why, we wonder, would sovereign politicians concede their power and authority in the first place?

The Question of Uniqueness

Held and McGrew (1999) aptly define globalization as a set of processes that transforms the spatial organization of social relations and transactions. Four transformations, they argue, characterize globalization, and thus presumably distinguish it from other phenomena. First, it stretches social, political, and economic activities across space. Second, it intensifies interconnectedness in finance, politics, culture, and investment. Third, it increases the rate at which goods, ideas, people, and information are diffused. Finally, and as a result of the other three changes, developments in one locale or region strongly affect conditions in others. In short, globalization means that policy decisions will have a wider and more immediate impact than ever before.

These changes not only define globalization, they represent some of the most dramatic and potentially consequential shifts of the last century. Decisions that a small group makes in Paris, Zurich, or New York City can immediately and substantially affect the lives of people throughout the world. No wonder that advocates and opponents of globalization alike express their views with zeal.

The increased scope, speed, and impact of highly intertwined decisions underline the need for democratic societies to make the right choices when deliberating issues associated with globalization, or when responding to the consequences of already-implemented policies. On that everyone will agree. However, these characteristics themselves say nothing about whether globalization poses new and unique decision-making challenges for citizens.

Consider the kinds of globalization-related questions that citizens have already faced: Will pending legislation designed to increase free trade help or hurt my country's workers? Which workers? Will a proposal to adopt a common currency weaken or strengthen the economies of the participating countries? Will it help some countries more than others? Will legislation encouraging the growth of regional and worldwide service providers reduce the costs of service delivery or lead to monopolies? To be sure, these questions are substantively unique to globalization, but finding answers to them poses no new and unfamiliar challenges. In the mid-1990s, for example, members of the U.S. Congress debated three separate bills designed to develop a national information infrastructure (Kuklinski and Hurley 1996). All of them contained pages of technical language. Sponsors of one bill cast its lot with the cable industry, sponsors of another with the telephone industry, and so forth. Which bill Congress ultimately adopted would affect people's lives for years. So which one should U.S. citizens have endorsed?

Pick this last question and then pick any of the globalization-related questions cited immediately before it. The obstacles to answering them will be identical. First is the lack of transparency. Citizens cannot expect to know every provision and stipulation of a current legislative bill or a policy agreement between two or more countries. Among active participants, the specifics found in such provisions and stipulations often generate the strongest and most heated disagreements because they define the stakes. Second, citizens are often judging policies whose consequences will be unknown for years or perhaps decades. Will adoption of the Euro have negative long-term effects? Some might offer more reasoned speculations than others, but speculation it nevertheless will be.

Finally, even when citizens have the benefit of observing actual consequences after implementation of a policy, they rarely will be able to assert confidently that the particular policy caused them. Suppose, for example, that citizens in several European Union countries find, ten years hence, that their purchasing power has fallen. Did adoption of the Euro cause the decline? Economists cannot convincingly answer the question; why assume that the typical citizen would even contemplate a possible connection between a policy passed years ago and the current state of affairs?

At least one of these three obstacles—lack of transparency, uncertainty arising from the time horizon, and difficulty of ascertaining cause and effect—

comes into play every time ordinary citizens evaluate the contents of a policy proposal or the consequences of an existing policy. Globalization highlights the difficulties, but, at least for citizens, it does not pose challenges that differ from those found in other domains. Therefore the existing literature on citizen decision making should offer insights into how citizens will fare when evaluating such issues, assuming they evaluate them at all.

Two Perspectives on Citizens and Democratic Governance

Although categorizing research is always perilous, we distinguish two perspectives on citizens and their roles in democratic governance. Whether the perspectives differ qualitatively or in degree is arguable, but, in either event, they point researchers in different directions. The first and currently dominant perspective emphasizes individual differences in political knowledge and cognitive capacity. Steeped in survey research, it places faith in the more politically sophisticated segments of nations' populations. The second emphasizes the structures of representative democracies and the nature of information flows within them. It speaks to the inherent limitations that apply to all citizens and declares differences in cognitive abilities largely irrelevant.

INFORMATION, COGNITION, AND POLITICAL SOPHISTICATION

Conceptually, to be politically sophisticated means to hold an extensive and cohesive mental representation of real-world politics. If we could look inside politically sophisticated people's heads, we would find many political cognitions, including values, beliefs, issue positions, and partisan attachments. These cognitions would be organized in politically logical ways (Luskin 1986). Politically sophisticated people might hold consistently liberal or conservative cognitions, for example.

Not surprisingly, the politically sophisticated also pay more attention to and express more interest in politics and policymaking. They can recite the major issues that Congress is debating. They more properly derive inferences from the available evidence.

Scholars typically do not measure political sophistication directly, but, rather, as the proportion of a set of factual items the survey respondent answers correctly. Examples of such items, as applied to the United States, include the following: Who holds veto power? How many justices sit on the Supreme Court? Which party controls the House (Senate)? Which party is more conservative? Who is Yassar Arafat?[2] By construction of the measure, those who correctly answer more items qualify as more politically sophisticated.

People vary markedly in their levels of political sophistication. Relatively few score high, the rest do not. This distribution is unfortunate, according to the theory of political sophistication, because only the more sophisticated can meaningfully guide politicians and policymakers.[3] They send the clear signal while the less sophisticated contribute most of the noise. Presumably this conclusion applies to globalization.

DEMOCRATIC STRUCTURES AND INFORMATION FLOWS

Proponents of the second perspective begin with the structure of contemporary political systems. It ensures, they assert, that most citizens cannot offer policymakers anything other than vague and general guidance. This is not to deny public opinion's presence or influence. But the contrast that students of public opinion make between more and less sophisticated citizens pales in comparison to the contrast between all citizens on the one hand and those who directly participate in the policy process on the other.

Anthony Downs's *An Economic Theory of Democracy* (1957) and E. E. Schattschneider's *The Semisovereign People* (1960), both written in the days before survey research dominated political behavior research, are the seminal works within this tradition.[4] Downs notes, in a rarely cited discussion, that although legislators publicly debate the general contours of proposed policies, they often fail to discuss the specific provisions that really matter. To take a current example, politicians have begun to debate whether to allow individuals to control the investments of part of their Social Security funds. But they have rarely discussed what provisions will exist to protect less business-savvy individuals from making bad investment decisions. On any major policy proposal, therefore, only the very small number of active participants—the insiders—can make informed and well-grounded judgments. Given the structure of contemporary representative democracies, most citizens will not be "well enough informed to influence directly the formulation of those policies that affect them" (259). To put it more bluntly, it is rational for the typical citizen to remain ignorant; and ignorant people cannot make good policy judgments.

Schattschneider echoes a similar theme. At best, he states emphatically, ordinary citizens can listen to the general arguments that competing partisan leaders make, and then support one or the other side. But politicians, not citizens, define the political discourse and the lines along which conflict will occur. In this sense, people are indeed only semi-sovereign.

Like Downs, therefore, Schattschneider does not distinguish more from less sophisticated citizens. To both authors, the distinction is meaningless; all citizens are necessarily too uninformed to guide policymaking.[5] But

Schattschneider goes further, chiding those scholars who use polls and survey data to determine what people know about politics. In his characteristically colorful language:

> The theory of the polls is essentially simplistic, based on a tremendously exaggerated notion of the immediacy and urgency of the connection of public opinion and events. The result is that sometimes we seem to be interviewing the fish in the sea to find out what the birds in the heavens are doing. (130)
>
> The public is far too sensible to attempt to play the preposterous role assigned to it by the theorists. We have tended to undervalue this attitude because we have labored under an illusion about democracy. (131)
>
> [Democracy is] a form of collaboration of ignorant people and experts. (136–37)

Whether the many survey studies falling under the political sophistication rubric have caused Schattschneider to roll over in his grave only he and God know for sure.

The Politically Sophisticated: Evidence and Assumption

We might simply acknowledge that political scientists are of two minds about the role of citizens in democratic governance and move on to other topics. A simple declaration of incompatibility will not do, however. The last four decades of research on public opinion, after all, has consistently distinguished between more and less sophisticated citizens for a reason. Surely there must be compelling evidence that the former will perform better, however that is defined. Is there? We think not.

First, scholars have found the more sophisticated to be better educated, more highly interested in politics, and more strongly partisan than the less sophisticated. Unfortunately, not one of these distinguishing characteristics directly measures performance. Second, these same scholars argue that the more knowledgeable perform better because they know more. This sounds tautological, and it is.

The seemingly most compelling evidence shows that less and more politically sophisticated citizens hold different opinions. Most convincing of all, in this regard, regression simulations in which researchers change the value on the knowledge variable from less knowledgeable to more knowledgeable demonstrate that the less knowledgeable would hold nearly the same opinions as the more knowledgeable if they knew more (Althaus 1998; Bartels 1996; Delli

Carpini and Keeter 1996; Gilens 2001). Uninformed liberal Democrats with eighth-grade educations, for example, would consistently take positions that look more like those of informed liberal Democrats with college educations.

These simulations make a key assumption, namely, that those who score higher on political sophistication measures hold the more democratically meaningful—the "right"—opinions. And how do we know this? We don't. Kuklinski and Quirk (2000) argued elsewhere that available evidence fails to support this assumption. Gilens (2001) has shown that general knowledge does not ensure policy-specific knowledge. Those who can recite civics-textbook facts, he found, did no better at knowing policy-specific facts.

Overall, then, the political sophistication thesis is based more on assumption than evidence. The assumption is understandable. After all, the more sophisticated trump the less sophisticated with respect to education and interest in politics; and these are the very factors one would expect to shape performance. But by what mental process do the more sophisticated reach their policy judgments? The answer to this question can provide a basis for anticipating how the presumably more capable segments of countries' populations, at least, will approach globalization-related issues.

Political Sophistication and Democratic Intelligence

Citizens perform many tasks in democratic societies. They vote, work on campaigns, post signs in their yards, and write letters to their representatives, among other things. Henceforth, we focus on a particular task: guiding democratic policymaking by expressing opinions for the purpose of endorsing or correcting existing policies. Citizens tell policymakers that they do or do not like what they see. We label this task democratic intelligence. Its importance to democratic societies becomes especially crucial when a policy's consequences become undeniably negative.

Why this task and not others? For one thing, democratic intelligence takes the form of a clear and explicit statement of approval or disapproval about a particular policy's consequences. It stands in contrast to election returns, for example, which simultaneously convey much and convey little. The removal of politicians from office likely reflects discontent, but beyond that, successful candidates can interpret the results as they see fit.[6] For another, democratic intelligence partially overcomes the structural and informational obstacles that led Downs and Schattschneider to their conclusions. People can see consequences in their daily lives. Finally, citizens will most likely evaluate globalization policies in terms of consequences. This will be especially true if, as Simmons and Freeman predict, initial globalization policy choices are increasingly made out of public view.

Democratic intelligence lies with aggregated public opinion; it is the public's collective voice. It begins with individual citizens, who, to render democratic intelligence workable, must meet four individually necessary and jointly sufficient conditions:

1. See a causal connection between a government policy and real-world conditions;
2. Know the relevant facts;
3. Update factual beliefs as real-world facts change;
4. Use changed beliefs to update policy assessments.

There are both structural and mental obstacles to meeting these conditions. The biggest structural obstacle is obvious: people might not be able to see a connection between a governmental policy and real-world conditions. Sometimes, however, they can. The president implements some widely discussed economic measures; they make things better or worse, or have no effect at all. The president undertakes educational reform; student performance increases, or it does not. The president declares war; there is a clear and quick victory, or troop casualties rise dramatically in a protracted engagement. How clearly citizens see the connection between a policy and its consequences will depend heavily on what the media and elected officials do. When the latter remain silent, there will be no democratic intelligence.

Less obvious are the mental obstacles. Steps 2–4 above assume that individuals strive to be rational updaters who consciously and objectively evaluate government policies. In short, the steps assume that citizens strive for accuracy. This assumption appears to underlie the theory of political sophistication. Otherwise, why care what people know?

Psychology suggests an alternative motivation: maintaining one's existing beliefs and opinions. Couched in the relatively new language of motivated reasoning (Kunda 1990), the idea is simple, intuitive, and familiar (see Festinger 1957). Essentially, people strive either to be accurate or to be consistent. The more strongly they feel about a particular domain in life, the more likely they will pursue consistency. Specifically with respect to politics, Lodge and Taber (2000) report that the politically sophisticated are the most emphatic in seeking to maintain their opinions. They seek out confirming evidence, counter-argue contrary information, and attribute more strength to arguments that match their existing opinions. Their strong partisanship serves as the motivation for opinion rationalization, and their general understanding of politics facilitates their mental efforts.

But how can strongly partisan Democrats and Republicans see the same world of policy consequences so differently when the facts are, supposedly, the facts? They could tune out so as to avoid learning the relevant facts. In politics, as in love, ignorance can be bliss. In addition, two features of American politics allow, if not encourage, differential perceptions: first, much of the partisan debate in politics centers on the future; and, second, all things political are open to interpretation. Suppose people learn that twenty troops are killed in Iraq on a single day. A strong and politically astute Republican might conclude that although twenty were killed today, chances are good that far fewer will be killed in the days ahead. Moreover, he or she might interpret the fatalities as not bad, given the nature of the Iraq conflict. Conversely, a strong Democrat might see the twenty fatalities as a harbinger of even worse things to come and conclude that, in any case, the loss of this many troops is deplorable. Should their own motivations not suffice to invoke this sort of reasoning, strongly (and weakly) partisan citizens can always heed and adopt their partisan leaders' pronouncements.

Our research group, which includes Brian Gaines and Jay Verkuilen as well as the current co-authors, has collected data that speak directly to these mental processes. To date, we have completed four panel studies, each consisting of three waves, on beliefs about and opinions toward the U.S. invasion of Iraq. The data we report herein come from the first and second panel studies, which cover fall to early winter 2003 and spring to early summer 2004, respectively.[7] We will refer to the remaining two panels when appropriate.

Figure 6.1 displays the major events that occurred during data collection. Most posed bad news for the Bush administration. Early on, these included the bombing of the Jordanian Embassy, the UN compound in Iraq, and the Red Cross headquarters; the rocket attack on the Al-Rasheed hotel; the downing of a Chinook helicopter; and the dramatic increase in the number of troops killed. The news for the administration continued to worsen. Both David Kay and Hans Blix publicly raised the possibility that weapons of mass destruction did not exist, after which the Bush administration began to admit as much. Highly visible bombings continued. Terrorists killed and mutilated four U.S. contractors in Fallujah (which, arguably, might have evoked strong support for the Bush administration, but it did not, at least among our sample). Perhaps most significant, the story about the torture of Iraqi prisoners broke. Democrats used these events to become even more

Figure 6.1 Timeline of Iraq events, August 2003–May 2004

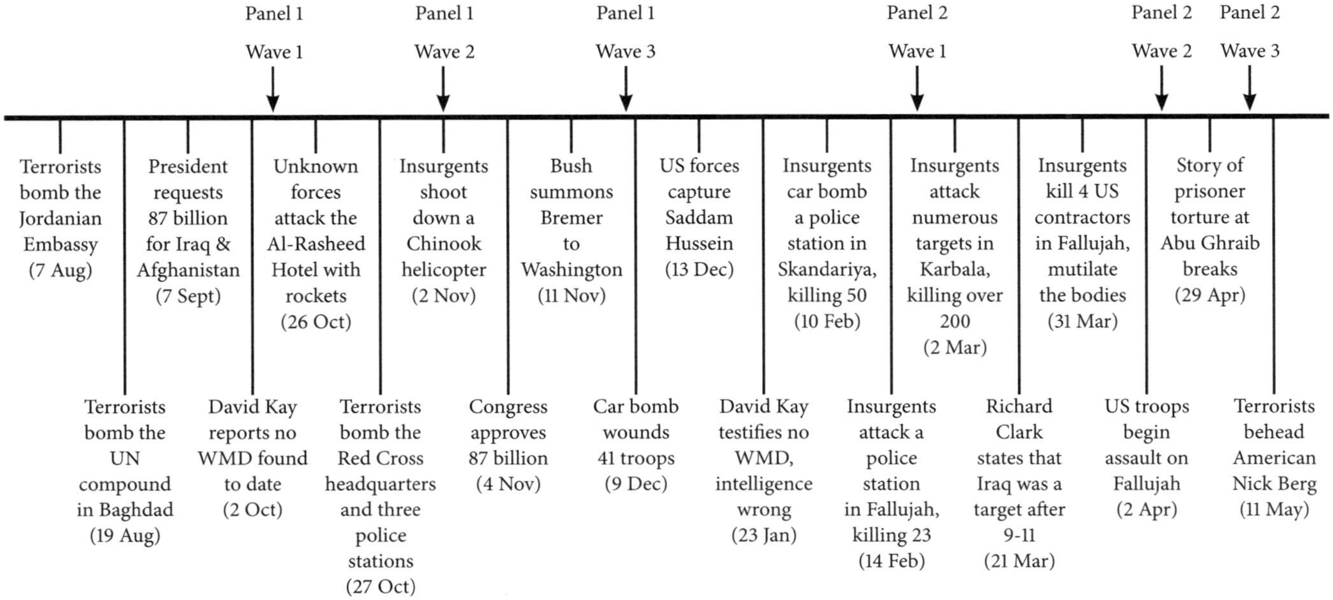

Panel 1 Wave 1
Panel 1 Wave 2
Panel 1 Wave 3
Panel 2 Wave 1
Panel 2 Wave 2
Panel 2 Wave 3

Terrorists bomb the Jordanian Embassy (7 Aug)
Terrorists bomb the UN compound in Baghdad (19 Aug)
President requests 87 billion for Iraq & Afghanistan (7 Sept)
David Kay reports no WMD found to date (2 Oct)
Unknown forces attack the Al-Rasheed Hotel with rockets (26 Oct)
Terrorists bomb the Red Cross headquarters and three police stations (27 Oct)
Insurgents shoot down a Chinook helicopter (2 Nov)
Congress approves 87 billion (4 Nov)
Bush summons Bremer to Washington (11 Nov)
Car bomb wounds 41 troops (9 Dec)
US forces capture Saddam Hussein (13 Dec)
David Kay testifies no WMD, intelligence wrong (23 Jan)
Insurgents car bomb a police station in Skandariya, killing 50 (10 Feb)
Insurgents attack a police station in Fallujah, killing 23 (14 Feb)
Insurgents attack numerous targets in Karbala, killing over 200 (2 Mar)
Richard Clark states that Iraq was a target after 9-11 (21 Mar)
Insurgents kill 4 US contractors in Fallujah, mutilate the bodies (31 Mar)
US troops begin assault on Fallujah (2 Apr)
Story of prisoner torture at Abu Ghraib breaks (29 Apr)
Terrorists behead American Nick Berg (11 May)

vocal in their criticism, while Republicans, lead by the administration, tried to minimize the events' cumulating effect.

So, did respondents change their beliefs and opinions in response to undeniably worsening conditions? In particular, did the highly partisan and more politically sophisticated take unfolding events into account, or did they rationalize their existing opinions? For purposes of answering these questions, we have divided our respondents into three categories: strong Democrats, strong Republicans, and weak partisans, which include self-proclaimed independents.[8]

We used two items to measure our respondents' opinions toward the war and another to measure their assessments of George Bush's performance with regard to the Iraq war. Table 6.1 shows the changes in opinions and assessments among the strongly and weakly partisan over the two panels. Responses to any one item look similar to those on the other two. Strong Republicans, confronted with more and more unwanted evidence, simply did not budge in their opinions; nor did strong Democrats. Not shown in Table 6.1, about 90 percent of strong Republicans supported the war and the Bush administration over the period of study, while about the same percent of strong Democrats opposed. Democratic intelligence, as we have defined it, did not emanate from strong partisans. Constancy and bifurcation, not change and consensus, tell the story of strong partisans.

Opinion change occurs far more frequently among the weak partisans. To be sure, a majority of them look like strong partisans, in that they held steady to their existing opinions and assessments. Nevertheless, about a quarter of them changed opinions and assessments over each of the two panels. Although not reported in Table 6.1, nearly all of the change represents increasing opposition to the war and the Bush administration's efforts. Also not shown: opinion change among weak Democrats and independents outdistances that among weak Republicans. In the third and fourth panels, however, weak Republicans became increasingly critical of the war and its handling.

To get a better sense of the mental processes that the partisan groups were using, consider the question of weapons of mass destruction (WMD) in Iraq. Recall that those who were in charge of finding such weapons began, early on, to suggest they did not exist. Nearly all of the respondents knew that WMD had not been found. Early on, strong Republicans were more inclined than others to say that the weapons had been found, but by the end of the second panel nearly 90 percent of them acknowledged that this was not the case. At least with respect to knowing this basic fact, partisan biases did not prevail. The massive media coverage probably precluded anything but accuracy.

Table 6.1. Percent who did not change attitudes and assessments from first to last wave of panel, by strength of partisanship

	Strong Democrats	Strong Republicans	Weak Partisans and Independents
Attitude toward the war 1[a]	91.5	88.9	73.8
Attitude toward the war 1[b]	91.7	92.3	83.3
Assessment of GWB policy on Iraq[c]	84.4	92.6	82.0
Spring 2004	**Strong Democrats**	**Strong Republicans**	**Weak Partisans and Independents**
Attitude toward the war 1[a]	90.6	95.0	82.2
Attitude toward the war 1[b]	84.4	100.0	88.0
Assessment of GWB policy on Iraq[c]	90.9	90.9	91.9

[a] Which of the following best describes your feelings about the U.S. invasion of Iraq?
[b] Do you think the U.S. made the right or wrong decision in using military force against Iraq?
[c] Do you approve or disapprove of the way President George W. Bush is handling policies toward Iraq?

Expectations about finding WMD in the future are a wholly different matter, however (Figure 6.2). Although strong Democrats and the weakly partisan overwhelmingly expected that WMD would not be found, a majority of strong Republicans, by completion of the second panel, still believed that they would. In fairness, it was still reasonable, at this time, to expect investigators to find the weapons.

By the time we completed the third and fourth panels, however, the Bush administration itself grudgingly began to concede that the weapons probably would not be found. Strong Republicans, in turn, became markedly less optimistic about finding the weapons. But they still found a way to rationalize their opinions. In these last two panels, we asked respondents why the United States had not found the weapons. About 90 percent of strong Democrats and weak partisans gave one answer: the weapons never existed. In striking contrast, the same percentage of strong Republicans offered one of three explanations: Iraq moved or destroyed the weapons, or the United States simply had not yet found them.

This mental rationalization occurred regarding more issues than weapons of mass destruction. On a series of factual items, we found that partisan motivations did not shape people's beliefs about the facts but did influence their interpretations of them and their expectations about what would happen in the future. For example, strong and weak partisans more or less agreed on the number of troops that had been killed; and they all updated their beliefs as the number of troops killed increased over time. However, strong Repub-

Figure 6.2 Expectations of finding WMD, by strength of partisanship

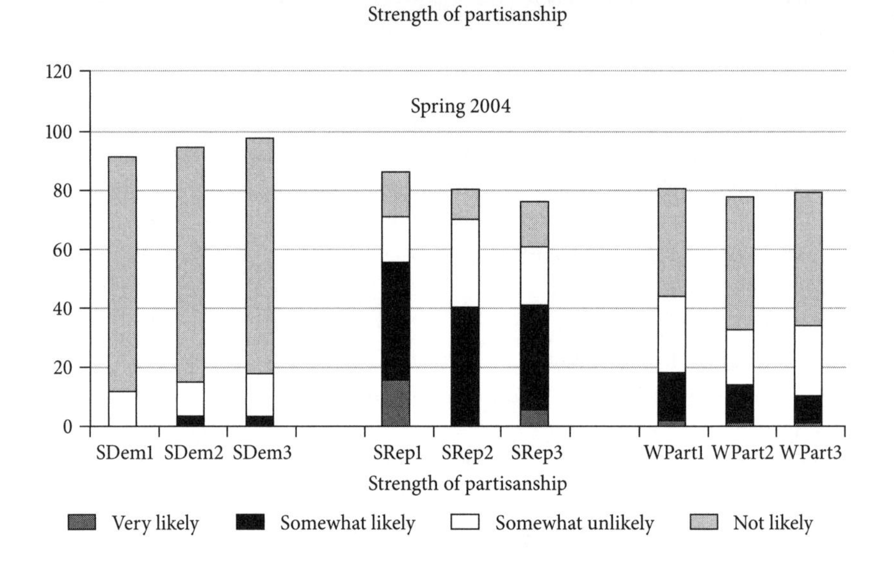

licans consistently interpreted the number as far less severe than anyone else and also predicted markedly fewer future casualties.

One might think that not seeing a connection between a policy and its consequences would serve as the biggest obstacle to democratic intelligence. It is indeed a necessary and perhaps the most fundamental condition. In the case of the Iraq war, however, people saw the connection. Nevertheless, the desire to maintain existing beliefs and opinions weakened the intelligence function, nowhere more so than among the highly partisan and politically sophisticated. Paradoxically, these are the very individuals who are best equipped to know and understand the facts, and thus perform the intelligence function.

The Iraq war occurred during a time of high partisan conflict. It undoubtedly contributed to that conflict. So what does the preceding discussion say, if anything, about likely citizen performance on globalization-related issues? By way of conclusion, we offer some speculations.

Citizens, Politicians, and Globalization

In the United States, Congress has already addressed globalization, most notably in the form of the 1993 North American Free Trade Agreement (NAFTA), which ultimately passed. Ordinary Americans watched and listened as congressional members debated the wisdom of eliminating trade barriers and promoting fair competition on the North American continent, which, to most Americans, represented a new idea with a lot of unknowns. President Clinton as well as former presidents Bush, Ford, and Carter made a strong case for NAFTA. Corporate America joined them. Former presidential candidate Ross Perot and leading Democrats such as Richard Gephardt strenuously argued against. Perot adopted an alarmist strategy, predicting that workers in potentially affected industries would lose their jobs. Labor and environmental groups sided with the opposition.

Like Iraq, NAFTA received unusually high media coverage, during congressional deliberations, especially, but also in the following years. Unlike Iraq, NAFTA required American citizens to enter new and unfamiliar terrain. Also unlike Iraq, arguments over NAFTA did not fall neatly along partisan lines.

Two types of data shed light on how Americans formed judgments about NAFTA during the time Congress debated it. Aggregate survey data show that a majority of Americans initially opposed NAFTA; by time of its passage, a small majority supported it. Many blue-collar workers endorsed the Perot-Gephardt position, while white-collar workers overwhelmingly supported the treaty. At the beginning of the debate, 34 percent of the populace said they had not heard enough about NAFTA to hold an opinion; by the end, a hefty 26 percent still proclaimed ignorance. People more easily grasp wars than they do international trade agreements, even when abundant information about the latter is readily available.

The aggregate data do not reveal the mental processes that individual citizens employed. Thus they do not allow us to determine whether more and less sophisticated citizens made their decisions in different ways and, if they did, whether the former made the "better" choices. Uslaner's study (1998), which uses September and November 1993 NBC-*Wall Street Journal* survey data, comes closer, although the data are not as complete as the Iraq data, which we collected with these questions in mind.

Uslaner's findings make clear that more and less politically sophisticated citizens, at least as measured roughly by education, coped with the new and unfamiliar policy proposal in similar ways. Not knowing all the details of the proposed policy and lacking a basis on which to make confident predictions about the policy's effects, people used their feelings toward the key actors in the NAFTA initiative as their primary criterion. Thus people who approved of Clinton and former presidents Bush, Ford, and Carter overwhelmingly supported the treaty. Conversely, those who liked Perot but not the presidents overwhelmingly opposed. In short, lacking experience on globalization issues, and facing much uncertainty, Americans optimized their choices by taking cues from political leaders they liked and trusted (Mondak 1993; Popkin 1991; Sniderman, Brody, and Tetlock 1991). Whether use of this heuristic was desirable is debatable; whether it was necessary is not.

During the decade following the passage of NAFTA, many American workers lost their jobs. Working-class incomes began and continue to stagnate. Although most Americans have continued to acknowledge the benefits of free trade, overall support has declined, with most of the change occurring among U.S. workers (Scheve and Slaughter 2007). Does it make sense for workers to attribute the job losses to NAFTA? In light of Perot's earlier predictions, as well as recent congressional deliberations on the trade agreement's consequences, their attributions make good sense. But are the attributions right? Professional economists, those best equipped to know, do not agree.

Liberalization is a fact of economic and political life. It will continue to affect the lives of citizens throughout the world. How will they respond? Will they make "good" judgments and evaluations? All of our answers, importantly, depend on what political leaders say and do. We assume, for the moment, that political leaders in countries throughout the world will debate proposed policies and openly discuss the consequences of existing policies, as U.S. leaders did on NAFTA.

If liberalization debates fall sharply along partisan lines, highly partisan and knowledgeable citizens will likely place their faith in one or another party, as our data on the Iraq war showed. In the U.S. context, for example, strong Republicans and strong Democrats will assume their parties to be protecting their interests and thus will stay the party line. The less politically astute will not ignore party positions, but neither will they rely on party alone. More directly and immediately affected by globalization policies, they will be more inclined to take their own well-being into account, and they will try to tell a causal story about how a particular policy caused that well-being. For them to succeed will require open political deliberation in which experts and politicians spin such stories. According to this prediction, the less politically sophisticated, as in the case of the Iraq war, will provide most of the signal for change. National debates about liberalization might not fall along established partisan lines, as NAFTA illustrates, in which case citizens will look to alternative cues, perhaps in the form of individual politicians whom they trust.

Notice the "hope and pray" character of all these possibilities. Citizens have no choice but to hope and pray that their parties or the leaders in whom they put their trust are pursuing the right liberalization policies. Similarly, they must hope and pray that they have adopted the right causal story.

Dire as this all sounds, it describes business-as-usual. Citizens, after all, are the outsiders, politicians the insiders. That is the essential message of Downs and Schattschneider.

Suppose, however, that Simmons, Freeman, and Orlie are right in suggesting that international organizations will gain proportionately more and more authority for globalization-related decisions. By implication, national legislators and executives will increasingly become outsiders, just as their citizens are now. Then all of the constraints that currently limit citizens will limit them as well. Presumably, public deliberation on globalization issues will decline. Those who value national sovereignty should shudder at the prospect.

We cannot help but wonder, however, why sovereign leaders would allow their power to slip away. On the surface, it makes no sense. Can they not harness the products of technological progress? Do they not see the developments that increasingly strip away their decision-making authority? The latter seems unlikely. Perhaps scholars exaggerate the changes and the potential dangers. That, too, seems unlikely, although more likely than politicians failing to see the impending threats to their sovereign power and authority. Or do most politicians in most countries see the rise of international organizations as a source of increased power? After all, many national leaders, on many occasions, have passed legislation creating international organizations. Knowing the implications of globalization for democratic governance requires more fully understanding the motives and incentives of national leaders. This might be one of the most important tasks facing students of globalization.

Notes

1. Rahn (chapter 7) documents that internationalization has also weakened people's allegiances to the countries in which they live.

2. Whether these factual items validly measure political sophistication would seem, on its face, to be questionable. However, Luskin (1986) makes a strong case in support of such items. In his creative study, Bartels (1996) uses interviewers' assessments of respondents' political knowledge as his measure of sophistication.

3. The overall level of political sophistication has remained constant over the past forty years (Delli Carpini and Keeter 1996).

4. Rarely do two books differ in style more than these two. Whereas Downs adopted a highly deductive approach that launched the use of formal theory and mathematical modeling in political science, Schattschneider offers rarely-seen insights and a lot of diatribe.

5. Schattschneider conveys the distinct impression that abolishing polls and surveys would benefit democratic societies.

6. Building on the retrospective voting literature, Nardulli (2005) argues that election returns send the needed signals. He provides strong evidence with respect to crime and unemployment.

7. Our respondents are University of Illinois students. Although it might seem a stretch to use students as respondents in the context of a discussion of citizen performance on globalization, the data serve our purposes. We feel confident that the processes we identify are universal.

8. That we could combine weak Democrats and weak Republicans in these two panels is an interesting story that we will not pursue here.

References

Althaus, Scott L. 1998. "Information Effects in Collective Preferences." American *Political Science Review* 92:545–58.

Bartels, Larry M. 1996. "Uninformed Votes: Information Effects in Presidential Elections." *American Journal of Political Science* 40:194–230.

Delli Carpini, Michael X., and Scott Keeter. 1996. *What Americans Know about Politics and Why It Matters.* New Haven, Conn.: Yale University Press.

Downs, Anthony. 1957. *An Economic Theory of Democracy.* New York: Harper.

Festinger, Leon. 1957. *A Theory of Cognitive Dissonance.* Palo Alto, Calif.: Stanford University Press.

Gilens, Martin. 2001. "Political Ignorance and Collective Policy Preferences." *American Political Science Review* 95:379–396.

Held, David, and Anthony McGrew. 1999. *Global Transformations: Politics, Economics, and Culture.* Cambridge: Polity Press.

Kuklinski, James H., and Norman Hurley. 1996. "It's a Matter of Interpretation." In

Political Persuasion and Attitude Change, ed. Diana C. Mutz, Paul M. Sniderman, and Richard A. Brody, 125–70. Ann Arbor: University of Michigan Press.

Kuklinski, James H., and Paul J. Quirk. 2000. "Reconsidering the Rational Public: Heuristics, Cognition, and Mass Opinion." In Lupia, McCubbins, and Popkin 153–82.

Kunda, Ziva. 1990. "The Case for Motivated Reasoning." *Psychological Bulletin* 108: 480–498.

Lodge, Milton, and Charles Taber. 2000. "Three Steps Toward a Theory of Motivated Reasoning." In Lupia, McCubbins, and Popkin 183–213.

Lupia, Arthur, Mathew D. McCubbins, and Samuel L. Popkin, eds. 2000. *Elements of Reason: Cognition, Choice, and the Bounds of Rationality.* New York: Cambridge University Press.

Luskin, Robert C. 1986. "Measuring Political Sophistication." *American Journal of Political Science* 31:856–99.

Mondak, Jeffery J. 1993. "Public Opinion and Heuristic Processing of Source Cues." *Political Behavior* 15:167–92.

Nardulli, Peter F. 2005. *Popular Efficacy in the Democratic Era: A Reexamination of Electoral Accountability in the U.S., 1828–2000.* Princeton, N.J.: Princeton University Press.

Popkin, Samuel L. 1991. *The Reasoning Voter: Communication and Persuasion in Presidential Campaigns.* Chicago: University of Chicago Press.

Schattschneider, E. E. 1960. *The Semisovereign People: A Realists View of Democracy in America.* New York: Holt.

Sheve, Kenneth F., and Matthew J. Slaughter. 2007. "A New Deal for Globalization." *Foreign Affairs:* 86:34–40.

Sniderman, Paul M., Richard A. Brody, and Philip E. Tetlock. 1991. *Reasoning and Choice: Explorations in Political Psychology.* Cambridge: Cambridge University Press.

Uslaner, Eric. 1998. "Trade Winds: NAFTA and the Rational Public." *Political Behavior* 20: 341–360.

7

Globalization, the Decline of Civic Commitments, and the Future of Democracy

WENDY RAHN

It's the end of the world as we know it.
It's the end of the world as we know it.
It's the end of the world as we know it and I feel fine.
—R.E.M.

We're on the road to nowhere.
—Talking Heads

According to a substantial number of people, the nation-state is under assault from both external and internal pressures.[1] The kinds of changes that have occurred in the global political economy in the last two decades are said to threaten the centrality of the nation-state as the primary unit of political organization. Collectively captured with the term "globalization," these forces are said to impinge on the capabilities—indeed, the very sovereignty—of even the strongest states, with perhaps problematic consequences for democracy as we have known it (see Simmons, chapter 8, and Freeman, chapter 9). My goal in this chapter is to discuss some of the manifold aspects of globalization as they bear on the loyalties and commitments of people who are implicated in, and affected by, these transformations.[2]

Notions of democracy and popular sovereignty are inextricably linked to the history of the nation-state (Benhabib 2002; Yack 2003; Williams 2004). Increasingly, however, intensifications in the cross-border movement of goods, people, and information have called into question the traditional historical formula. Citizenship has become decoupled from territory (Soysal 1994; Jacobson 1997; Sassen 2004); global flows of capital and labor challenge states' authority to control their borders and to deliver the goods of state membership; and international travel and worldwide communications systems make the world available to everyone, not just the few. There are vigorous theoretical debates about the implications of this "turbulence" (Rosenau 1990) for democracy, but to a remarkable degree, these debates have been unanchored by large-scale quantitative investigations of the impact of globalization on individual-level identities and orientations.[3] In addition, even though many discussions of globalization treat it as an irresistible force that is happening everywhere, there is, in fact, enormous variation across countries in the degree of their participation in the economic, cultural, and political dynamics of globalization. In this chapter, I seek to put this variation to productive use in order to provide a more systematic overview of the much-ballyhooed consequences of globalization. If, according to many a prophecy, it is the end of the world as we know it, we should have some idea of what might await us in the next one.

A glimpse into democracy's future is made possible by the recent release of the International Association for the Evaluation of Educational Achievement (IEA) Civic Education Study (Civ-Ed). Comprising some ninety thousand students in more than four thousand schools across twenty-eight established and new democracies interviewed in the late 1990s, the IEA data set provides a unique crystal ball in which to peer. The attitudes and orientations of democracy's youngest members are our tea leaves, for they will "come to dominate institutions and infuse politics as older generations quietly or not so quietly leave the population" (Rahn 1998, 1). Exploiting the power of this enormous data set, I will examine in this chapter between-nation differences in national attitudes and civic commitments, attempting to relate these to various themes discussed in the enormous literature on globalization and the future of the nation-state. In the end, I conclude that the future of democracy appears troubled; from the vantage point provided by the IEA data, it is apparent that many of the elements of globalization are compromising the continued viability of democratic nation-states as objects of attachment for young people. Furthermore, this denationalization weakens commitments to conventional civic virtues—without, however, a corresponding increase in commitments to so-called cosmopolitan forms of democratic action.

Research Design and Measures

INDIVIDUAL ORIENTATIONS: THE IEA DATA

The IEA is a consortium of nearly sixty countries that collaborate in the collection of data on student knowledge in a variety of different areas, including science and mathematics. Spurred by international developments, a group of interested countries called on the IEA to undertake a cross-national study of civic education. After some initial development phases, in 1999 the IEA fielded a survey study of nationally representative samples of fourteen-year-olds in twenty-eight countries. A follow-up study in sixteen countries followed in 2000, focusing on older upper-secondary students ages sixteen to nineteen (Torney-Purta and Amadeo 2003). Because of its greater coverage of countries, I make use of the study of fourteen-year-olds.[4] Table 7.1 lists the participating countries in the study of fourteen-year-olds and the number of students surveyed.

One advantage of the IEA data set is that it includes nations that differ tremendously on a number of dimensions, including levels of economic development, population size, age of democracy, continent, and heterogeneity. While not strictly a random sample of the world's democratic nation-states, the diversity of the cases does help to maximize variation on my independent variables of interest, increasing my confidence in the generality of my findings. This variation is discussed in greater detail in the next section.

Students were asked to answer a variety of different types of questions, including their understanding of concepts of democracy, their attitudes toward their nation and government, feelings about immigrants, and assessments of the classroom climate for political discussion. A substantial portion of the questionnaire was given over to measuring political and civic knowledge. Some of the civic knowledge questions were of a factual nature: "Which of the following is an accurate statement about laws?" Others required skills in "political interpretation" of common forms of political communication such as editorial cartoons and campaign platforms.

DEPENDENT VARIABLES

NATIONAL IDENTITY As I have argued elsewhere, psychological sense of national identity has several dimensions and is distinct from, although related to, patriotism (Rahn, Kroeger, and Kite 1996; Rahn 2004). The psychological centrality of national identity is our term for "the significance that the individual invests in his or her national membership" (Rahn, Kroeger, and

Table 7.1. Countries in the IEA Civ-Ed study

Country	N of students
Australia	3,301
Belgium (French)	2,075
Bulgaria	2,857
Chile	5,677
Colombia	4,889
Cyprus	3,102
Czech Republic	3,599
Denmark	3,192
England	3,011
Estonia	3,418
Finland	2,776
Germany	3,685
Greece	3,448
Hong Kong (SAR)	4,993
Hungary	3,165
Italy	3,808
Latvia	2,570
Lithuania	3,494
Norway	3,310
Poland	3,372
Portugal	3,234
Romania	2,993
Russian Federation	2,129
Slovak Republic	3,460
Slovenia	3,064
Sweden	3,061
Switzerland	3,096
United States	2,786

Kite 1996) and should be measured by questions that ask not about how one feels about the country, but rather about the explicit importance of the identity to one's self-concept (Ashmore, Deaux, and McLaughlin-Volpe 2004). Fortunately, the IEA questionnaire included two questions that appear to be reasonable measures of this notion. Students were asked to indicate their level of agreement or disagreement with the statements, "The flag of [name of country] is important to me," and "The national anthem of [name of country] is important to me." The correlation of these two items is quite high (.69), and so I simply averaged responses to create a measure of national identity.[5] The resulting variable was rescaled to a 0–to-1 range.

Figure 7.1 arrays the twenty-eight countries on the measure of national identity centrality. While all country averages, save Switzerland's, exceed .5, there is still considerable variation in the degree to which young people in various countries consider their national membership important to them. Interestingly, and perhaps contrary to the expectations of some, the U.S. mean, at .71, is just slightly below the international average of .72.

CIVIC COMMITMENTS Students were asked a series of fifteen questions about their definitions of "good adult" citizenship attributes and behaviors. From these items, two citizenship scales were constructed that correspond to different aspects of political engagement. The study architects labeled these scales "conventional" and "social-movement-related" citizenship (see Schulz and Sibberns 2004).[6] It is clear from the items' content in Table 7.2 that the former corresponds to those virtues we associate with traditional democratic citizenship, while the latter clearly emphasizes more elite-challenging forms of participation (Inglehart 1997) and the kind of postnational citizenship captured in the bumper sticker, "Think Globally/Act Locally." The citizenship scales were rescaled to 0–1 range. The international mean for social movement citizenship, .63, is appreciably higher than that for conventional citizenship, .53. At the country level, national identity centrality is correlated .74 with the conventional commitments scale and .71 with the social movement scale. In other words, psychological investment in national-state member-

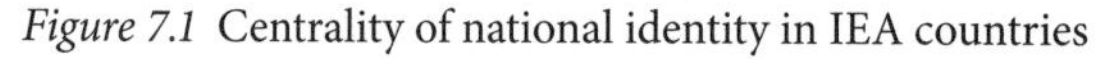
Figure 7.1 Centrality of national identity in IEA countries

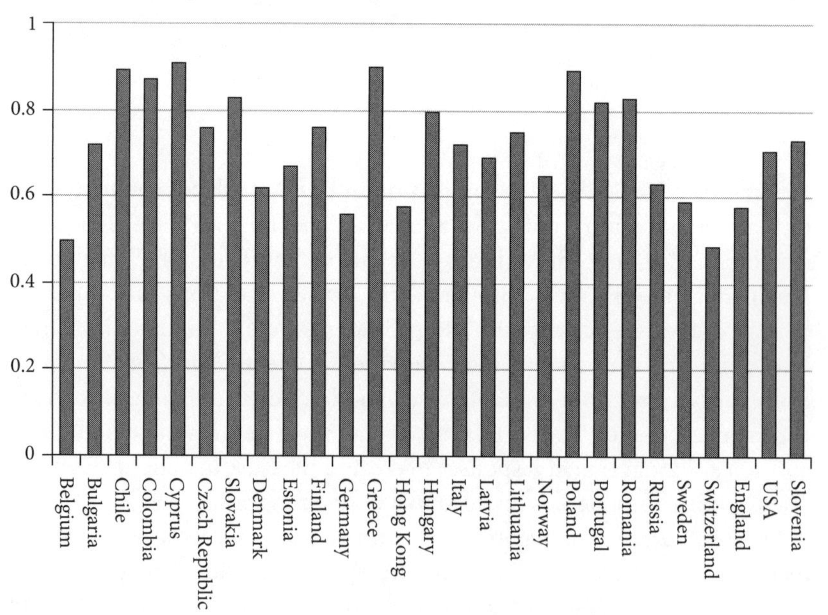

Table 7.2. Item wording for citizenship scales

Importance of conventional citizenship
An adult who is a good citizen . . .
Votes in every election
Joins a political party
Knows about the country's history
Follows political issues in the newspaper, on the radio, or on TV
Shows respect for government representatives
Engages in political discussion
Importance of social-movement-related citizenship
An adult who is a good citizen . . .
Would participate in a peaceful protest against a law believed to be unjust
Participates in activities to benefit people in the community
Takes part in activities promoting human rights
Takes part in activities to protect the environment

Note: Response categories—not important, somewhat unimportant, somewhat important, very important

ship appears to correspond highly with commitments to various kinds of civic virtues, both "old-fashioned," such as voting, and newer forms, such as involvement in human rights issues.

DEFINING AND MEASURING GLOBALIZATION

In my view, it is important to consider globalization as a multifaceted phenomenon that impinges on nation-states to different degrees and in different ways. It is for that reason that I favor understandings of globalization that emphasize the interconnections among political, social, economic, and technological forces. For measurement purposes, however, it is convenient to disaggregate the catch-all term into more distinct components, although these groupings should be viewed as heuristic rather than analytical.

ECONOMIC GLOBALIZATION World Bank economist Milan Brahmbhatt (1998) proposes a working definition of economic globalization as the "increasing freedom and ability of individuals and firms to undertake voluntary economic transactions with residents of other countries, a process entailing a growing contestability of national markets by foreign suppliers" (1). Other definitions of economic globalization (or integration) are said to involve (essentially) the sharply rising movement of labor and capital across national borders that sharply accelerated after the end of the cold war.[7]

Political economists who study economic globalization tend to rely on three different measures of the phenomenon: international trade or trade openness, direct foreign investment, and capital market flows. All show increasing levels of global interconnection through the end of the 1990s. In Figure 7.2, I chart some of the indicators that are frequently employed in the globalization literature as signs of growing world economic interdependence. The end of the twentieth century brought with it a crisis in Asian financial markets and the collapse of the tech bubble in the American stock market; barely into the twenty-first century, the United States suffered from deadly terrorist attacks. These events seemed to have slowed the relentless march of economic integration somewhat; two of the three indicators evince retreats from their end-of-century high points.

This growing economic integration was experienced unevenly across different parts of the world (Garrett 2004), and even within the twenty-eight IEA countries, economic globalization did not proceed at the same pace. Figure 7.3 compares four of the advanced democracies in the IEA set—Sweden, Switzerland, the United States, and Australia—on one measure of economic integration: international trade (the ratio of imports + exports to total economic output). Not only do levels of trade differ among them, but Switzerland and Sweden, compared with the United States and Australia, have a much more volatile trajectory. As small countries heavily reliant on export markets, they are much more vulnerable to world economic conditions than their larger counterparts (Katzenstein 1985).

Less often included in discussions of economic integration is the globalization of labor, registered by the unprecedented migration of peoples across borders. As Massey (1999) points out, based on a synthesis of hundreds of

Figure 7.2 Economic globalization, 1990–2002

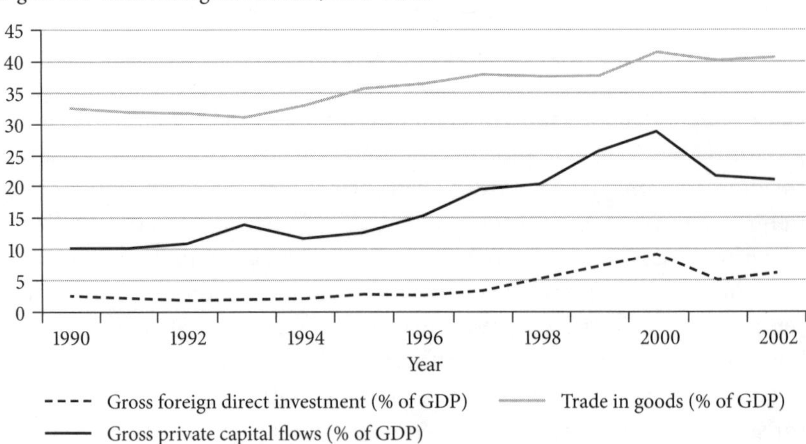

Figure 7.3 International trade in four IEA countries

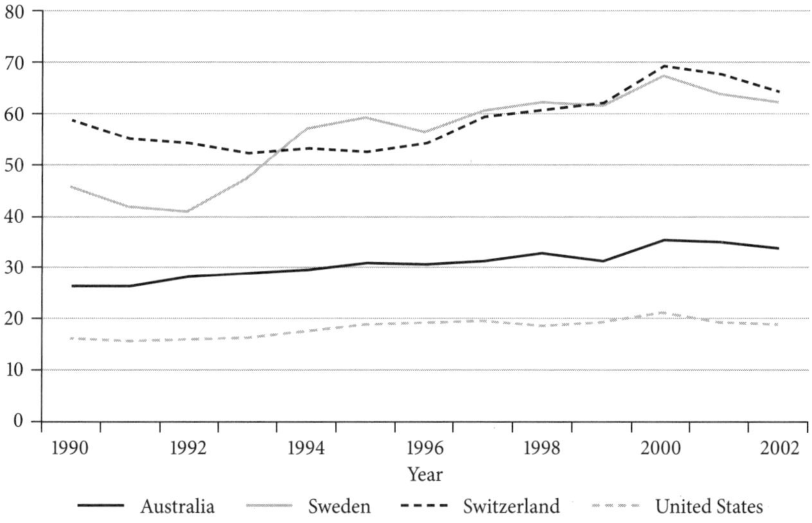

studies across different social science disciplines, "international migrants tend not to come form poor, isolated places that are disconnected from world markets, but from regions and nations that are undergoing rapid economic change and development as a result of their incorporation into global trade" (48). The economies, politics and cultures of sending and receiving countries are profoundly affected by these movements. For example, Adams and Page (2003) conclude that the remittances sent home by migrants play a large role in reducing poverty levels in many of the world's less-developed countries. The economic clout that migrants wield is making them increasingly powerful players in the politics of both their countries of origin and their host countries (Thompson 2005; Cornelius and Rosenblum 2005). In addition, the new international migration has given rise to the phenomenon of transnational communities "whose identity is not primarily based on attachment to a specific country. They therefore present a powerful challenge to traditional ideas of national belonging" (Castles 2002, 1157).

Migration, whether in the form of legal immigration, illegal immigration, asylum-seeking, or refugee flows, presents clear challenges to nation-states (Joppke 1998), leading some writers, such as Jagdish Bhagwati (2003), to conclude that "the reality is that borders are beyond control and little can be done to really cut down on immigration" (Bhagwati 2003, 99; emphasis added). Others are not so ready to view states as hopeless in the face of economic imperatives. Freeman (1998), for example, argues that states do have the capacity to control their borders, but they often lack the political will to do so because of powerful domestic forces. Thus, even though mass publics in democracies consistently oppose more liberal immigration policies (Scheve and Slaughter 2006), business interests, migrant lobbies, and the insulation of elite decision makers from popular pressure (Tichenor 2002) have often meant that immigration policy has been more expansionist than public opinion would dictate.

International law, particularly in the area of human rights, also influences domestic policy regarding migration issues. The rights and privileges that once were reserved for citizens are now granted to resident aliens in the name of universal personhood (Soysal 1994), enabling migrants to press rights-based claims against nation-states. Extensions of voting rights to noncitizens in some democracies, including some localities in the United States (Earnest 2003), calls into question the very idea that citizenship is a status reserved exclusively for nationals (Williams 2004). The value of territorially based citizenship, therefore, may have declined (Jacobson 1996).

As a consequence of a world on the move, ethnic, religious, and linguistic diversity has dramatically increased in parts of the developed world. The debates over the appropriate political response to this growing heterogeneity have racked many a polity. Should difference be celebrated, protected, even subsidized by state resources? Or should older notions of assimilation prevail?[8] Is it possible to reconcile the universalistic aspirations of democracy with the particularism essential for maintaining an idea of national distinctiveness? However resolved, one likely outcome of the frequent, public, and noisy arguments surrounding these issues is to create uncertainty about what it means to be "an X," where X is Romanian, Hungarian, Polish, American, or British, especially for people whose collective identities are not yet solidified.

As the discussion of international migration indicates, increasing economic integration has much more than just material and distributional consequences for the people who are experiencing it. As John Tomlinson (1999), among others, avers, the more radical consequences of global economic interconnectedness may be cultural, "the ways in which people make their lives, individually and collectively, meaningful by communicating with each other" (18; see also Boli and Thomas 1997). Although the debates about the impact of economic globalization on economic growth, living standards, and income inequality are vitally important, I will not examine them here. Rather, this chapter is an attempt to assay the consequences of global economic integration for the psychology of nationalism and democratic citizenship.

POLITICAL GLOBALIZATION In the present era of globalization, political authority is said to be "migrating" (Gerber and Kollman 2004) away from its traditional locus in the nation-state. Some of this movement is "upward" toward organizations, institutions, and agreements that are multinational in character. The growing size and institutionalization of the European Union is perhaps the most conspicuous example of such a transformation, but centralization at supranational levels has occurred in all parts of the world in many different institutional forms as detailed by Beth Simmons in her chapter.

Political authority has also migrated downward. Devolution, the popularity of subsidiarity rhetoric, and the federalization of former unitary states, such as Belguim, for example, illustrate that the authority of the nation-state is being "hollowed out," to use a common phrase, from below as well as above.

Authority migration also involves the transfer of public power to private entities. John Freeman (chapter 9) discusses how democracy may be threatened by the privatization of political authority. Underlying the views of many critics of economic globalization, for example, is the belief that multinational firms have the ability to shape states' domestic policies (such as corporate tax rates) while at the same time being less accountable to national policymakers and regulators (Naveretti and Venables 2004).

In addition to firms, other nonstate actors appear to be increasingly influential sites of political authority in a global world. The presence of international nongovernmental organizations (INGOs) grew enormously during the twentieth century (Boli and Thomas 1997). While these organizations have the power neither to make nor enforce law, they "carry and re-frame ideas, insert them into policy debates, pressure for regime change, and enforce existing international norms and rules" (Keck and Sikkink 1998, 199). According to world-polity theorists, such as Boli and Thomas, INGOs are the "primary carriers of world culture," a cosmopolitan worldview that is often at odds with national allegiances (Calhoun 2002; Huntington 2004; Lasch 1995; Reich 1991; Rosenau et al. 2003) and nation-state–centered sovereignty (Fonte 2004).

CULTURAL AND INFORMATIONAL GLOBALIZATION Many scholars of national identity point to the essential role played by cultural institutions, particularly communications systems, in developing national consciousness (Anderson 1983; Deutsch 1966; Gellner 1983). Anderson's (1983) notion of imagined communities, for example, ties the development of national identity to the spread of what he calls print capitalism, of which the newspaper was a primary product. The reading of the newspaper, Anderson argued, involves millions of people in a daily mass ceremony, creating a community even in the midst of anonymity.

But communication systems may remake allegiances. Smaller numbers of people in the developed world are engaged in the rituals that forged national consciousness in earlier ages, largely because older citizens, whose habits were acquired before the spread of the global communications revolution, are being replaced by younger generations who have grown up with CNN and the Internet. The "e-world" has helped to promote the obliteration of place as a meaningful distinction.

Advancing technologies in communication and transportation mean for many that the world is just a keystroke, phone call, or cheap flight away. Northwest Airlines, for example, has advertised on its ticket jackets, "No borders." The Asian tsunami in late 2004 demonstrated just how close faraway places have become. For many less-developed countries, international tourism powers the national economy (Hazbun 2004; Martin 2003). Even within developed states, international tourism is viewed as key sector of export growth. In response to the hit that international tourism took in the wake of 9/11, both the U.S. and Australian national governments in 2003 formulated new policies and agencies to boost travel to their countries. President Bush signed into law an appropriation that authorized the Secretary of Commerce to make grants in support of an international advertising and promotional campaign to encourage travel to the United States and authorized the creation of the U.S. Travel and Tourism Advisory Board. In December 2004, the first commercials of a multiyear international marketing campaign were unveiled in the United Kingdom.[9] A similar effort, "Brand Australia," was launched in May 2004 as a result of the Tourism White Paper issued by the Prime Minister of Australia.[10]

The increasing competition for the international traveler may unleash forces that have the effect of strengthening nation-state capacities, a process Hazbun (2004) calls "re-territorialization." Re-territorialization, however, is only a viable economic development strategy to the extent that there are enough people desiring to visit "foreign" destinations. These "frequent travelers, easily entering and exiting polities and social relations around the world" (Calhoun 2002, 872), have become more numerous. The "other" WTO, the World Tourism Organization, reports that outbound tourism increased by an annual percentage rate of over 4 percent during the 1990s. During this period, interregional travel (e.g., Europe to Asia) grew much faster than intraregional travel (e.g., Sweden to Germany).[11] The increased cultural contact manifested in tourism statistics, among other things, has fueled discourses of cosmopolitanism and global citizenship, a rhetoric that frequently views territorially based identities, such as nationalism, with deep suspicion, if not downright derision (Calhoun 2002).

MEASURES: INDEPENDENT VARIABLES

Table 7.3 details the indicators that I employ to explain country-level variation in the dependent variables. These variables are grouped under the headings described in the previous section. While globalization as a whole phenomenon is certainly more than just these specific parts, these are measures that are routinely employed in the economic, political science, and sociology literatures, as I foreshadowed in the preceding section.

Table 7.4 presents the correlations among my measures of globalization. The most striking thing about the table is the relative weakness of the interrelationships. With the exception of international calls and international departures, which display a correlation in excess of .8, and membership in IGOs and nongovernmental organizations, which are correlated a .7, most of the correlations are near zero or only slightly positive.

The hefty correlation between international calls and international departures suggests that these two variables can be usefully combined into one measure of "cultural contact." Similarly, intergovernmental nongovernmental organizations can be pooled into a single indicator of "political globalization." I rescaled each of these composite measures to lie within a 0 to 1 range. All other variables in Table 7.4 are similarly rescaled. Coding all variables to a similar metric will facilitate interpretation of the coefficients in multivariate analysis, to which I now turn.

Analysis

Two variables, population size and GDP per capita measured in purchasing power parity (PPP), serve as control variables, while the variables in Table 7.4 are designed to tap the economic, cultural, and political aspects of globalization. The two controls are necessary because many aspects of globalization, such as trade openness, are also associated with country size and levels of economic development. As a rule, small states rely on international trade more than their larger counterparts to compensate for what they cannot produce at home (Katzenstein 1985), and many of the world's smaller democracies seem to have pursued integration with the global economy more aggressively than others (Garrett 2000). The correlation between population (logged) and trade openness is –.31 in the IEA set of countries—negative, as expected, al-

Table 7.3 Indicators used to explain country-level variation in dependent variables

Variable	Data source	Year	N of cases	Min	Max	Mean
Controls						
GDP per capita as Purchasing Power Parity (PPP) in constant 1995 dollars	World Bank World Development Indicators (WDI)	1999	28	$5,226.33	$31,626.76	$16,023.20
Total population	World Bank WDI	1999	28	754,000	279,000,000	31,160,393
Economic globalization						
Foreign born % of total population	United Nations Common Data Base Series 30030	2000	27	.30%	26.20%	7.99%
Trade in goods (imports + exports) % of PPP GDP	World Bank WDI	1999	27	9.30%	239.20%	50.73%
Cultural globalization						
Internet usage per 1,000 population	World Bank WDI	1999	28	10.9	413.70	152.46
Outgoing international calls (min/person)	World Culture Report, 2000 UNESCO	1997	27	1.00	276.00	54.6
Departures of nationals abroad (per 100 people)	World Culture Report, 2000 UNESCO	1998	27	1.9	164.0	37.9
Political globalization						
IGOs	Union of International Organizations	1995	28	13	90	56.7
INGOs	Union of International Organizations	1995	28	389	3061	867.8

ıble 7.4. Correlations among indicators

	Economic openness	% Foreign born	Internet use	International calls	International departures	NGOs	INGOs
onomic openness	1.00						
Foreign born	.22						
	(26)	1.00					
ternet use	26	.02	1.00				
	(27)	(27)					
ternational calls	.27	.21	.02	1.00			
	(26)	(26)	(27)				
ternational departures	.30	.10	.02	.83***	1.00		
	(26)	(27)	(27)	(27)			
Os	.14	.00	.34*	.23	.28	1.00	
	(27)	(27)	(28)	(27)	(27)		
GOs	.16	−.13	.18	.30	.52***	.87***	1.00
	(.43)	(27)	(28)	(27)	(27)	(28)	

Note: Table entries are bivariate correlations with the number of cases in parentheses.
***p < .01, **p < .05, *p < .10, two-tailed

though not overwhelmingly so. The correlation between economic openness and economic development is somewhat stronger at .41.

It is particularly important to control for economic development in order to distinguish processes of modernization more generally from the specific dynamics associated with globalization. Inglehart (1997), for example, has argued that as levels of affluence rise around the world, individuals can increasingly take human survival for granted. As a consequence, prosperity brings with it a change in worldview wherein traditional sources of authority, such as family, religion, and the state, are de-legitimated. And indeed, the correlation between national wealth and national identity is negative (−.58), just as we would expect according to the postmodernization thesis.[12] By controlling for the impact of economic development on adolescents' orientations, I can more cleanly parse globalization's distinctive contribution.

Table 7.5 displays the unstandardized coefficients (with their associated standard errors) obtained by regressing my three dependent variables on GDP per capita, logged population size, and each of the indicators of economic, cultural, and political globalization.

There are several noteworthy patterns in Table 7.5. Beginning first with the control variables, we see that neither population size nor country wealth has consistently significant effects, although the signs are always in the same direction. Population size, in general, is negatively related to my measures

Table 7.5. Multivariate results

	National identity centrality	Conventional citizenship	Social-movement citizenship
GDP per capita	2.48×10^{-6}	1.6×10^{-6}	4.6×10^{-6} *
	(.000)	(.000)	(.000)
Population (logged)	–.08**	–.01	–.02
	(.04)	(.02)	(.02)
Trade openness	–.63**	–.15	–.28**
	(.23)	(.11)	(.13)
Migration	–.19***	–.04	–.08**
	(.06)	(.03)	(.03)
Internet penetration	–.07	–.07**	–.10**
	(.07)	(.03)	(.04)
Cultural contact	–.06	–.04	–.01
	(.08)	(.04)	(.05)
Political globalization	–.04	–.03	–.04
	(.10)	(.05)	(.06)
R2	.75	.60	.40
N	25	25	25
SEE	.07	.03	.04

*p < .10, **p < .05, ***p < .01, two-tailed

of civic orientations, but its coefficient reaches statistical significance only in the case of national identity centrality. All else equal, adolescents in more populous countries have weaker national identities, a result perfectly consistent with decades of research on the impact of group size on group cohesion (see, for example, Mullen and Copper 1994). I will revisit the question of polity size in the conclusion.

Interestingly, while its bivariate correlations with the three dependent variables are negative, in the multivariate model the impact of economic development is positive, and in one case, that of social-movement citizenship, it is statistically significant. While this finding is consistent with Inglehart's thesis of postmaterial value change and its implications for elite-challenging forms of political participation, the remaining globalization-specific variables are all negatively signed.

In fact, the most striking regularity in Table 7.5 is that every one of the independent variables I use to measure globalization is negative, and, in several cases, significantly so.[13] Trade openness, in particular, shows large effect sizes across the three equations. For example, its coefficient of –.63 in the national identity equation means (given the coding of the variables) that moving from the least open economy (Colombia) to the most open economy (Belguim)[14] explains fully 63 percnt of the range of the dependent variable.

Integration with the global economy explains more than one-quarter of the range of social-movement citizenship, which does not look very impressive when compared to nearly two-thirds, but by absolute standards it would still be considered a very large substantive effect.[15]

The coefficients for cultural and political globalization do not match those for economic globalization, but they nonetheless have the correct sign, and one, Internet penetration, is significant in two of the three equations. Ironically, even though the Internet is seen as crucial for the development of transnational collective action (della Porta and Tarrow 2004) and its organizational forms and diffusion (Bennett 2004), its penetration into national societies seems to weaken commitments to those causes that are at the core of these movements.

The results in Table 7.4 are easy to summarize: not only is globalization associated with weaker nation-state identities, but the concept of citizenship itself also seems to be rendered less meaningful in an increasingly interconnected world.

Discussion

National identity rests on instrumental and symbolic supports that reinforce each other (Kelman 1997). Globalization reduces the benefits of national membership at the same time that its processes make it increasingly difficult to construct a compelling national story. Weakened national identities may reduce commitments to the kinds of virtues associated with democratic citizenship as exercised in the territorially delimited nation-state. William Damon (2001), an influential developmental psychologist, has argued that sustained engagement with a community requires emotional investment in the group, commitments that are powered by identity: "In order to understand a person's behavior, we must know not only what he or she believes but also how important that belief is to the person's sense of self—that is, why (or even whether) it is important for the person to act according to the belief" (135). To the extent that national identities, or a sense of peoplehood, to use Smith's (2002) phrase, are also interwoven with notions of citizenship (Conover, Searing, and Crewe 2004), then the kinds of factors that affect the intensity of national attachments will have implications for the strength with which people endorse commitments to citizenship behavior. And this is precisely what I have found.

What size should the polity be? As Dahl and Tufte made so very plain in their Size and Democracy, there is no ready answer, for size is differently related to two essential criteria for political system performance: system capacity and citizen effectiveness. The nation-state in its current form seems "too small" in the face of many global problems, which has led some (Habermas 2001, for example) to argue for larger political entities, such as the EU, as a means for coping with global complexity. But, as both Frank Bryan (2004) and Eric Oliver (2001) show in their studies of local participation in the United States, the bigger the polity, all else equal, the less willing are its citizens to participate in its governance. Turnout in EU elections, as Beth Simmons (chapter 8) notes, has declined at the same time that its membership has enlarged and its powers increased. "Democratic deficits" appear to be part and parcel of the new global order, leading many (see Melissa Orlie, chapter 10, for a summary) to question whether democracy and global integration can ever be fully compatible.

The same sorts of trade-offs exist at the psychological level as well. Human beings have two fundamental needs that need to be reconciled. On the one hand, their need for self-protection and self-transcendence propel them to become parts of larger units. At its maximum, this "need for assimilation" is met when everyone is a member of the same group. On the other hand, people's needs to differentiate themselves from others in order to have a meaningful sense of self move them in the opposite direction. This "need for distinctiveness" is maximized when everyone is their own group, an "empire of one." Marilynn Brewer (1991) argues in her theory of "optimal distinctiveness" that group identity provides a mechanism for harmonizing these two contrary tendencies. Groups need to be big enough to provide for assimilation needs but small enough to allow for some intergroup distinctiveness. There is, then, some "goldilocks" point, and groups that find it will be the ones in which individuals are more willing to invest their identities.

By this account, the modern democratic nation-state may be "too big." With the collapse of the Soviet Union, democracies have become more common (less distinctive) as a form of political organization. At the same time, according to the logic of the democratic peace hypothesis, the greater proportion of democracies has made the world in general a much safer place, perhaps reducing people's felt need to assimilate for security reasons. Democracy in the nation-state form has become, ironically, the victim of its own success. No longer "just right," the nation-state has lost its psychological attraction as people search for new group forms in which to be optimally distinct.

Political authority is moving up, down, and sideways at the same time (Gerber and Kollman 2004). These authority migrations are a sign that the nation-state is no longer a viable solution to the contradictory impulses outlined above. But whether concepts of democratic citizenship and popular sovereignty can outlive the nation-state seems to remain an open question.

Notes

1. So many have made this argument in both popular and academic writings that it is impossible to provide a complete listing. Among the works I consulted include Axtmann (2004), Benhabib (2002), Castles and Davidson (2000), Croucher (2004), Griffin (2003), Friedman (1999), Garrett (2000; 2004), Habermas (2001), Held et al. (1999), Keck and Sikkink (1998), Jusdanis (2001), Poole (1999), Reich (1991), Sassen (1996), Schnapper (1998), Spruyt (2002), and Tambini (2001). The contributors to the Paul, Ikenberry, and Hall (2003) volume, on the other hand, demur, arguing that the erosion of state capacity has been greatly exaggerated.

2. This section draws some of the arguments advanced in Rahn (1998) and Rahn and Rudolph (2001).

3. An exception is the work on the impact of globalization on citizens' electoral choices and preferences for public policies, such as immigration and trade. See, for example, Aldrich et al. (1999), Hellwig (2001), Hiscox (2004), Mayda and Rodrik (2001), Rankin (2001), Scheve and Slaughter (2001; 2004), and Freeman (chapter 9). In addition, Franklin (2004) has recently argued that globalization may be one of the factors accounting for the decline in voter turnout that has occurred among most of the advanced democracies (see also Rahn and Rudolph 2001).

4. Both studies can be accessed online at http://www.iea.nl/cived.html. A technical report edited by Schulz and Sibberns (2004) also available at the IEA site. It provides essential details about the sampling procedures, construction of the sampling weights, and computation of assorted scales.

5. In an ideal world, I would have preferred a measure of identity importance that did not involve national symbols. However, both these items are closer to the concept than the alternatives available on the IEA, such as "This country should be proud of what it has achieved."

6. The average reliability of the two citizenship scales is .68 and .63, respectively (Schulz and Sibberns 2004).

7. There is also an earlier period of economic globalization in the late nineteenth century that has many hallmarks of today's economic integration, including falling trade barriers, massive migrations of people across borders, and restrictionist and protectionist backlash. For an especially informative historical perspective on the last great wave of globalization, see James (2002). Kahler and Lake (2004) discuss how the two periods of globalization have important differences.

8. Both Brubaker (2004) and Joppke (2004) have recently argued that assimilation is making a comeback.

9. Office of Travel and Tourism Industries, http://tinet.ita.doc.gov/about/us_promo_campaign/omnibus_appr.html. The ad shows scenes from several American

movies, including Thelma and Louise and Maid in Manhattan, and ends with the tag line: "You've seen the movie, now visit the set."

10. http://www.tourism.australia.com/AboutUS.asp?sub=0304.

11. Regional reports are available at http://www.world-tourism.org/facts/tmt.html.

12. The correlations between GDP per capita and traditional and social movement citizenship are –.47 and –.35, respectively.

13. With only twenty-five cases for the multivariate models, I have limited statistical power to detect effects at conventional levels of significance. For this reason, I believe it is more informative to focus on the pattern of relationships and also the effect sizes of the independent variables.

14. Hong Kong actually has the highest levels of international trade, but it is missing data on migrant stock and therefore is an excluded case in the multivariate analysis.

15. The cross-sectional nature of the research design gives rise to legitimate concerns about simultaneous relationships or the possibility that some of my independent variables are actually endogenous to levels of national identity or citizenship commitments. It seems quite plausible that rather than, say, trade openness undermining national and civic orientations, the relationship is the reverse. In other words, it may be the case that states are permitted to pursue economic liberalization precisely because levels of attachment and civic commitments are already relatively low.

References

Adams, Richard H. Jr., and John Page. 2003. *International Migration, Remittances and Poverty in Developing Countries.* World Bank Policy Research Working Paper #3179. World Bank.

Aldrich, John, Claire Kramer, Peter Lang, Renan Levine, Laura Stephenson, and Elizabeth Zechmeister. 1999. Raising the Titanic: Globalization, Insecurity, and American Democracy. Presented at the annual meeting of the American Political Science Association, Atlanta, September 2–5.

Anderson, Benedict. 1983. *Imagined Communities.* London: Verso.

Ashmore, Richard D., Kay Deaux, and Tracy McLaughlin-Volpe. 2004. "An Organizing Framework for Collective Identity: Articulation and Significance of Multidimensionality." *Psychological Bulletin* 130:80–114.

Axtmann, Roland. 2004. "The State of the State: The Model of the Modern State and Its Contemporary Transformation." *International Political Science Review* 25:259–79.

Benhabib, Seyla. 2002. "Political Theory and Political Membership in a Changing World." In *Political Science: State of the Discipline,* ed. Ira Katznelson and Helen V. Milner, 404–32. New York: Norton.

Bennet, W. Lance. 2004. "Social Movements beyond Borders: Understanding Two Eras of Transnational Activism." In della Porta and Sidney, *Transnational Protest and Global Activism,* 203–27.

Bhagwati, Jadish. 2003. "Borders beyond Control." *Foreign Affairs* 82 (1): 98–104.

Boli, John, and George M. Thomas. 1997. "World Culture in the World Polity: A Century of International Non-Governmental Organization." *American Sociological Review* 62:171–90.

Brahmbatt, Milan. 1998. "Measuring Global Economic Integration: A Review of the Literature and Recent Evidence." http://www1.worldbank.org/economicpolicy/globalization/documents/measuring.pdf. Accessed March 3, 2005.

Brewer, Marilynn B. 1991. "The Social Self: On Being the Same and Different at the Same Time." *Personality and Social Psychology Bulletin* 10:585–95.

Brubaker, Rogers. 2004. *Ethnicity without Groups.* Cambridge, Mass.: Harvard University Press.

Bryan, Frank. 2004. *Real Democracy: The New England Town Meeting and How It Works.* Chicago: University of Chicago Press.

Calhoun, Craig. 2002. "The Class Consciousness of Frequent Travelers: Toward a Critique of Actually Existing Cosmopolitanism." *South Atlantic Quarterly* 101(4): 869–97.

Castles, Stephen. 2002. "Migration and Community Formation under Conditions of Globalization." *International Migration Review* 36 (Winter): 1143–68.

Castles, Stephen, and Alastair Davidson. 2000. *Citizenship and Migration: Globalization and the Politics of Belonging.* New York: Routledge.

Conover, Pamela Johnston, Donald D. Searing, and Ivor Crewe. 2004. "The Elusive Ideal of Equal Citizenship: Political Theory and Political Psychology in the United States and Great Britain." *Journal of Politics* 66:1036–68.

Cornelius, Wayne A., and Marc R. Rosenblum. 2005. "Immigration and Politics." *Annual Review of Political Science* 8:99–119.

Croucher, Sheila L. 2004. *Globalization and Belonging: The Politics of Identity in a Changing World.* Lanham, Md.: Rowman.

Dahl, Robert. A., and Edward R. Tufte. 1973. *Size and Democracy.* Stanford, Calif.: Stanford University Press.

Damon, William. 2001. "To Not Fade Away: Restoring Civic Identity Among the Young." In *Making Good Citizens: Education and Civil Society,* ed. Diane Ravitch and Joseph P. Viteritti, 122–42. New Haven, Conn.:Yale University Press

della Porta, Donatella, and Sidney Tarrow. 2004. "Transnational Processes and Social Activism: An Introduction. In della Porta and Sidney, *Transnational Protest and Global Activism,* 1–20.

———, eds. 2004. *Transnational Protest and Global Activism.* Lanham, Md.: Rowman.

Deutsch, Karl W. 1966. *Nationalism and Social Communications.* 2nd ed. Cambridge, Mass.: MIT Press.

Earnest, David C. 2003. "Noncitizen Voting Rights: A Survey of an Emerging Democratic Norm." Paper presented at the 2003 annual meeting of the American Political Science Association, August 27–31.

Fonte, John. 2004. "Democracy's Trojan House." *National Interest* (Summer): 117–27.

Franklin, Mark N. 2004. *Voter Turnout and the Dynamics of Electoral Competition in Established Democracies since 1945*. Cambridge: Cambridge University Press.

Freeman, Gary P. 1998. "The Decline of Sovereignty? Politics and Immigration Restriction in Liberal States." In Joppke, *Challenge to the Nation-State*, 86–108.

Friedman, Thomas L. 1999. *Lexus and the Olive Tree: Understanding Globalization*. New York: Farrar.

Garrett, Geoffrey. 2000. "The Causes of Globalization." *Comparative Political Studies* 33 (6/7): 941–91.

———. 2004. "Globalization's Missing Middle." *Foreign Affairs* 83 (6): 84–96.

Gellner, Ernest. 1983. *Nations and Nationalism*. Ithaca, N.Y.: Cornell University Press.

Gerber, Elisabeth R., and Ken Kollman. 2004. "Introduction—Authority Migration: Defining an Emerging Research Agenda." *PS: Political Science and Politics* 36 (3): 397–401.

Griffin, Keith. 2003. "Economic Globalization and Institutions of Global Governance." *Development and Change* 34(5): 789–807.

Habermas, Jürgen. 2001. *The Postnational Constellation: Political Essays*. Translated and edited by Max Pensky. Boston, Mass.: MIT Press.

Hazbun, Waleed. 2004. "Globalisation, Reterritorialization, and the Political Economy of Tourism Development in the Middle East." *Geopolitics* 9(2): 310–14.

Held, David, Anthony McGrew, David Goldblatt, and Jonathan Perraton. 1999. *Global Transformations: Politics, Economics, and Culture*. Stanford, Calif.: Stanford University Press.

Hellwig, Timothy T. 2001. "Interdependence, Government Constraints, and Economic Voting." *Journal of Politics* 63:1141–62.

Hiscox, Michael J. 2004. "Through a Glass Darkly: Attitudes toward International Trade and the Curious Effects of Issue Framing." Manuscript, Department of Government, Harvard University.

Huntington, Samuel P. 2004. "Dead Souls: The Denationalization of the American Elite." *National Interest* (Spring): 5–18.

Inglehart, Ronald. 1997. *Modernization and Postmodernization: Cultural, Economic, and Political Change in 43 Countries*. Princeton, NJ: Princeton University Press.

Jacobson, David J. 1996. *Rights Cross Borders: Immigration and the Decline of Citizenship*. Baltimore, Md.: Johns Hopkins University Press.

James, Harold. 2002. *The End of Globalization*. Cambridge, Mass.: Harvard University Press.

Joppke, Christian. 1998. *Challenge to the Nation-State: Immigration in Western Europe and the United States*. Oxford: Oxford University Press.

———. 1998. "Immigration Challenges the Nation-State." In Joppke, *Challenge to the Nation-State*, 5–48.

———. 2004. "The Retreat of Multiculturalism in the Liberal State: Theory and Policy." *British Journal of Sociology* 55(2): 237–57.

Jusdanis, Gregory. 2001. *The Necessary Nation.* Princeton, N.J.: Princeton University Press.

Kahler, Miles, and David A. Lake. 2004. "Governance in a Global Economy: Political Authority in Transition." *PS: Political Science and Politics* (July): 409–14.

Katzenstein, Peter J. 1985. *Small States in World Markets: Industrial Policy in Europe.* Ithaca, N.Y.: Cornell University Press.

Keck, Margaret, and Kathryn Sikkink. 1998. *Activists beyond Borders: Advocacy Networks in International Politics.* Ithaca, N.Y.: Cornell University Press.

Kelman, Herbert C. 1997. "Nationalism, Patriotism, and National Identity: Social-Psychological Dimensions." In *Patriotism in the Lives of Individuals and Nations,* ed. Daniel Bar-Tal and Ervin Staub, 165–89. Chicago: Nelson-Hall.

Lasch, Christopher. 1995. *The Revolt of the Elites.* New York: Norton.

Martin, Lisa L. 2003. "The Leverage of Economic Theories: Explaining Governance in an Internationalized Industry." In *Governance in a Global Economy: Political Authority in Transition,* ed. Miles Kahler and David A. Lake, 33–59. Princeton, N.J.: Princeton University Press.

Massey, Douglas S. 1999. "Why Does Immigration Occur? A Theoretical Synthesis." In *The Handbook of International Migration: The American Experience,* ed. Charles Hirschman, Philip Kasinitz, and Josh DeWind, 34–52. New York: Russell Sage Foundation.

Mayda, Anna Maria, and Dani Rodrik. 2001. "Why Are Some People (and Countries) More Protectionist than Others?" NBER working paper #8461. Available at http://www.nber.org/papers/w8461.

Mullen, Brian, and Carolyn Copper. 1994. "The Relationship between Group Cohesiveness and Performance: An Integration." *Journal of Personality and Social Psychology* 115:210–27.

Navaretti, Giorgo Barba, and Anthony J. Venables. 2004. *Multinational Firms in the World Economy.* Princeton, N.J.: Princeton University Press.

Nezlek, John B. 2001. "Multilevel Random Coefficient Analyses of Event- and Interval-Contingent Data in Social and Personality Psychology Research." *Personality and Social Psychology Bulletin* 27:771–85.

Oliver, J. Eric. 2001. *Democracy in Suburbia.* Princeton, N.J.: Princeton University Press.

Paul, T. V., G. John Ikenberry, and John A. Hall. 2003. *The Nation-State in Question.* Princeton, N.J.: Princeton University Press.

Poole, Ross. 1999. *Nation and Identity.* London: Routledge.

Rahn, Wendy M. 1998. "Generations and American National Identity: A Data Essay." Paper presented at the Communication in the Future of Democracy Workshop, Annenberg Center, Washington, D.C., May 8–9.

———. 2004. "Being and Doing: Public Mood, American National Identity and Participation." Paper presented at the 2004 annual meeting of the Midwest Political Science Association, Chicago, April.

Rahn, Wendy M., Brian Kroeger, and Cynthia Kite. 1996. "A Framework for the Study of Public Mood." *Political Psychology* 17:29–58.

Rahn, Wendy M., and Thomas Rudolph. 2001. "National Identities and the Future of Democracy." In *Mediated Politics,* ed. Robert Entman and Lance Bennett, 453–67. Cambridge: Cambridge University Press.

Rankin, David M. 2001. "Identities, Interests, and Imports." *Political Behavior* 23:351–76.

Reich, Robert B. 1991. "What Is a Nation?" *Political Science Quarterly* 106:193–209.

Rosenau, James. 1990. *Turbulence in World Politics: A Theory of Change and Continuity.* Princeton, N.J.: Princeton University Press.

Rosenau, James N., David C. Earnest, Yale H. Ferguson, and Ole R. Holsti. 2003. "On the Cutting Edge of Globalization." Paper presented at the 2003 annual meeting of the American Political Science Assocation, Philadelphia.

Sassen, Saskia. 1996. *Losing Control? Sovereignty in an Age of Globalization.* New York: Columbia University Press.

———. 2004. "Transforming Citizenship? Transnational Membership, Participation, and Governance." Available at http://www.maxwell.syr.edu/campbell/Citizenship.htm.

Scheve, Kenneth, and Matthew J. Slaughter. 2001. "What Determines Individual Trade-Policy Preferences?" *Journal of International Economics* 54(2) (August): 267–92.

———. 2004. "Economic Insecurity and the Globalization of Production." *American Journal of Political Science* 48:662–74.

———. 2006. "Public Opinion, International Economic Integration, and the Welfare State." In *Globalization and Egalitarian Redistribution,* ed. Pranab Bardlan, Samuel Bowles, and Michael Wallerstein, 217–60. Princeton, N.J.: Princeton University Press.

Schnapper, Dominique. 1998. *Community of Citizens: On the Modern Idea of Nationality.* New Brunswick, N.J.: Transactions.

Schulz, Wolfram, and Heikko Sibberns, eds. 2004. The IEA Civic Education Study Technical Report. http://www.iea.nl/cived-datasets.html.

Smith, Rogers. *The Politics of Peoplehood.* Cambridge: Cambridge University Press.

Soysal, Yasemin Nuhoğlu. 1994. *Limits of Citizenship: Migrants and Postnational Membership in Europe.* Chicago: University of Chicago Press.

Spruyt, Hendrik. 2002. "The Origins, Development, and Possible Decline of the Modern State." *Annual Review of Political Science* 5:127–49.

Tambini, Damain. 2001. "Post-National Citizenship." *Ethnic and Racial Studies* 24:195–217.

Thompson, Ginger. 2005. "Mexico's Migrants Profit from Dollars Sent Home." *New York Times*, February 23, A1.
Tichenor, Daniel J. 2002. *Dividing Lines: The Politics of Immigration Control in America*. Princeton, N.J.: Princeton University Press.
Tomlinson, John. 1999. *Globalization and Culture*. Chicago: University of Chicago Press.
Torney-Purta, Judith, and Jo-Ann Amadeo. 2003. "A Cross-National Analysis of Political and Civic Involvement among Adolescents." *PS: Political Science and Politics* (April): 269–74.
Williams, Melissa. 2004. "Of Peoples and Constitutions, Sovereignty and Citizenship." Paper presented at the annual meeting of the American Political Science Association, Chicago, September 2–5.
Yack, Bernard. 2003. "Nationalism, Popular Sovereignty and the Liberal Democratic State." In Paul, Ikenberry, and Hall, *The Nation-State in Question*, 29–50.

8

Globalization, Sovereignty, and Democracy

The Role of International Organizations in a Globalizing World

BETH SIMMONS

An important part of the globalization process has been the internationalization of political authority. International organizations are an attempt to respond to, as well as to further, the development of transnational relationships, private and public. Democracies have been the most ardent participants in international organizations, which raises some intriguing issues: What does the transfer of authority imply for democratic governance? Are citizens losing control as decision making becomes more and more removed from local control? Or are threats of an impending democratic deficit greatly exaggerated?

The first section of this chapter documents the growth of international organizations over time, with special attention to democratic participation in these institutions. An interesting irony emerges: governments based on the will of "the governed" are more likely than others to delegate decision-making authority to institutions over which "the governed" effectively cannot participate. The second and third sections examine the effects of such extensive delegation on the quality of self-rule. Briefly, international organizations tend not to operate according to democratic principles. Serious challenges here include bureaucratic independence, the dominance of the powerful, and a general lack of transparency surrounding how decisions are made. On the other hand, these same institutions can have a positive influence on their newly democratizing membership. The final section concludes that the most serious threats to democratic governance accrue not to the major democracies, which tend to dominate these institutions, but to the small and emerging democracies, where hopes for self-governance are increasingly disappointed by the reality of decision making above their heads. Realistic solutions are tough but require a commitment to transparency as well as a serious look at how to guarantee input from the full range of stakeholders, and not just the noisiest segments of the wealthiest countries.

Democracy and the Growth of International Organizations

Two trends stand out starkly in the twentieth century: the spread of democracy and the trend toward the institutionalization of international authority. More citizens have gained meaningful input into the national laws and policies that govern their lives; at the same time, their governments have increasingly delegated aspects of policymaking to international organizations. Figure 8.1 shows the way this relationship has generally evolved over time. While the causal story is undoubtedly complex, it is clear that the spread of democracy and the growth of international authority have increased side by side.

For a number of reasons, democratization and the internationalization of authority are likely to be causally related (Plattner 2002). Research suggests that in their mutual relations with one another, democratic countries enjoy

Figure 8.1 Democracies and international organizations in the twentieth century

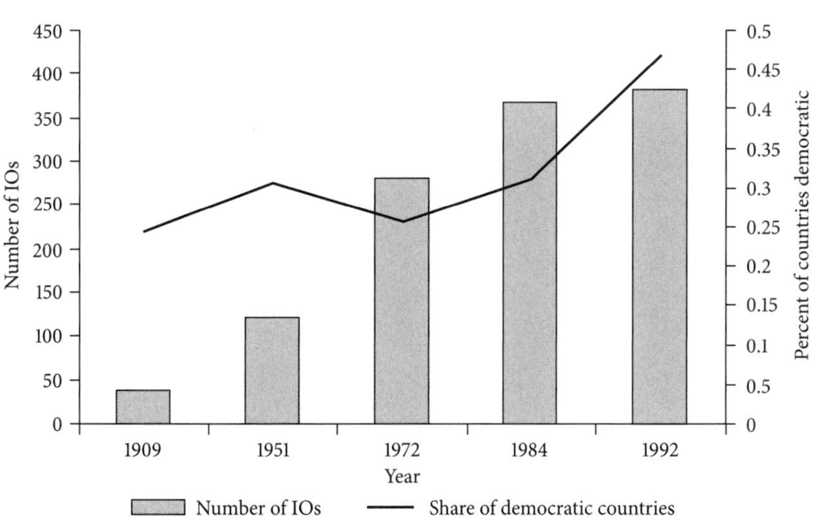

especially pacific relationships (Russett 1993). Indeed, the leading democracies have been at the forefront this century in the creation of an elaborate set of institutions meant to bolster international peace and security. After each of the world wars, democratic countries led the way in founding institutions that were designed to enhance collective security, though in practice it has typically proven difficult for these institutions to avert serious military conflicts. The original signatories of the League of Nations were just about as democratic on average as the countries that did not participate. But by the time the United Nations—the most ambitious project to date to attempt to instill in the international community a commitment to collective security—was founded in 1945, the world's democratic leadership was disproportionately behind it. On average, the original signatories were much more democratic (average polity score of 1.2 on the –10 to +10 scale) than were those that initially opted to stay out (average polity score of –4).

Liberal democracies are characterized by their highly developed systems of constitutionally based rule of law, and many scholars have argued that this accounts for their unusual international behavior (Burley 1992). The spread of democracy has been accompanied by a striking growth in international judicial and quasi-judicial institutions over the course of this century (Figure 8.2).

Democracies are primarily responsible for the rise of international court-like institutions. For example, while any member state of the United Nations may use the International Court of Justice (ICJ), this institution has been largely sustained by its democratic members. It is the world's democracies that are most likely to delegate the ultimate power—the power to render a decision on the legality of a sovereign policy—to the ICJ. Indeed, the sixty-two countries that have made a precommitment to accept the court's jurisdiction in the form of an optional clause declaration are far more democratic (averaging 5.6 on the –10 to +10 polity scale) than those that refuse to make such a declaration (average score of 1.5). Thus, democracies have been much more willing to delegate the power to render authoritative decisions on the legality of their policies to international adjudicative bodies than have less democratic governments.[1]

Moreover, for most of the ICJ's history, the more democratic countries have also been the most willing to use its adjudicative mechanisms. In the late 1940s and 1950s, complainants tended to be much more democratic on average than were countries accused of various forms of international law violation (see Figure 8.3). Very few cases were filed in the 1960s and 1970s. But when use of the court came back into vogue in the 1980s and, especially the 1990s (Henkin 1995), this situation was reversed: democracies found

Figure 8.2 Growth in international judicial, quasi-judicial, and dispute settlement bodies

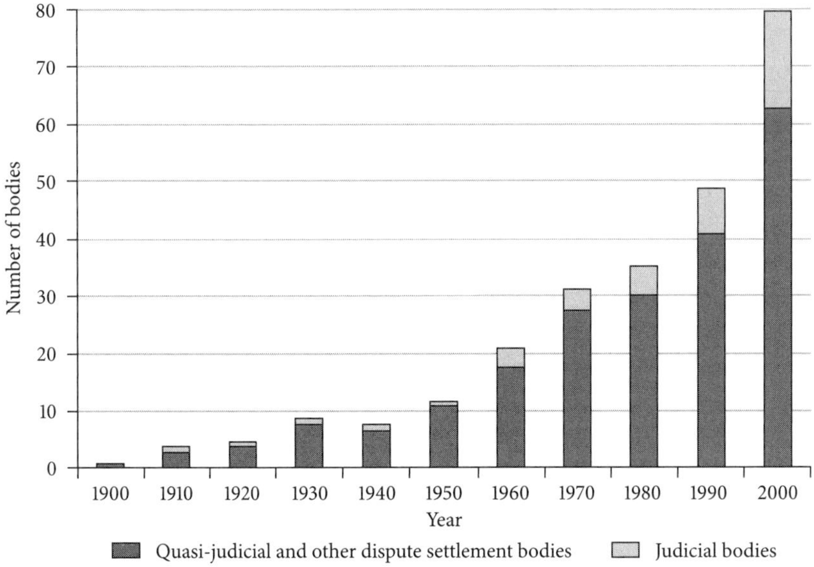

Source: The Project on International Courts and Tribunals: The International Judiciary in Context, http://www.pict-pcti.org/publications/synoptic_chart2.pdf.

themselves more frequently on the defensive, with the more autocratic regimes (on average) in the complainant's seat.

Many have noted that liberal democracies are more likely than other clusters of countries to allow for intensive civil society interactions that lead to a broad range of interdependencies, many of which transcend political boundaries (Moravcsik 1997). With their emphasis on property rights and market economy arrangements, liberal democracies are more likely to develop intensive trading relationships that in turn give rise to demands for rules to facilitate such transactions. Figure 8.4 demonstrates that international trade has followed the same general upward path as citizen participation and international institutionalization has. A host of careful studies shows that democracies are especially likely to trade intensively with one another.

The history of the postwar period is largely the history of the major democracies' efforts to reconstruct the world economy—and hence to protect their trading interests—through the creation of international economic regimes. The United States and the United Kingdom were the architects of the Bretton Woods institutions—the International Monetary Fund and the World Bank—that have had such a profound impact on the international monetary

Figure 8.3 Average polity scores for complainants and defendants in ICJ cases

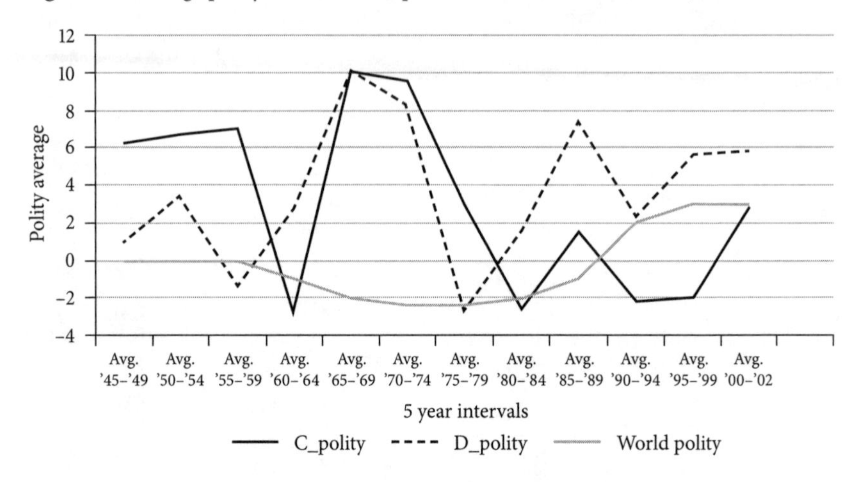

Figure 8.4 Trade and international organizations in the twentieth century

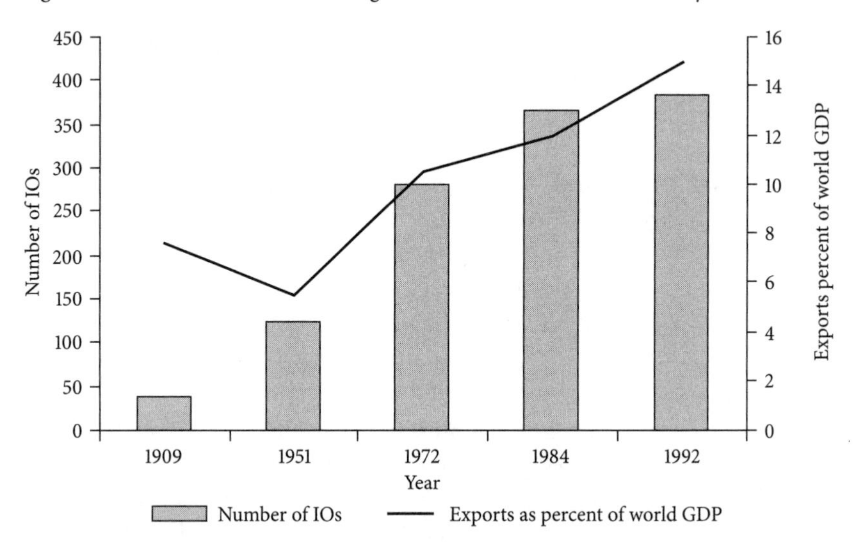

system and development assistance for the past five decades. These institutions involved historically unprecedented sovereign concessions regarding the right to establish and maintain exchange rates (Simmons 2000) and the right of the international community to engage in "surveillance" of members' macroeconomic policies.

As intense traders, democracies have a clear interest in international trade institutions (Mansfield, Milner, and Rosendorff 2002). The democratic governments took a leadership role in creating the General Agreement on Tariff and Trade in the late 1940s[2] and have since become the most active—some would say the dominant—force in the WTO's operation.

Figure 8.5 shows that countries joining the GATT and the WTO are more democratic on average than the rest of the world (especially in the early years of this institution) and much more democratic on average than nonmembers. Even more clearly, countries that have actually used the Dispute Settlement Mechanism (DSM) of the GATT and WTO are significantly more democratic than the rest of the GATT or WTO membership.[3] Those who tend to accept the legally authoritative decisions of the panels formed to rule on violations of international trade law are the most democratic states—those with polity scores in the +8 to +10 point range. Also, on average, a complainant is just as likely to be highly democratic as a defendant. There is practically no change in the average democracy score of DSM participants after 1995, when the whole settlement procedure became more binding. What this figure shows is that the most highly democratic countries in the world are increasingly delegating important economic policy decisions to a "higher" legal authority.

Finally, consider the area of international human rights protection. Many of the smaller democracies led the way after World War II to ensure that human rights protections were included in the UN founding documents, early resolutions, and eventually in treaty law (Korey 1998; Waltz 2001). One of the

Figure 8.5 GATT/WTO average polity score

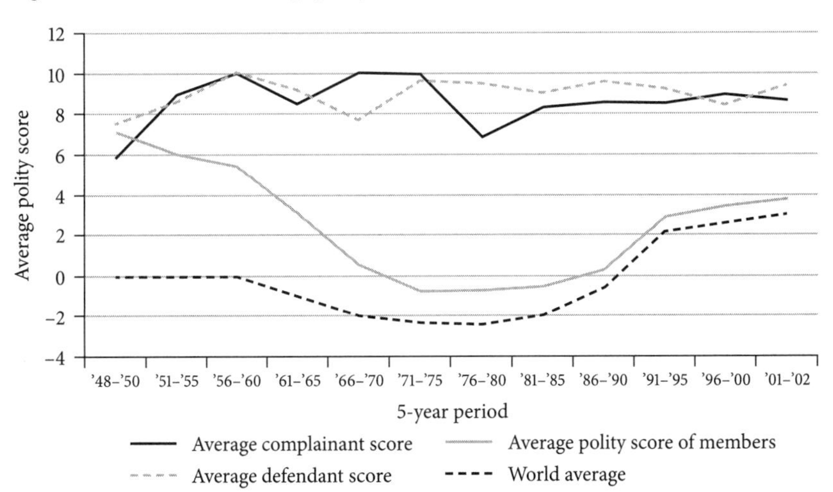

major early accomplishments in this regard was the negotiation and passage of the International Covenant on Civil and Political Rights (ICCPR) (1966). In its early years, the apparatus to enforce this rights agreement was weak. But governments could indicate their willingness by signing Optional Protocol I to allow the treaty's oversight committee, the United Nations Human Rights Committee (UNHRC), the right to hear and render authoritative judgments on complaints of individuals that their own governments had violated aspects of the ICCPR. The countries that agreed to recognize the authority of the UNHRC to hear individual complaints were overwhelmingly the more democratic: those who have so agreed have polity scores of +5.6 while those who have not agreed have polity scores on average below zero (−0.1). Among those countries that do recognize the authority of the UNHRC to hear individual complaints, the most highly democratic governments—those that score a perfect +10—have been subject to the largest number of complaints of rights violations of their own citizens (Figure 8.6).[4]

Data in this section have underscored the fact that international organizations have taken root and spread dramatically during the twentieth century. At the same time, we have witnessed the dramatic spread of democratic domestic institutions. This correspondence is not coincidental: the evidence presented here demonstrated that the most highly democratic states in the world have been the most ardent participants in the organization of international authority. Perhaps this is because liberal democracies privilege civil

Figure 8.6 Average number of individual complaints to the UN Human Rights Committee

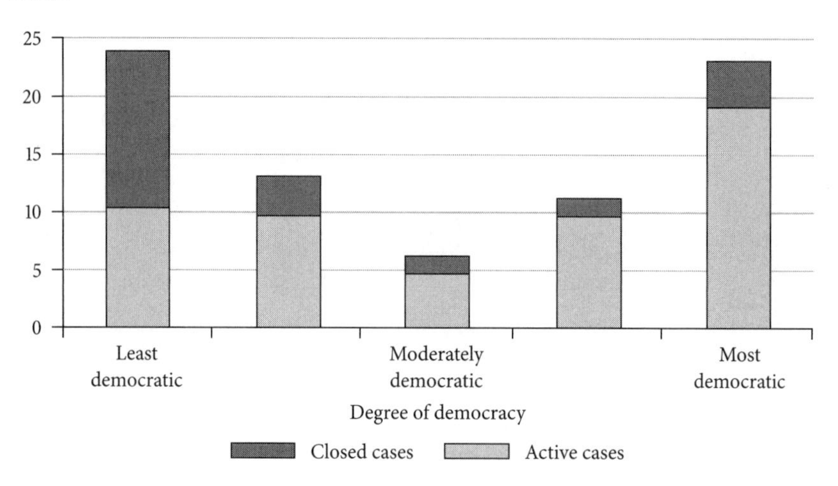

society and free markets, leading to dense transnational contacts that require some kind of coordination. Liberal democracies also privilege the rule of law. Apparently, their governments are more likely to believe that law-based institutions will in the long run protect their interests and are a better guarantor of international order than are the alternatives.

The Downside of Delegation: The Threat of a Democratic Deficit

Liberal democracies have had a strong influence on the globalization of the past century. The individual rights, the market relationships, and civil society contacts they foster have accelerated the unification of markets, technological innovation, and the rise of transnational civil society contacts that enhance a subjective attitude of global interconnectedness. And, as we have seen, democratic polities have increasingly delegated aspects of national sovereignty to international organizations, largely to deal with the consequences of the transnational interconnectedness to which liberal governance tends to give rise.

But globalization puts liberal democracies in an uncomfortable position: the transnational linkages to which they naturally give rise challenge the value they place on local democratic control (Nye and Trilateral Commission 2003; Stein 2001). This is painfully evident in the creation of regional and global markets. What civil societies have created—and their democratically elected governments have supported through rules protecting property rights—now clearly transcends the ability of a single government to effectively regulate transactions. The irony is that liberal democracy has created the very conditions that decouple political space from functional space. Transnational actors' demands for congruence requires delegation; locally rooted citizens and communities often have interests in the converse (Scheve and Slaughter 2001).

Has this trend weakened or strengthened local democratic decision making? One school of thought insists that local control has been threatened by delegation of authority to institutions beyond the nation-state. Any shift of authority further from the local conditions it influences damages the ability of citizens to participate effectively in self-governance. In the American context, proponents of strong states' rights have decried the assertion of federal authority in education and other areas as an intrusion by Washington bureaucrats unfamiliar with local circumstances into local affairs. Similarly, in Europe, decisions made in Brussels are criticized as removed from local control. Delegation in this view inevitably lengthens the chain of relationships between the principals (individual citizens) and their agents (governmental bodies), allowing greater opportunities for "agent slack" and the frustration of self-rule.[5]

The problem is exacerbated by decision-making procedures in international organizations that lack clear modes of accountability. Many of the institutions that have been delegated authority are not democratic institutions. Some of them, such as judicial and quasi-judicial institutions, were obviously intended not to be. Courts operate domestically in balance with popularly controlled branches of government. The only real check on an international court, however, is the principle of consent: governments cannot be bound by adjudicative procedures in which they have not agreed to participate. Governments have taken care to develop legal doctrines to prevent tribunals from rendering decisions far beyond their competence, though arguably some of these control mechanisms are in need of strengthening (Reisman 1992).

International organizations can also be undemocratic due to the strength and independence of an international bureaucracy that agents—member governments—find difficult to control effectively. This gives rise to a principal-agent problem in which many principals (member governments) face the problem of delegating to and then controlling an agent (the international civil service). All members potentially face the risk that the bureaucracy will escape effective control. The threat to democratic participation in this case flows from citizens' double delegation problem: they delegate decision making to their national government, which then delegates some portion of that to an international bureaucracy (e.g., commission, secretariat, etc.). The longer the delegation chain, the more room exists for agent slack and loss of effective citizen voice.

The dominance of a handful of powerful states over decision-making procedures of an international organization is another factor that can lead these organizations to operate in an undemocratic fashion. This case need not involve new actors, formal delegation, or troublesome principal-agent chains. The problem here is institutional weakness relative to the political power of a few large players. The citizens of powerful democracies can find their interests magnified by these kinds of arrangements; their views are reasonably aggregated by their national government, which is then in a position to press these interests internationally. On the other hand, citizens of less powerful democracies have practically no representation in power-based international institutions. Because many international arrangements do nothing to alleviate extreme power asymmetries, the citizens of powerful democracies may be rewarded, while those of smaller democracies are effectively disenfranchised.

Both bureaucratic and power threats to democratic governance are common in well-known international organizations. Perhaps the prime example of a perceived bureaucratic threat is the European Union, and most especially, the European Commission. Because the commission has accumulated more of what used to be considered "sovereign" authority than any other regional or international institution—at least since 1992—it has been criticized as possessing more governing power than political accountability. The "growing gap between the power and authority" (Baun 1996) is the reason some worry about a democratic deficit in European institutions. Probably no region of the world has seen quite as swift and intense a transfer of authority from nation-states to region-wide institutions as has Europe. Recent institutional changes have tried to address the democratic deficit by strengthening the European Parliament, but detractors note that these powers have yet to rival those of the European Commission. Disenchantment with their effective ability to control European decisions is reflected in European citizens' waning interest in European parliamentary elections (Figure 8.7).

Many institutions have been similarly criticized for the power residing in unaccountable bureaucracies. Regional trade arrangements—and particularly their provisions for the protection of private foreign direct investment—potentially pose similar challenges to local democratic rule. Following a

Figure 8.7 Percent voter turnout, E.U. and U.S. elections

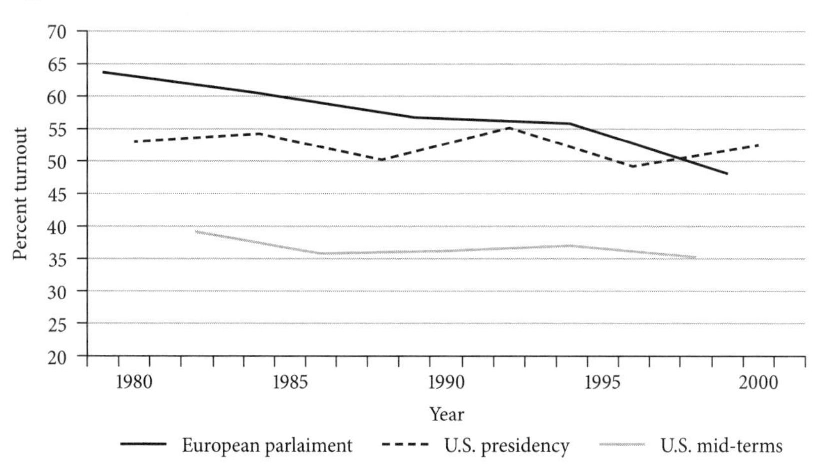

pattern that had been developed in U.S.-model bilateral investment treaties, the North American Free Trade Agreement (NAFTA) contains a clause for the protection of foreign investments that many claim creates a clear tension with the ability of national and local governments to regulate business activities within their jurisdiction.[6] This provision allows an investor in the event of a dispute involving direct or indirect expropriation to pursue legal remedies through international arbitration rather than local host-country courts. While this option is meant to protect investors from unreasonable interference from host governments, it also raises the difficult issue of where investors' rights end and the legitimate regulatory goals of the local community begin. Cases involving unfair competition and environmental protection laws have been taken away from communities and sent to nonpublic and unaccountable international arbitration panels, unintentionally compromising local democratic and judicial processes.[7]

Examples of threats to democratic representation due to power asymmetries in international organizations are also easy to find. The World Trade Organization is a case in point. Here the problem is not a difficult-to-control agent; the secretariat's power certainly does not rival that of the powerful members.[8] The problem is that rulemaking is dominated by a few powerful states. Many of the key decisions this organization makes are taken in informal meetings to which a small number of countries—"key" producers and consumers—are invited. It is hard to know exactly what takes place at these meetings because records of the proceedings are not public. Indeed, no votes have been taken on substantive issues at the WTO since 1959. These practices allow the larger states to set the agenda in ways that make eventual agreement much more predictable (Steinberg 2002). As a result, largely through nontransparent processes, the international trade agenda has grown recently to encompass not only trade in goods, but investment, competition policy, and government procurement practices. Almost every serious analysis of the content of the international trade regime concludes that the regime's coverage reflects the interests of the major industrialized states. American, European, and Japanese citizens' interests are pretty well represented in this process. The same cannot be said of the interest of citizens in small democracies such as Costa Rica or Botswana, or even larger but less powerful ones, such as India.

Some international organizations are subject to both bureaucratic and power-based sources of democratic frustration. The international financial institutions—the International Monetary Fund and the World Bank—both have large, independent, well-funded, and technically competent bureaucracies. In the IMF, the staff's autonomy flows primarily from its ability to propose loan packages, on which the members then vote at executive board meetings. The ability to propose gives the staff tremendous agenda-setting power. The executive board rarely, if ever, amends a staff proposal, though they do have the power to vote them up or down. Since many loans have already been negotiated between the staff and the potential recipient, the executive board may reject a loan, but it rarely influences the terms of a loan (Martin 2002).

Moreover, international financial institutions' formal decision-making rules heavily favor the wealthy creditors. When decisions are not made by consensus in these institutions, a system of weighted voting is used that gives the largest contributors (roughly based on the size of their economy) by far the largest say in lending and policy decisions. Economic clout is a voting principle that no democracy in the world openly tolerates, yet it is the basis for voting in the international financial institutions.

One final challenge to democratic governance relates to a lack of transparency. Some international institutions operate in ways that their ultimate principals—citizens—cannot easily observe, therefore making the institutions impossible to monitor. The IMF is often cited as an example, and it has made some efforts to address the transparency issue by making more information available on certain aspects of its business. Governments have also been encouraged to authorize publication of staff reports on yearly Article IV consultations, to release letters of intent for countries' use of resources, and to make public some policy papers.[9] Despite these recent efforts, the IMF makes decisions very much behind closed doors. Discussions and decisions of the executive board remain confidential. The charge of opacity has been leveled at other international organizations as well: the arbitration panels formed pursuant to investment clauses in regional and bilateral trade agreements are closed to the public; the proceedings of informal meetings among the major WTO members are not disclosed to the public; even the UN Human Rights Committee until recently declined to make its "views" on alleged violations of international obligations on civil and political rights public. In the European setting, exactly how member states interface with the European Council to vet proposals and set agendas remains the largely secretive work of the Permanent Representatives Committee (COREPER).[10] Demands for greater transparency over the past decade have helped in some of these cases, but the utter opacity of some proceedings renders democratic participation a chimera.

IOs and the Promotion of Democracy

Bureaucracy, power asymmetry, and opaqueness in international organizations (IOs) all potentially frustrate democratic decision making. But something should be said on the other side of the ledger. International organizations have also been a force on the side of democratization in some cases. The shortcomings listed above may compromise the quality of democracy in those countries that already have open participatory governing institutions; after all, the criticisms leveled against IOs really do bite when a citizenry is accustomed to genuine participation in national governance. But what about the effects of international organizations on less democratic polities? The net impact of international delegation is much less dire for polities that do not enjoy popular participation in their own governance. In fact, as Bruce Russett shows (chapter 4), there are good reasons to think that international organizations can contribute at the margins to the local process of democratization, at least in some circumstances. In this section I consider four ways in which IOs could make a positive net contribution to democratization among less democratic or transitioning democratic regimes.

CONTINGENT CONTACTS

One mechanism by which international organizations can encourage democracy is to make membership or other kinds of partnerships contingent on national democratization. If the benefits of these contacts are perceived to be strong enough, the prospect of entry could in some circumstances improve the attraction of a proliberalization coalition. Certainly, the lure of membership in the European Union has contributed to the momentum toward democratization in Eastern Europe over the past decade. Since 1992 the EU has included a controversial "democracy clause" in most of its agreements with third-world countries, in an effort to link deeper economic relations with the EU to respect for human rights, democracy, and the rule of law (Sanahuja 2000; Schimmelfennig, Engert, and Knobel 2003).[11]

INSTITUTIONAL DEVELOPMENT

Some international institutions have projects aimed specifically at supporting the development of local democratic and other "good governance" institutions (Carothers 1999). The European Union's PHARE program is an example. The purpose of this financial assistance program is to assist new and prospective members to "fulfill the requirements of the Copenhagen political criterion: the stability of institutions guaranteeing democracy, the rule of law, human rights and respect for and protection of minorities."[12] The World Bank is obviously not in the democratization business, but its relatively new concern with governance suggests an approach potentially supportive of democratic consolidation.[13] Many of its main goals (reduction of corruption, public sector decentralization and competition, greater transparency and accountability of the public sector, judicial independence and reform) are at least compatible with democratic consolidation. The bank's new approach emphasizes "voice" and "partnership" between the public and private sectors in the provision of public services. Furthermore, since early 2003, the World Bank has begun to promote the idea that unions should participate in the development and implementation of economic adjustment initiatives.[14] Unfortunately, neither broad statistical studies nor individual case studies can confirm that foreign aid generally—at least the way it has been used until recently—has a direct, significant impact on democracy among recipients (Knack 2000; Tuozzo 2004). It still may be too early to tell whether a "governance approach" to development assistance will contribute substantially to democratic institutions on the local or national level.

SOCIALIZATION

Some recent research suggests that international organizations—especially regional organizations—can have an important socializing effect on their members. Governments that join IOs dominated by democratic members over time begin, to a limited extent, to internalize the values of the other members of the organization. IOs may create opportunities for members to teach and to persuade, and new members to learn and become socialized into the values of the group. Some studies suggest that membership in regional organizations that are made up primarily of democracies has a clear effect—controlling for other influences—on the probability of a member's successful transition to democracy (Pevehouse 2002). Other studies have shown that membership in regional organizations can socialize leaders to understand their interests in ways fundamentally different from those they originally brought to the organization. This, again, suggests the potential for IOs to gradually socialize "outliers" to the values of the group (Johnston 2002).

AUTHENTICATION

Finally, IOs are increasingly legitimizing democratic practices by monitoring national elections. Democratizing but somewhat polarized polities may be better able to accept the legitimacy of an election if "neutral" observers indicate it was (for the most part) fairly conducted. Such observers can also vouch for the authenticity of these processes to the international community. In anticipation of such disclosure, more serious efforts may be made to conduct a free and fair election.

Certainly, IOs are not the only institutions able to authenticate national elections, but they do have some comparative advantages. Organizations are likely to be viewed as less biased than individual countries and better able to render fair assessments. Regional organizations especially are likely to have more legitimacy than either an individual foreign government or a global international organization. The latter may be viewed as less in tune with local values and practices. And intergovernmental organizations may have some advantages over nongovernmental observers, especially if politicians in the newly democratized state desire peer acceptance of the results of their election. These considerations may help to explain the large-scale expansion in national election monitoring by regional governmental organizations over the past few decades (see Figure 8.8).

Figure 8.8 Regional election monitoring, 1962–2001

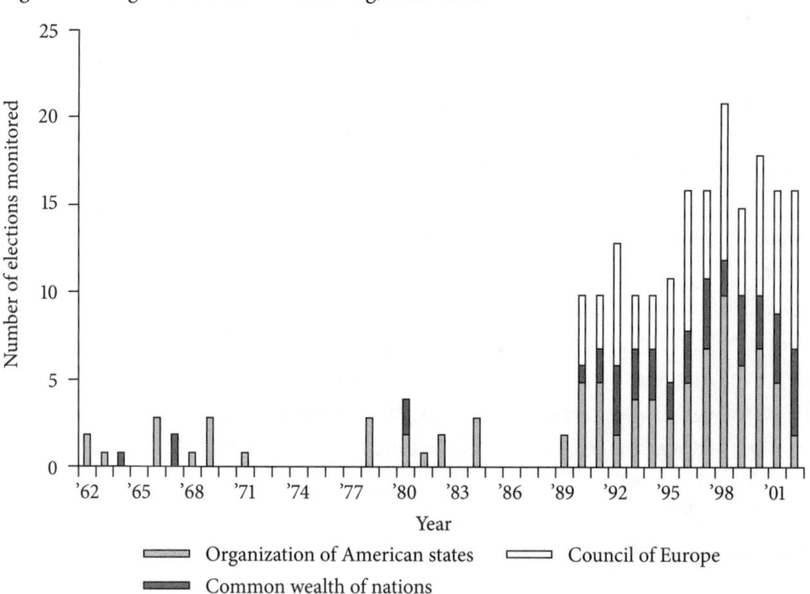

Conclusion: Discussion and Policy Responses

International organizations are a pervasive fact of international life. New ones proliferate while a few die out (Shanks, Jacobson, and Kaplan 1996). A sense of their intrusiveness into the traditional sovereign functions of the state—judicial functions, developmental decisions, social policy—raises concerns of an alarming gap between these entities' power and their authority. The inability to extract meaningful accountability from many of these organizations gives rise to concerns that governments have given away too much. The situation is especially ironic, since relatively democratic states, whose very legitimacy derives from input from below, lead the way in delegating decision-making authority.

None of this is to suggest of course that national democracies are perfectly representative institutions. The litany of imperfections in representative governance in even the most democratic countries suggests we must not compare intergovernmental organizations with local ideals that exist only in theory. Scholars have long recognized the pathologies of even the most democratic countries: elections alone do not guarantee accountability (Manin, Przeworski, and Stokes 1999); distant and unrepresentative bureaucracies undermine local democracy (Krislov and Rosenbloom 1981); and special interests often dominate the pubic good (Olson 1965). Besides, highly democratic governments delegate a good deal of authority to local or national nonmajoritarian institutions (e.g., the judiciary, central banks, independent regulatory bodies) (Pollack 2002). Indeed, John Freeman persuasively argues (see chapter 9) that we really know very little about how well national governments are satisfying public preferences in the face of growing and intensifying global markets.

Still, the delegation to international bodies raises these old concerns in a new context. Many of these bodies are increasingly making the kinds of decisions in which people imbued with democratic values rightly expect to have some say. In trade, for example, the move from discussing tariff levels to discussing intellectual property rights, environmental regulations, and consumer and labor protection standards rouses concern that we have moved from implementing consensus trade liberalization to legislating whole new areas of intergovernmental coordination. Arguably, all but the most powerful democratic governments have traded the people's sovereign self-rule in areas previously defined as domestic for the benefits of international cooperation.

Liberal democracy itself seems to contain its own contradictory impulses in this regard. The people are regarded, theoretically, as sovereign. Globalization internationalizes and transnationalizes the interests of important segments of civil society so that demand increases for governance structures that protect and facilitate international transactions. This is a natural consequence of a polity type that celebrates civil society and market-based economic transactions, and that depends on the rule of law to prosper. We have seen that democracies delegate "upward" liberally; we have also seen that public sentiment in at least one major democracy is generally supportive of such delegation.

International organizations have improved the prospects for meaningful participation in self-governance for some of the world's population and endangered it for others. Despite the recent growth in the number of democracies world wide, it is important to remember that some 42 percent of the world's population has no popular sovereignty to lose. If there is some chance that IOs exert some positive influence in insisting on respect for democracy in their external relations, extending developmental aid aimed at institutional improvements, socializing their membership toward participatory forms of governance, and authenticating national elections, then for at least this segment of the currently disenfranchised world the net effects of such institutions are likely to be positive.

The threats are greatest where local participation in self-governance has some meaning, or at least some potential meaning. And, despite the noise from NGOs in Europe and America, the potential risks of democratic deficits are insignificant for the largest democratic players. To believe that supranational authority poses a serious risk to self-governance in these regions is to swallow the idea that the U.S. government has not managed to protect American interests in these organizations, and that the Europeans are unable to hold the European Commission accountable for its actions. Neither is supported by the facts. By its sheer size and financial clout, the United States has probably too much influence in most institutions to which it belongs. It even exerts a shadow influence on those institutions—such as the International Criminal Court—that it refuses to join. WTO protestors may have a point about transparency, but can we not assume that citizen interests are taken seriously by the U.S. Congress, to whom the Office of the U.S. Trade Representative (USTR) is responsible (McGillivray 2000)? And surely there is little doubt that the position of the USTR gets a serious hearing at the WTO (Steinberg 2004).

Talk of a democratic deficit in Europe has been preemptive rather than reflective. The talk has been productive, and has set in train the ongoing negotiations meant to improve the democratic performance of that institution. But much of the criticism of the EU flows from holding this and other international institutions to unrealistic and highly idealized standards of democratic participation—standards that we do not even observe in most domestic settings that pass as liberal democracies (Moravcsik 2004). Recently, for example, the British press worried that democracy in European institutions was threatened by low voter turnout for European parliamentary elections. It turns out that until 2000, turnout for the European parliament exceeded voter turnout for U.S. presidential elections. Historically, it has ranged 30–40 per cent higher than turnout in midterm congressional elections in the United States (see Figure 8.8).[15] Thanks to the fact that the EU is composed of democratic states, leaders in that region have heard the complaints and summoned the political will to consider seriously the democratic legitimacy in revamping European institutions.

The most serious challenges to democracy posed by international organizations affect neither Americans nor Europeans. The most serious compromise of democratic ideals involves those democracies that try to play by international rules, but whose input is drowned out by the most powerful governments whose exercise of power in some institutions goes unchallenged or is even legitimated. Indeed, about 44 percent of the world's populations live in less powerful democracies (see Figure 8.9).[16] Yet their governments are regime takers rather than regime makers. It is precisely in these cases that genuine local decision making is being compromised by the "globalization" of political authority. For the less powerful democracies, joining international organizations usually does involve a net loss in self-rule.[17] For the world's politically repressed, international organizations may offer some succor in their efforts to gain meaningful participation in national politics. But the sad truth is that there is a growing class of (largely) self-governing

Figure 8.9 Share of world's population in the less-powerful democracies

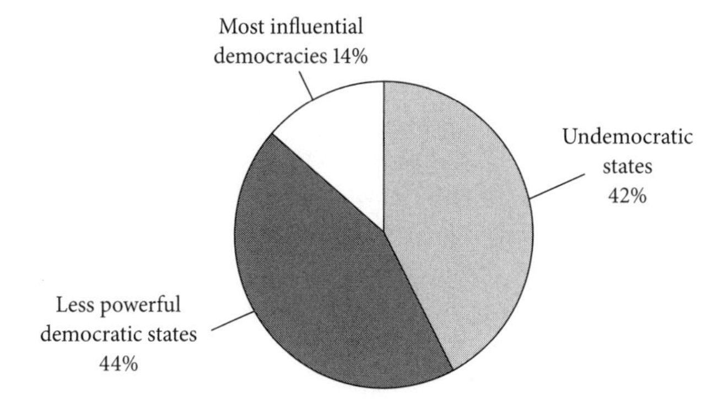

but second-class global citizens whose expectations for participation have been raised—only to be frustrated by opaque institutions that favor their more powerful foreign counterparts.

Efforts to reform the most important international institutions should take much more seriously the 44 percent of the world's population that live in less powerful democracies. We can envision various solutions. Radically, one might call for the parliamentarization of international organizations so that individuals directly elect their representatives in something like a transnational legislative body. This would be the European solution on a functional, regional, or global scale. Of course, governments of all regime types can be expected to oppose such an end run around their authority. To the extent that directly elected transnational parliaments might be expected to "work," they would be resisted in the anticipation that their legitimacy would make irrevocable the secession of state authority. Even so, given the flagging turnout in European parliamentary elections, it is hard to imagine such a solution ending in anything but voter fatigue as transnational parliaments proliferate on a regional and global scale.

If formal parliaments are not the answer, perhaps a solution lies in the virtual world. Can we envision developing a virtual public discourse, stimulated and to a great extent organized by "issue entrepreneurs" who articulate grassroots concerns? Perhaps it is not far-fetched to imagine widespread participation in a global discourse organized around particular issue areas as a way to empower nonstate interests in an egalitarian fashion. The spread of the Internet (see Figure 8.10) gives rise to the hope that soon most of the world's population will have instant access to the information and the resources they need to mobilize to articulate their interests directly. The image of a global "town hall" is attractive, but it can be nothing but a cacophony in the absence of some way to aggregate and articulate popular views. This model tends to rely on nongovernmental organizations to take up the global public interest. Increasingly, NGOs have regularized status in a number of international governmental organizations, such as the United Nations Economic and Social Council and the World Bank (Scholte 2004). But why should states listen? And what guarantees that these organizations legitimately represent broad societal interests? From a developing country's point of view, do Western environmentalists and labor and consumer protection groups do much to further their citizens' most urgent interests?[18]

The most realistic solution to the threats to democratic governance outlined in this chapter maintain the presumption that the most legitimate institution to represent a people's interests is their own government. Measures should

Figure 8.10 Number of Internet users, in millions, 1995–2002

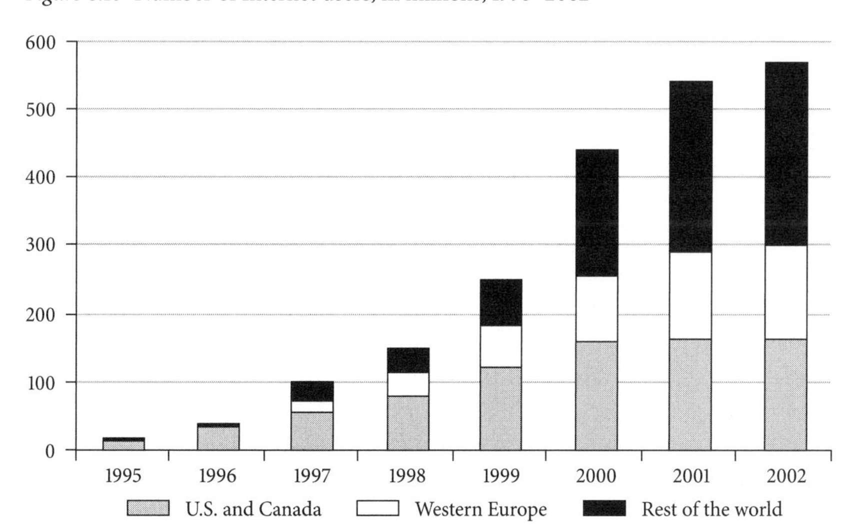

be taken to take this representative function far more seriously. A starting point would be to create fair representation in international organizations. The model should not be one-country–one-vote, as in the UN General Assembly, but some formula for weighted voting based on population, enhanced by an index of representative government. Small democracies should get extra weight for being democratic; large autocracies' voices should be discounted for their lack of representative institutions at home. In this way, the small democracies would have an enhanced voice, and the large autocracies would have some incentives to improve local democratic institutions.

Such a scheme would have to be accompanied by much greater decision-making transparency than is now the case in most international institutions. Bigger and better Internet sites are great, but they are not enough. Too often, these merely post after-the-fact press releases or already-adopted policy statements. Proposals should be posted whenever possible before they are decided on—preferably with six months' notice before a decision is taken—so that meaningful national debates can inform governments of the preferences of their people. We should not be surprised, however, to find that national governments themselves might oppose moves toward greater transparency. As Miles Kahler (2004,143) writes with respect to the global economic multilaterals, "A major obstacle to enhanced transparency at the GEMs has been the resistance of national governments" who themselves value secrecy and tactically attempt at times to shift blame to these institutions.

While the creation of a series of international parliaments is a premature idea, the idea of better empowering national parliaments is not. International institutions should consider adopting procedures that require regular reporting directly to national parliaments—and especially reporting on items to be considered, and not just the most recent list of faits accomplis. Even if they are not themselves flawless institutions, national parliaments should be able to debate the major proposals under consideration by the IOs of which they are members. In the meantime, the project of democratization at home should continue. It would be an irony, indeed, if attention to globalization's alleged tendency to create democratic deficits were to fasten exclusively on international governance structures.

Notes

1. Democracies are also much more likely to have domestic judicial review. Some scholars have argued that this is because of the uncertainty new democracies face as they liberalize (see Ginsburg 2001). Other scholars note that democracies are more likely to involve third parties (though not necessarily international courts) in the settlement of their international disputes generally (see Dixon 1993).

2. Though the initial proposal for an International Trade Organization could not gain support in the United States Senate in 1947.

3. For a more detailed examination of how democracies use WTO dispute settlement, see Busch 2000.

4. Note that this is despite the fact that the highly democratic European cases tend with much greater frequency to be taken to the better known European Court of Human Rights (ECHR); see Heffernan 1997.

5. For a skeptical discussion of international organizations' accountability problem, see Kahler 2004.

6. North American Free Trade Agreement, Chapter 11. The text can be found at: http://www.dfait-maeci.gc.ca/nafta-alena/chap11–en.asp.

7. Examples of cases include: the California-based Metalclad company successfully challenged the denial of a construction permit by a Mexican municipality for the building of a toxic waste facility; environmental and health bans of suspected toxins have been challenged, with one case already resulting in reversal of a Canadian government ban on the gasoline additive MMT; Canada's implementation of two international environmental agreements has been successfully challenged, and Canada will soon be ordered to pay damages to U.S. investors in both cases; foreign corporations have taken two lawsuits they lost in U.S. domestic courts to be "reheard" in the NAFTA investor-to-state system, one challenging the concept of sovereign immunity regarding a contract dispute with the City of Boston and the other challenging the rules of civil procedure, the jury system, and a damage award in a Mississippi state court contract case; the American company United Parcel Service (UPS) has

filed a suit challenging the governmental provision of parcel and courier services by the Canadian postal service; and a Canadian steel fabrication company challenged a federal "Buy America" law for highway construction projects in the United States.

8. In fact, of the global economic multilateral organizations, the ratio of WTO staff to the staff of national delegations in Geneva is one of the lowest for any of the global economic multilateral organizations. See Henderson 1998.

9. For the IMF's explanation of their transparency policies and improvements, see http://www.imf.org/external/np/exr/facts/transpar.htm.

10. For a description of COREPER's "pivotal" role (but no evidence of how it conducts its business), see http://www.dip-badajoz.es/eurolocal/entxt/eu/institut/coreper.htm.

11. See the Joint Statement on EC Development Policy, Council and Commission, 10 November 2000; described in document at http://europa.eu.int/comm/external_relations/human_rights/doc/com01_252_en.pdf.

12. A description of the PHARE program can be found at http://www.seerecon.org/romania/ec/phare.htm.

13. The World Bank for example has local governance projects in to promote grassroots democracy in East Timor. See http://www.etan.org/lh/bulletin04.html#CEP.

14. http://www.worldbank.org/mdf/mdf1/democra.htm, http://web.worldbank.org/WBSITE/EXTERNAL/NEWS/0,contentMDK:20091472~menuPK:34457~pagePK:34370~piPK:34424~theSitePK:4607,00.html.

15. See http://news.bbc.co.uk/1/hi/world/europe/3224666.stm.

16. Less powerful democracies, comprising 44 percent of the world's population, are those countries that score above +5 on the –10 to +10 polity scale, excluding the United States, Canada, Japan, and all countries of the EU.

17. Norway's history of resistance to the EU reflects such a concern. The Norwegian people have turned down EU membership twice, in 1972 and 1994. Recently, Norway's popular support reached record levels (58 percent of those polled; Financial Times Information, January 14, 2003), but only after the EU threatened the EFTA countries with a twentyfold increase in the dues to access the Single Market (EUObserver.com, January 10, 2003). This arguably reflects a sense of powerlessness among Norwegians regarding their ability to resist decisions being taken in the EU.

18. Claude Barfield notes that Western NGOs often have more resources to influence policy in global intergovernmental organizations than do many developing countries. See Barfield 2001.

References

Barfield, Claude E. 2001. *Free trade, sovereignty, democracy: The future of the World Trade Organization.* Washington, D.C.: AEI Press.

Baun, Michael J. 1996. *An imperfect union: The Maastricht Treaty and the new politics of European integration; The new Europe.* Boulder, Colo.: Westview Press.

Burley, Anne-Marie. 1992. *Law among liberal states: Liberal internationalism and the Act of State Doctrine.* Columbia Law Review 92:8.

Busch, Marc L. 2000. Democracy, consultation, and the paneling of disputes under GATT. *Journal of Conflict Resolution* 44 (4): 425–446.

Carothers, Thomas. 1999. *Aiding democracy abroad: The learning curve.* Washington, D.C.: Carnegie Endowment for International Peace.

Dixon, William J. 1993. Democracy and the management of international conflict. *Journal of Conflict Resolution* 37 (1): 42–68.

Ginsburg, Tom. 2001. Economic analysis and the design of constitutional courts. *Theoretical Inquiries in Law* 3 (1): 1–39.

Heffernan, Liz. 1997. A comparative view of individual petition procedures under the European Convention on Human Rights and the International Covenant on Civil and Political Rights. *Human Rights Quarterly* 19 (1): 78–112.

Henderson, David. 1998. International agencies and cross-border liberalization: The WTO in context. In *The WTO as an international organization,* edited by A. O. Krueger and C. Aturupane, 97–132. Chicago: University of Chicago Press.

Henkin, Louis. 1995. *International law: Politics and values.* Vol. 18, *Developments in international law.* Dordrecht: Nijhoff.

Johnston, Alastair Iain. 2002. The social effects of international institutions on domestic (foreign policy) actors. In *Locating the proper authorities: the interaction of domestic and international institutions,* edited by D. Drezner, 145–96. Ann Arbor: University of Michigan Press.

Kahler, Miles. 2004. Defining accountability up: The global economic multilaterals. *Government and Opposition* 39 (2): 132–58.

Knack, Stephen. 2000. Does foreign aid promote democracy? In IRIS Center Working Paper Series, No 238. Washington, D.C.: World Bank—Development Economics Research Group.

Korey, William. 1998. *NGOs and the Universal Declaration of Human Rights : A curious grapevine.* 1st ed. New York: St. Martin's.

Krislov, Samuel, and David H. Rosenbloom. 1981. *Representative bureaucracy and the American political system.* New York,: Praeger.

Manin, Bernard, Adam Przeworski, and Susan Carol Stokes. 1999. Elections and representation. In *Democracy, accountability, and representation,* edited by A. Przeworski, S. C. Stokes, and B. Manin, 29–54. Cambridge: Cambridge University Press.

Mansfield, Edward D., Helen V. Milner, and B. Peter Rosendorff. 2002. Why democracies cooperate more: Electoral control and international trade agreements. *International Organization* 56 (3): 477–514.

Martin, Lisa. 2002. Distribution, information, and delegation to international organizations: The case of IMF conditionality. Manuscript, Harvard University, Cambridge Mass.

McGillivray, Fiona. 2000. Democratizing the World Trade Organization. In *Hoover Institution essays in public policy.* Stanford, Calif.: Hoover Institution.

Moravcsik, Andrew. 1997. Taking preferences seriously: A Liberal Theory of International Politics. *International Organization* 51 (4): 513–53.

———. 2004. Is there a "democratic deficit" in world politics? A framework for analysis. *Government and Opposition* 39 (2): 336–63.

Nye, Joseph S., and Trilateral Commission. 2003. The "democracy deficit" in the global economy: Enhancing the legitimacy and accountability of global institutions. Triangle papers 57. Washington, D.C.: Trilateral Commission: [distributed by the Brookings Institution Press].

Olson, Mancur. 1965. *The logic of collective action: public goods and the theory of groups.* New York,: Schocken.

Pevehouse, Jon C. 2002. Democracy from the outside in? International organizations and democratization. *International Organization* 56 (3): 515–49.

Plattner, Marc F. 2002. Globalization and self-government. *Journal of Democracy* 13 (3): 54–67.

Pollack, Mark A. 2002. Learning from the Americanists (again): Theory and method in the study of delegation. *West European Politics* 25 (1): 200–219.

Reisman, W. Michael. 1992. *Systems of control in international adjudication and arbitration: breakdown and repair.* Durham, N.C.: Duke University Press.

Russett, Bruce. 1993. *Grasping the democratic peace: Principles for a post–cold war world.* Princeton N.J.: Princeton University Press.

Sanahuja, Jose Antonio. 2000. Trade, politics, and democratization: The 1997 global agreement between the European Union and Mexico. *Journal of Interamerican Studies and World Affairs* 42 (2): 35–62.

Scheve, Kenneth F., and Matthew J. Slaughter. 2001. What determines individual trade policy preferences? *Journal of International Economics* 54:267–92.

Schimmelfennig, Frank, Stefan Engert, and Heiko Knobel. 2003. Costs, commitment and compliance: The impact of EU democratic conditionality on Latvia, Slovakia and Turkey. *Journal of Common Market Studies* 41 (3): 495–518.

Scholte, Jan Aart. 2004. Civil society and democratically accountable global governance. *Government and Opposition* 39 (2): 211–33.

Shanks, Cheryl, Harold K. Jacobson, and Jeffrey H. Kaplan. 1996. Inertia and change in the constellation of international governmental organizations, 1981–1992. *International Organization* 50 (4): 593–627.

Simmons, Beth A. 2000. The legalization of international monetary affairs. *International Organization* 54 (3): 573–602.

Stein, Eric. 2001. International integration and democracy: No love at first sight. *American Journal of International Law* 95 (3): 489–534.

Steinberg, Richard H. 2002. Consensus-based bargaining and outcomes in the GATT/WTO. *International Organization* 56 (2): 339–74.

———. 2004. Judicial lawmaking at the WTO: Discursive, constitutional, and political constraints. *American Journal of International Law* 98 (2): 247–75.

Tuozzo, Maria Fernanda. 2004. World Bank, governance reforms and democracy in Argentina. *Bull Latin American Research* 23 (1): 100–118.

Waltz, Susan. 2001. Universalizing human rights: The role of small states in the construction of the Universal Declaration of Human Rights. *Human Rights Quarterly* 23 (1): 44–72.

9

Democracy and Markets in the Twenty-first Century

An Agenda

JOHN R. FREEMAN

The direction of global economic change in this century is relatively clear. State-owned enterprises are being privatized and new capital markets are emerging in many countries. These and existing markets are becoming increasingly liberalized and interconnected. A truly global financial system is emerging, one in which huge sums of money and capital are continuously and rapidly transferred from one location to another. This system is composed, in part, of large, privately owned financial institutions. These institutions construct and rapidly adjust portfolios composed of assets from many locations with the aim of maximizing a worldwide rate of return. They and the intermediaries through which they deal constantly are inventing new financial products and services as well as new technologies with which to process their transactions. The information revolution contributes to these developments.[1]

We care about privatization and economic globalization because of the widespread belief that markets enhance the welfare of people throughout the world. We attribute to markets the tremendous rise in the standards of living of many of the world's inhabitants over the past two hundred years (see Figure 9.1). In the minds of people who are committed to privatization and globalization, markets produce justice both intergenerationally and intragenerationally.[2]

In contrast to the direction of economic change, that of political change is unclear. Political authority is "migrating." New supranational institutions like the European Union (EU) have been created. At the same time, the re-

Figure 9.1 World population and production

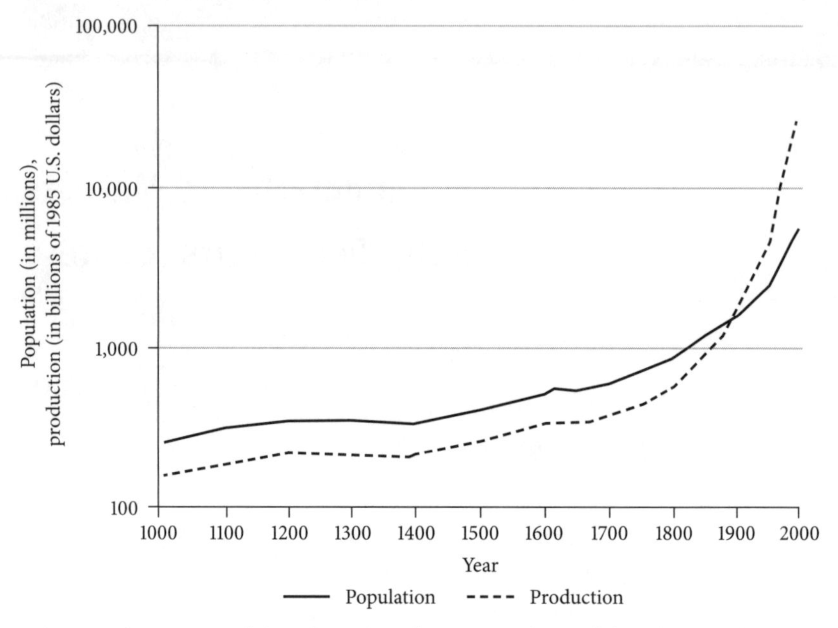

Source: Robert H. Lucas, "The Industrial Revolution: Pat and Future" from the Annual Report of the Federal Reserve Bank of Minneapolis.

sponsibilities for many public tasks are being transferred to subnational units of government. Some nation-states are disintegrating. Meanwhile, national political authorities struggle to retain some influence over their economies. For example, concerning privatization, national authorities try to retain influence through "golden shares" and restrictions on the resale of shares in formerly state-owned firms. Their efforts in this regard pale in comparison to the institutional innovations that are occurring in global markets. Moreover, public authorities do not seem able to exploit the information revolution as effectively as international traders and investors. While information technologies have revolutionized international economic dealings, these same technologies appear to have had little impact on democratic governance at least at the national level. Teledemocracy, for instance, is in its infancy.[3]

We care about the direction of political change, particularly within democratic nation-states, because their political institutions confer and protect rights. They also serve as channels of popular sovereignty. Through democratic political institutions, civil, political, and, increasingly, social rights are provided to citizens. Through elections, citizens exercise some influence over their economic well-being and the well-being of their children.[4] This notwithstanding, there is evidence that as privatization and globalization have progressed, democratic citizens have lost faith in their governments' capacities to manage their economies. In several major industrialized democracies there has been a decline in the number of citizens who hold their national governments responsible for jobs and prices (see Table 9.1). More to the point, almost half of French and British citizens believe economic globalization leaves their national governments little room to create preferred macroeconomic outcomes (French National Election Study 1997; Heath, Jowell, Curtice 2002) (see Tables 9.2 and 9.3). This may be why, at the time of their respective surveys, 49 percent of French respondents and about 27 percent of British respondents indicated they were unsatisfied with the way democracy works in their countries. More recent surveys show that many citizens in these and other European countries do not feel their governments have enough influence over economic globalization (see Table 9.4).

Table 9.1 Citizen attitudes toward government responsibility

	Germany (West)	Great Britain	Italy	Sweden	Mean
Provide jobs					
1974	94	85	94	89	91
1985	82	72	89	—	81
1990	74	63	85	75	74
1996	75	69	77	65	72
Control prices					
1974	96	—	95	—	96
1985	76	93	98	—	89
1990	70	89	96	86	85
1996	71	86	93	86	84
Provide health care					
1974	93	95	96	86	93
1985	98	99	100	—	99
1990	95	100	99	97	98
1996	93	99	99	96	97
Provide for the elderly					
1974	93	88	92	90	91
1985	97	98	100	—	98
1990	95	99	99	97	98
1996	94	98	98	98	98

Notes: 1974: Summed percentages of respondents who think policy domain is "essential for the government to do" or "that the government has an important responsibility to do." 1985, 1990, 1996: Summed percentages of respondents who think policy domain is "definitely" or "probably" the government's responsibility to do.

Sources: Timothy Hellwig (PhD diss., University of Minnesota, 2004).

Table 9.2 French public opinion on government control of economy under globalization

	Respondents (%)
Very much	5
Somewhat	37
Not very much	43
Very little	11

Question: In your opinion, does globalization still leave the French government room to maneuver in the economy?

Original question: "Selon vous, est ce que la mondialisation laisse encore au gouvernement français dans le domaine économique de marges de manœuvre très grandes, assez grandes, assez faibles, ou très faibles?"

Source: Centre d'Etudes de al Vie Politique FranHansie (CEVIPOF), Centre d'Informatisation des Donnes Socio-Politiques (CIDSP) and Centre de Recherches Adminitsratives, Politiques et Sociales (CRAPS) 2001. French National Election Study, 1997 [Computer file]. ICPSR version. Ann Arbor, MI: Inter-university Consortium for Political and Social Research [distributor].

Table 9.3. British public opinion on government influence on economy under globalization

	Respondents (%)
A great deal	9
Quite a lot	44
Not very much	38
Hardly any	5

Question: In today's worldwide economy, how much influence do you think British governments have on Britain's economy?

Source: Heath, Anthony, Roger Jowell, and John Curtice. 2002. British Election Panel Study, 1997–2001; Waves 1 to 8 [computer file]. UK Data Archive version, University of Essex, Colchester.

Table 9.4 European public opinion on national influence on globalization

	BASE	Too much influence (%)	Not enough influence (%)	Just the right level of influence (%)	DK/NA (%)
EU 15	**7,515**	**10**	**54**	**32**	**4**
Belgium	498	5	64	29	3
Denmark	501	3	59	31	7
Germany	501	6	57	35	2
Greece	500	18	73	7	2
Spain	503	13	38	42	8
France	500	10	57	33	1
Ireland	500	5	69	24	2
Italy	501	15	53	29	3
Luxemburg	503	5	56	36	3
Netherlands	500	6	61	31	2
Austria	500	2	78	15	4
Portugal	500	7	61	25	7
Finland	501	1	68	28	4
Sweden	500	6	52	27	15
United Kingdom	507	16	45	35	4
Gender					
Male	3,654	10	55	33	3
Female	3,861	11	54	31	4
Age					
15–24	1,114	12	44	43	2
25–39	2,145	13	56	28	3
40–54	1,941	11	58	28	4
55+	2,311	8	55	33	5
Education					
15 years and less	1,420	13	49	33	6
16–20 years	3,327	11	55	32	3
21+ years	2641	8	57	32	2
Occupation					
Self-employed	692	9	57	31	3
Non-manual employee	2,466	10	56	31	3
Manual worker	10,001	10	56	31	3
Without prof. activity	3,309	11	52	33	4
Locality Type					
Metropolitan zone	1,972	11	53	33	3
Other town urban center	2,923	11	55	30	4
Rural zone	2,620	9	54	34	4
Position on globalization					
In favor	4,690	10	52	36	2
Opposed	2,134	12	63	22	3
Level of Openness of EU					
Too protectionist	1,749	13	55	31	1
Too liberal	1,618	10	58	30	2
Neither too prot., too lib.	3,373	11	52	34	4

(Question: For each of the following actors, tell me, if in your opinion, it has too much influence, too little influence or the just the right level of influence on the process of globalization . . .
Actor in question: "j) our country")

Source: European Commission (2003).

Nor do citizens express much faith in the authority of their newly created supranational institutions. Turnout in recent EU elections, for example, has been below fifty percent. And the European Parliament is populated by an increasing number of Euro-skeptics, the so-called "awkward squad."[5]

Is this decline in efficacy, and perhaps popular sovereignty, the price of privatization and economic globalization? To enjoy the material benefits provided by global private markets, must we surrender national rights and national management of our economic futures? Can subnational or—as is more likely—supranational governments restore these protections and assert popular sovereignty over regional or the international economy? I submit that, while political economists have devoted much time and energy to studying how economic change affects political authority, they have not adequately addressed, let alone answered, these important questions about democracy's future.

The first part of this chapter criticizes extant treatments of democracy and markets. It argues there are five key questions that must be answered to determine if democracy and market globalization are compatible. Political economists have addressed only the first two. Moreover, many of the research designs they have used to address these two questions have been flawed. The second part of the chapter calls for studies of the remaining questions and proposes a preliminary research agenda composed of six projects. This agenda rests on the contention that in order to demonstrate the compatibility of democracy and economic globalization, we must accomplish two things: establish the democratic bona fides of "expert democracy" as it applies to monetary technocracies both at the levels of national and supranational government, and show that citizens not only have a conception of government capacity vis-à-vis global market constraints, but also that citizens are content with the consequences of adhering to these constraints.

Markets, Government, and Welfare

That markets impose constraints on government, and hence limits on the macroeconomic outcomes public authorities can create, is well recognized. Over the long term, trends in material standards of living depend on technological change and on the fertility choices populations make (Lucas 2003, 2002). Governments, by protecting property rights (Olson 1993) and providing care for older generations, may accelerate the pace of these trends. However, because these trends are driven, over the long term, by technological change and fertility decisions, trends in per capita growth presumably are out of governments' hands.[6]

Over the medium and short terms, government can use economic policy to foster certain macroeconomic outcomes. Consider monetary policy. Through their monetary authorities, governments can influence the operations of global markets. In particular, their open market operations and/or foreign exchange interventions affect the money supply and this, in turn, affects the real exchange rate. From a macroeconomic point of view, financial openness and capital mobility actually enhance the effectiveness of some monetary policies. All things being equal, monetary contractions lead to increases in interest rates, capital inflows, currency appreciation, and slowdowns in economic activity. In other words, over the medium and short terms, central banks actually have an easier time fighting inflation in financially open as opposed to closed economies. What financial openness constrains is government's ability to influence the *allocation of credit* within its jurisdiction. Today, governments have less ability to influence the location and type of investments within their economies. This, in turn, limits their ability to pursue industrial policies and to influence the distribution of income within their jurisdictions.[7]

With regard to fiscal policy, there is an emerging consensus that globalization limits governments' abilities to raise revenue through certain kinds of taxes. Globalization also affects the price governments must pay to borrow and, in some cases, their ability to borrow. Over the past several decades international companies and financial institutions have developed methods to avoid taxation. Through the skillful manipulation of tax treaties, multinational firms and transnational banks reduce their tax liabilities. The increasing integration of capital markets and the proliferation of financial service firms make it easier for them to do this. To raise revenue, governments therefore rely more and more on consumption, payroll, and property taxes. Since globalization makes it increasingly easier for buyers of luxury goods to evade taxation, these consumption taxes fall increasingly on basic necessities.[8]

In addition, global markets now "discipline" governments when it comes to borrowing. For example, markets demand higher bond yields from governments that, in traders' views, engage in excessive spending. At some level, markets simply refuse to finance government spending. The "hot money segment" of these markets punishes governments with capital flight when they judge the authorities' policies are unsound. Mexico's experience in the mid 1990s is illustrative.[9]

Global markets also pose regulatory challenges for governments. For instance, there is much concern about the ability of national authorities to cope with international financial crises, that is, to ensure the soundness of what is increasingly global banking system. To this end governments are attempting to establish international accounting standards for international financial institutions.[10]

Economic Globalization, Democracy, and Political Economy Research

Political economists have devoted a good deal of attention to two important questions about the compatibility between economic globalization and democracy:

1. Do governments have the capacity, through different mixes of monetary and fiscal policies, to produce genuinely distinct macroeconomic outcomes for their citizens?
2. What are the welfare costs of violating the monetary and fiscal constraints that markets impose?

Most work in macro and international political economy in political science focuses on the first question. The dominant view is that governments in the industrialized democracies still have much "room to maneuver." Despite economic globalization, policies are not converging and, more important, neither are macroeconomic variables. Political economists study these distinct policy mixes and resulting welfare outcomes under such guises as liberal market versus social corporatist systems (Garrett 1998) and liberal market versus coordinated market economies (Hall and Soskice 2001). One scholar, Torben Iversen (1999) goes so far as to argue that decentralized monetarism—a combination of technically proficient, insulated central banks and intermediate forms of wage bargaining—produces the most preferred blend of growth, prices, and jobs.[11]

Students of economics and elections add that governments still have the capacity to create short-term changes in real disposable income immediately after, and in the run-up to, national elections (Krause 2004; see also Lohman 1999). Political economists studying privatization argue that through "golden share mechanisms," deliberate "ownership fragmentation," and other forms of "protectionist liberalization," national governments can retain some degree of influence over national industrial development (Etchemendy 2004). In general, the recent political economy literature is replete with studies that claim there are major differences in the tax, wage, and spending policies of governments in advanced industrialized countries (Steinmo 2002; Boix 2001, Mosley 2000, Garrett 1998, Swank 1998)—as well as major differences in wage equality, employment, and prices (Pontusson, Rueda, and Way 2002; Rueda and Pontusson 2001; Traxler, Blaschke, and Kittel 2000, 2001; Franzese 2002; Wallerstein 1999; Iversen and Wren 1998). Some of these studies claim that it is this room to maneuver that explains the liberal economic order—citizens agree to open their economies to trade and capital flows because they can rely on their government's policies to cushion the impacts of global markets (see Scheve and Slaughter 2004a).

A handful of scholars contend that monetary and fiscal policies of advanced industrial countries are becoming more similar. For instance, there are well-established schools of thought about how monetary policy ought to be formulated (Woolley 1984; Kapstein 1992). And there is a clear trend toward making central bankers independent of elected officials. Political economists are hard at work explaining how democratic institutions ought to be modified to insure that this independence is preserved (Bernhard 2002; Bernhard, Broz, and Clark 2003b). Iversen's case for decentralized monetarism—a key component of which is, in effect, monetary technocracy—implies that eventually all countries will settle on a similar set of institutions because that set produces, over the short and medium terms, the most socially preferred policies in world markets. In a piece entitled "How Far Will International Economic Integration Go?" Dani Rodrik (2000) goes further, characterizing the constraints that global markets now impose on governments as a "golden straitjacket." Rodrik downplays the room to maneuver in policy and variance in macroeconomic outcomes across countries. In his mind, only world federalism will produce significant policy autonomy (Figure 9.2).[12]

Economic Globalization, Democracy, and Voids in Political Economy Research

Despite the different conclusions produced concerning the first two questions related to the compatibility of economic globalization and democracy, neither camp addresses three equally fundamental questions:

3. Does "room to maneuver" achieved through monetary technocracy come at the expense of popular sovereignty, or does monetary technocracy fit in a democracy?
4. Is the degree of policy flexibility that governments still enjoy over the short and medium terms sufficient to satisfy the mass publics' preferences for certain macroeconomic outcomes?

Figure 9.2 Pick two, any two

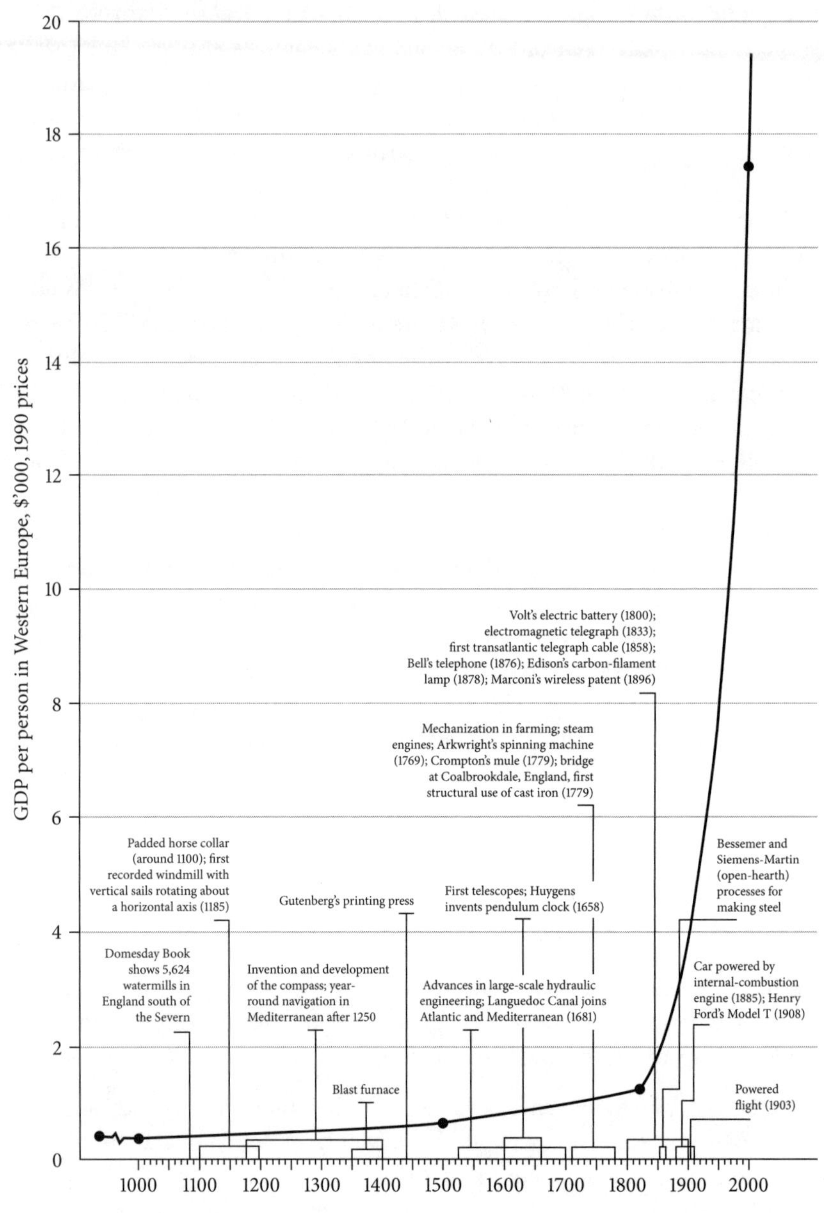

Source: Dani Rodrik, "How Far Will International Economic Integration Go?" *Journal of Economic Perspectives* 14(1), 2000, p. 181.

5. Does world federalism, or some other form of supranational government, enhance democratic governments' "room to maneuver" to a degree that mass preferences are more fully realized than at the national level?

Most political economists paper over, or ignore, question 3; they accept the rationale for monetary technocracy and assume that, in practice, monetary authorities adopt socially benign policies. With regard to questions 4 and 5, political economists posit public preferences for macroeconomic outcomes rather than demonstrate—say, through survey research—that mass publics are happy with these outcomes. Nor does Rodrik, or any other scholar, show that, in the minds of mass publics, globalization's straitjacket is "golden"[13]

Monetary technocracy is, in important respects, incompatible with democracy. For this reason, distinguished *economists* for years have questioned its justification. For example, Joseph Stiglitz (1998, 216–17) argues, "The ostensible reason for delegating responsibility to a group of experts is that the decisions are viewed to involve largely technical matters in which politics should not intrude. But the decisions made by the central bank are not just technical decisions; they involve trade-offs, judgments about whether the risks of inflation are worth the benefits of lower unemployment. These trade-offs involve values." James Tobin simply states that "monetary policy is politics." He advocates institutional changes that will hold central bankers more accountable to citizens.[14]

The assertion that existing policy flexibility allows public authorities to satisfy the preferences of mass publics also is problematic. For example, political economists cannot explain survey results like those reported in Tables 9.1 and 9.2. If governments, including their central banks, are using their room to maneuver to bring about distinct macroeconomic outcomes, why do more and more citizens believe governments are not responsible for jobs and prices? Why, if their governments enjoy substantial policy flexibility, do almost half of the citizens in Britain, France, and other European countries believe their governments do not have enough influence over their national economies?[15] And, if governments have so much power to buffer citizens from the welfare effects of global markets, how can we explain that so many citizens in countries like France are dissatisfied with their democracy and that European citizens in general show so little interest in making their voices heard in the newly created supranational institutions of Europe? For instance, Rodrik characterizes welfare mixes in industrial democracies as "golden." His political trilemma predicts a rise, not a decline, in mass politics in the

EU. Until we can reconcile these survey results with the claims of macro and international political economists, we will not know if, in fact, there is any meaningful degree of popular sovereignty over advanced industrial economies. And we will not be able to gauge the compatibility between markets and modern democracy.[16]

Can the *micro* political economists help us here? Unfortunately, the answer is no. There is almost no work on the values of central bankers, how central bankers view their role in democracy, or on citizens' conceptions of central bank insulation vis-à-vis democracy. There is more work on how citizens view their government's economic management. The responsibility attribution genre is illustrative. The problem with this research is the priming in the survey questions on which it is based, and the fact that it too rarely asks directly about the room-to-maneuver controversy. For example, Thomas Rudolph's (2003) research on responsibility attribution in the United States uses a question that asks respondents who is *most* responsible for the economy, not if officials have any room to maneuver. This question does not probe the reasons subjects give for answering "Don't Know." Nor does it attempt to sort out the macroeconomic outcomes that citizens believe government does and does not influence.[17]

The same problem plagues studies of "elite responsiveness" and of macroeconomic priorities. National election studies frame the questions about elites so that nonresponsiveness is due to "crookedness," a lack of concern for voters' welfare, or some (venal?) desire for votes. The possibility that international market constraints limit elites' abilities to respond to mass preferences is not included among the responses on survey questions. In the same vein, many survey researchers frequently ask citizens a pair of questions that *imply* governments do have room to maneuver. They first ask respondents to tell them the most important economic problem facing the respondent's country, and then ask if the respondent's government should (or has made) the solving of this problem a priority. This, of course, presumes that the government is unconstrained. Thus, like macro and international political economists, survey researchers simply *assume* governments have the capacity to influence macroeconomic outcomes. Survey researchers seem unaware of the debate described above and of citizens understanding of this debate.[18]

The literature on economic voting usually takes as axiomatic the idea that citizens hold governments responsible for the economy, including outcomes in the open economy. But, as we shall see, when it inquires whether trade openness makes it easier for citizens to evaluate the competency of incumbents, researchers obtain conflicting results (Scheve 2004b; Hellwig

2001). Also, the economic voting literature contains perplexing results, like the finding that voters reward incumbents for long-term growth trends—trends that most economists think government has no control over (Suzuki and Chappell 1996).

Returning to the macro and international political economy literature, what should we make of the large number of statistical results that supposedly demonstrate the influence of elections and political institutions on policy and macroeconomic outcomes? First, regarding the political business cycle literature, note that even when these studies find impacts of elections, these impacts are very small. Consider Krause's (2004) important contribution on political business cycles. Krause's *point estimates* for the immediate impact of electoral forces on real per capita GDP growth are less than 1 percent. He contends that under an infinite period of incumbency ("dynamic effects") these impacts would be somewhat larger. But it is unclear what infinite incumbency represents. Also, like many other scholars who write about this subject, Krause calls these effects "distortionary" (15). However, if elections are channels of popular accountability and sovereignty, we expect parties to create some (minor) alterations in economic outcomes as a result of the natural workings of democratic institutions.[19]

In addition, like much of the existing work in political economy, much of the literature on electoral effects on the economy relies on single-equation, cross-sectional, pooled time-series models. Such models ignore endogeneity in economies and polities within and between countries. Conceptually, ignoring feedback from popular opinion to policy to outcomes to popular opinion also ignores the political accountability that we hope for in democratic market systems. Thus, most of these works are plagued by endogeneity bias. Concomitantly, they are oblivious to the normative concern that motivates us in studying democracy and markets: the feedback from policy outcomes to policy choice, as revealing of popular evaluations of those outcomes.[20] Finally, much of the empirical research ignores the important temporal distinction between long-, medium-, and short-term economic forces. As explained above, the conventional wisdom in economics is that long-term trends in growth and demographics are largely beyond the control of government. If this is the case, these long-term trends need to be filtered out of our macro economic, and perhaps also macropolitical, series *before* we conduct our analyses. Failure to detrend our series may lead to mistaken inferences about the impact of short- and medium-term policy choices.[21] These criticisms apply with equal force to studies of the first and second questions about democracy and markets. To determine if democracy and markets are compatible in the twenty-first century, these design flaws must be corrected. But our agenda needs also to be expanded to include questions 3, 4 and 5. The following section proposes an agenda and sets forth projects to address these questions.

A Three-Pronged Agenda

TECHNOCRACY AND DEMOCRACY

QUESTION 3: *Does "room to maneuver" achieved through monetary technocracy come at the expense of popular sovereignty, or does monetary technocracy fit in a democracy?*[22]

One approach to use in addressing this question involves the use of the idea of expert democracy. Even though they care a great deal about inflation and related macroeconomic outcomes, citizens might be unable or unwilling to decide how monetary policy ought to be formulated. They therefore may choose to defer to technocrats to make this kind of policy. The identities of these technocrats are less important than their scientific training and presumed commitment to the public interest. If necessary, a small, highly informed segment of the citizenry together with a select group of legislators who periodically appoint and interact with monetary officials can provide oversight.[23]

Unfortunately, it is not clear that, for their part, citizens grasp—let alone support—this concept. On the one hand, attribution surveys show that citizens are able to assign responsibility for economic performance to monetary authorities as opposed to elected officials. For example, consider the results of a survey conducted in 2001 by Hart and Teeter Research Companies for the *Wall Street Journal.* A combined 41 percent of respondents attributed the economic boom of the 1990s to the productivity of business and workers, and to business cycles; 19 percent gave the credit to Alan Greenspan and the Federal Reserve; and only a combined 28 percent said the Clinton Administration or the Congress were responsible. Also, Adolph (2002) recently uncovered a connection between the partisan identity of government and the career patterns of the central bankers they appoint.[24]

On the other hand, new research in political science raises questions about citizens' willingness to defer to monetary technocrats. Hibbing and Theiss-Morse (2002) find that "perceived consensus" best characterizes Americans views on many issues. That is, U.S. citizens believe that, with regard to inflation and other variables, they and their counterparts agree about what is desirable. For this reason citizens might be willing to defer to experts, as these experts are willing and able to choose the best policies to achieve mutually preferred ends.[25] But, in fact, Hibbing and Theiss-Morse (2002) present data that indicate the American electorate is uncomfortable with deference to nonelected officials. Their data also provide little support for the idea of public-spirited veto players who guard the independence of central banks—a key idea in the political science literature on the subject (Bernhard, Broz, and Roberts 2003b).

Moreover, the consensus that Hibbing and Theiss-Morse found in the United States may not exist in other countries. For example, in a sophisticated study of the macroeconomic preferences of mass publics in Organization for Economic Cooperation and Development (OECD) countries, Scheve (2004a) found significant differences both within and across countries. Conceivably, these differences explain some of partisan the appointment patterns that Adolph (2004) discovered. But, in fact, Adolph reports that, for unemployment, the impact of partisan appointments is less than 1 per cent. Thus, the implication is that elected officials have not delegated authority to monetary authorities (Bernhard 2002) as much as they have abdicated their responsibility to use monetary policy to satisfy the heterogeneous preferences of their constituents.

With respect to the values and beliefs of technocrats, political scientists have long recognized differences in state administrative traditions.[26] Some have studied the values of bureaucrats in Western countries (Aberbach, Putnam, and Rockman 1981), while others have focused on the beliefs and attitudes of central bankers. Within this literature central bankers are recognized as an epistemic community (Kapstein 1989; McNamara 2002). There is anecdotal evidence that some central bankers harbor a notion of perceived consensus in terms of the objectives of monetary policy,[27] and the recent behavior of leading central banks suggests that their members are striving for greater and more direct channels of public accountability. Finally, it is clear that many view their mission as much wider than price management, as evidenced by the Bank of England's Inflation Attitude survey and the Minneapolis Federal Reserve's writings and high school essay contest. The fact remains, however, that we know very little about how central bankers view their roles in democracies generally or in adjudicating what are heterogeneous preferences for prices, jobs, and income equality. Political scientists have not inquired about these matters, perhaps because they themselves are so mystified by monetary economics.[28]

Project 1a: Conduct comparative survey research that asks citizens:

1. If their monetary authorities provide them with room to maneuver in the face of international economic forces;
2. If they are willing to defer to central banks to make monetary policy in return for the distinctive macroeconomic outcomes that insulated central bankers are able to create;
3. If the room to maneuver achieved through monetary technocracy actually serves the interests of some groups more than others; and
4. What their views are regarding the economic tradeoffs monetary technocrats make.

Concerning the first two points, it is important to learn if British and French citizens feel that their respective central banks have no room to maneuver. With regard to Iversen's case for decentralized monetarism, we need to probe the opinions of citizens in countries like Austria to learn if people see monetary technocracy as a necessary complement to their system of intermediate wage bargaining.[29] Questions along the lines of points 3 and 4 above might show that, while citizens agree monetary technocracy affords their government room to maneuver, citizens oppose this type of insulated economic policy making. These are plausible results because citizens may believe that the policies pursued in such a policy-making environment serve the interests of citizens who are especially inflation-averse at the expense of those who are unemployment-averse.

Project 1b: Conduct comparative research that focuses on central bankers and asks

1. About their understanding of the expectational mechanisms and other key features of the *political economy;*
2. If and how they are (or should be) held accountable to other (living) citizens for their policies;
3. Whether they believe they achieve a distinctive mix of welfare outcomes that best serves the interests of their citizens vis-à-vis countries with alternative political institutions;
4. How they perceive the level of consensus within living generations over the relative importance of prices, jobs, and income distribution; and
5. What monetary policy can they implement to expand the range of welfare outcomes that are possible vis-à-vis the preferences of different groups of citizens.

The founders and users of the new accountability studies of the Bank of England deserve special attention in this study. Why and how the Bank of England has taken the lead in these matters needs to be explained. Why the bank frames its questions in ways that paper over the distributional conflict Scheve illuminates also needs to be explained. Finally, the welfare consequences of synchronizing popular elections and appointments of central bank officials, as is the practice in Sweden (Adolph 2002), needs to be analyzed.[30, 31]

THE SATISFACTION OF MASS PREFERENCES

QUESTION 4: *Is the degree of policy flexibility that governments still enjoy over the short and medium terms sufficient to satisfy publics' preferences for certain macroeconomic outcomes?*

Consider a citizen who agrees with most macro political economists in our discipline that her government has policy flexibility in the face of global market constraints. To gauge the degree of popular sovereignty, at least three facets of this citizen's reasoning must examined. The first is her conception of *government capacity.* It is important to know that, even if she has difficulty awarding credit (or placing blame) for particular policy choices and macroeconomic outcomes, this citizen believes her government has the capacity to bring about her preferred blend of social welfare. The issue therefore is deeper than "the clarity of responsibility." A citizen might be unable to discern who is responsible for actual outcomes but still be convinced that, despite global market forces, (non)elected officials could improve macroeconomic performance.

In this regard, this individual could understand that government's capacity to change long-term growth rates is limited (Lucas 2003); recognize that in the aftermath of and run-up to elections elected officials manipulate the short-term growth rate (Krause 2004); and believe that public officials are free to choose the mix, if not the level, of public spending (Mosley 2000). Where privatization has occurred, she also might believe that golden shares and ownership fragmentation allows her government to retain influence over economic activity (Etchemendy 2004). Second, this citizen may comprehend the costs of departing from international constraints. She may also understand the constraints that apply to inflation and deficits, and that excessive prices and deficits are likely to produce higher interest rates that, in turn, will depress her government's economy (Mosley 2000, esp. 764). Third, this citizen, who believes public officials enjoy policy flexibility, is perhaps satisfied with her democracy, at least insofar as the management of economic life is concerned.

But, again, it is possible that she is unhappy with her democracy because, in her judgment, (non)elected public officials are not using their room to maneuver to bring about the macroeconomic outcomes she prefers.

Political science offers few insights into the reasoning and disposition of this first kind of citizen. Steinmo's (2002) research suggests that Swedes appreciate the room for maneuvering, that they are satisfied both with the macroeconomic policies their government chooses and, concomitantly, with the way their democracy holds their government accountable for these choices. Tax policy may be one of those about which citizens are satisfied. But, in fact, we have no survey data that shows Swedes agree that the limits of policy flexibility have been reached, or that they believe some kind of social optimum has been achieved.[32]

In an important study of economic voting in open economies, Scheve (2004b) shows that trade makes it easier for citizens to ascertain the "competency" of their elected officials. He does not attempt to characterize the policy content of "competency," let alone what competency means vis-à-vis international market constraints. Scheve's work suggests that, where there is clarity of responsibility and strong parties, citizens reward incumbents for exercising their room to maneuver. But, again, no survey data are supplied by Scheve to support this result; nor does he show that citizens in his sample of countries are satisfied with the growth rates they observe. Moreover, he does not probe the understanding of "competency" among citizens either in terms of policy choice or policy limits. Regarding satisfaction with democracy, there is evidence that the workers in geographically concentrated industries display more political efficacy when it comes to voting, campaign contributions, and lobbying (Busch and Reinhardt 2000). These workers may be satisfied with the way their democracy responds to calls for assistance, but no surveys I could find confirm that they were, in fact, satisfied.[33]

Political science offers a few insights into the identities of this first kind of citizen. For instance, skilled workers generally are more favorably disposed to trade and financial openness than unskilled workers (Scheve and Slaughter 2001).[34] Skilled workers may believe that their government retains enough room to maneuver in order to shelter them and other workers from the effects that global markets have on their well-being. The popular support for retraining schemes for affected workers is consistent with this possibility. With regard to the survey evidence reported earlier about the beliefs in room to maneuver, the only breakdowns available are for the French case. And, unfortunately, there is not enough variance in these data to generate hypotheses about the impact of gender, age, education, and occupation on this belief.[35]

Finally, studies of comparative political economy like Iversen and Wren (1998) suggest that, despite recent trends in globalization, first wave democracies have made, in recent years, distinct institutional choices about how to cope with economic change (i.e., with the transformation of the industrial economy into a service economy). The citizens in these countries—especially those where the choices have been most "radical," like Britain—should perceive that their government enjoys room to redesign political and economic institutions thereby manifesting popular sovereignty over economic life. In fact, citizens should perceive their governments as having made distinct pairs of choices from the "trilemma of the [new] service economy."[36]

Consider, in contrast, the citizen who believes his government has no room to maneuver, like those who responded negatively in the surveys in France in 1997 and in the United Kingdom in 2001. In this individual's mind, because of the constraints global markets impose, certain policies and macroeconomic outcomes can no longer be achieved. These outcomes could include, as Mosley (2000) suggests, inflation and public deficits. But it is unlikely that these are the only outcomes on the mind of such an individual. The outcomes could also include employment, short- and medium-term growth, and income equality. This citizen reasons that there are causal connections between prices, public spending patterns, and the outcomes he desires, causal connections such that once interest rates and spending levels are determined, some spending *profiles*—and hence macroeconomic outcomes—are ruled out.

For this individual, ironically, the power of governments to create a neoliberal model (Iversen and Wren 1998) actually is a decision to eliminate room to maneuver, akin to the decision to abdicate power to monetary technocrats.[37] Such a person might be opposed to privatization. He might consider golden shares and ownership fragmentation inadequate to preserve government influence over his country's economy. In addition, this citizen probably considers the costs of violating market constraints to be intolerable. He envisions dire scenarios if (non)elected officials fail to adhere to market constraints; conceivably this is how he understands incompetence. His belief in limited capacity of government probably means he is dissatisfied with democracy. It could be, however, that he believes other kinds of public policies compensate for what is, in his mind, the loss of government influence over economic life.

The political economy literature offers even fewer insights into how this second type of citizen reasons and who he is. This is because, as noted above, almost all the literature takes policy flexibility as a given. Once more, in their study of economic voting, Suzuki and Chappell (1996) actually show that citizens reward elected officials for long-term trends in growth—trends that Lucas and other economists contend are out of the hands of governments. This result is anomalous.[38] Hellwig (2001) suggests that trade dampens economic voting for individuals who are more educated, do not belong to unions, and work in the private sector in tertiary industries. His findings therefore are the opposite of Scheve's (2004b). Hellwig's results also are inconsistent with Kuklinski, Peyton, and Quirk's (2004) idea that the more educated use "motivated reasoning" to justify their partisan preferences.[39]

Concerning privatization, Spanish governments attempted to maintain influence over their economy through golden shares and especially through ownership fragmentation. And the Austrians still refuse to privatize a comparatively large number of their state-owned firms. Whether citizens in Spain or Austria consider their governments' policies an effective means of maintaining room to maneuver in the global economy is unclear. Survey results suggest they are not, particularly in Austria, where 78 percent responded in 2003 that their country did not have enough influence over the process of globalization. But, again, we lack direct survey results on this issue.[40] We also lack survey data on whether citizens who believe their governments have no room to maneuver are satisfied with their democracy.

Project 2a: Conduct comparative survey research that explicitly probes citizens understanding of

1. The capacity of their governments to bring about, in the face of international market forces, macroeconomic outcomes like employment, price stability, and growth;
2. The costs of violating these constraints—what scenarios might ensue if (incompetent) governments violate market constraints;
3. The effectiveness of government attempts to retain some national control over privatized firms through golden shares and/or ownership fragmentation; and
4. The link between these evaluations and satisfaction with democracy.

The Swedish case is especially important in this project because of the distinctiveness of the spending mix and welfare outcomes in Sweden vis-à-vis others (like the U.S.). Comparison of the British, Spanish, and Austrian experiences) with respect to privatization would be especially useful for understanding citizens' evaluations of privatization. Britain privatized with few restrictions; Spain engaged in "protectionist liberalization" and tried to retain some control over their economy through golden shares and ownership fragmentation; and Austria not only engages in the same policies but also still has a good number of publicly owned firms.[41]

Project 2b: Macro political economic research is needed that

1. Explicitly models the causal connections between macroeconomic variables within and between countries (i.e., that models simultaneity within a key set of political and economic variables);
2. Uses various filters and accounts for long-term trends in variables like growth, trends that may be outside governments' control even in closed economies; and
3. Allows for the possibility of *multiple, dynamic (moving) equilibria* suggestive of the room to maneuver (Steinmo 2002, 857).

The analyses suggested here could be of the traditional, simultaneous equation type (Chappell and Keech 1983; Alesina, Rosenthal, and Londregan 1993), reduced form-multiple time series variety (Freeman and Alt 1994; Franzese 2002), or computational type (Freeman and Houser 1998; Houser and Freeman 2001). Using these models, we need to probe, counterfactually, how much change public policies can make in what are dynamic, complex, interdependent political economies.[42]

AUTHORITY MIGRATION AND POPULAR SOVEREIGNTY

QUESTION 5: *Does world federalism, or some other form of supranational government, enhance democratic governments' "room to maneuver" to a degree that mass preferences are more fully realized than at the national level?*[43]

The logic here is simple. Enlarging the size of the government jurisdiction loosens the constraints on public policy. For instance, the ability of firms and banks to exit one jurisdiction in order to enjoy a lower tax rate than in another is diminished if both jurisdictions are absorbed into a supranational one.[44] Presumably, such a supranational entity has a monetary authority that exercises greater control over prices and other macroeconomic outcomes than its counterparts in smaller member governments. Citizens might continue to believe in expert democracy. Only now they feel their supra-technocrats have more influence over economic activity than their national technocrats. Hence, they presumably take a greater interest in the appointment of the respective monetary officials and in the oversight exercised by supranational, legislative institutions over the new monetary authority. Because citizens comprehend the increased capacity of supranational institutions to affect economic activity generally, they are more efficacious and hence more engaged in the democratic process. In turn, as Rodrick's trilemma suggests (Figure 9.2) supranational, mass politics has a greater direct and substantial impact on their economic lives than national-level mass politics.

The recent experience of Europe provides perhaps the best test of these ideas. Unfortunately, the results of the European experience are not encouraging.[45] There is little doubt that the supranational technocrats in the European Central Bank (ECB) have greater capacity to affect economic activity than the technocrats in member, national central banks. And there is evidence that some citizens believe the EU is better able to cope with the problems posed by globalization than member governments. For example, more than 50 percent of the same French citizens who participated in the 1997 National Election Survey agreed with the statement, "With the European Union, France will be best protected against the risks of economic globalization." In the European Commission's (2003) survey on globalization, 58 percent of the EU15 citizenry judged the EU as having too much (21 percent) or the right level (37 percent) of influence over the process of globalization (Q10, p. 39).

However, in a more recent survey, 49 percent of French respondents said the EU now does not have enough influence over globalization. Moreover, most observers agree that the EU itself suffers from a "democracy deficit." For instance, the ECB is considered one of the most insulated in the world (Berman and McNamara 1999; McNamara 2002). Its first head, Wim Duisenberg, expressed distain for democratic oversight of his bank's policies.[46] Overall, for various reasons, the supranational institutions of the EU discourage rather than encourage popular sovereignty (Wallace and Smith 1995). Whether the European Constitution—even if it is adopted—will rekindle popular efficacy and foster the kind of "mass politics" Rodrik (2000) envisions is unclear. The abandonment of the European stability pact, low turnout in recent EU elections, and growing support for Euro-skeptic parties suggest the opposite. In fact, a recent survey by *The Economist* (September 25, 2004) argues that the EU's biggest problem is a "lack of popular understanding and enthusiasm." *The Economist* predicts the transformation of the EU into core and aligned groups of nation-states.

Project 3a: The citizens of the EU should be surveyed about the capacity of the ECB to influence macroeconomic outcomes in Europe and about how the ECB figures in their vision of supranational democracy. We need to know from citizens about whether

1. They appreciate the greater capacity the ECB has given Europe to achieve particular macroeconomic outcomes;
2. They are willing to defer to ECB technocrats in this regard; and
3. They understand the weakening of the EU as a reduction in capacity for policy flexibility in Europe as a whole and in their own country.

A split in the aftermath of the constitutional deliberations would provide a natural experiment: citizens in the countries who become the core states should perceive greater capacity to maneuver vis-à-vis global economic constraints than those in aligned states. With regard to the latter, it will be interesting to learn what trade-off these citizens (those who vote to reject the constitution in referenda, for example) perceive in relation to diminished government capacity.

Project 3b: We need to ask officials in the ECB questions aimed at determining

1. Whether and how they believe the ECB achieves greater room to maneuver in the face of globalization;
2. If they see the costs of departing from international economic constraints as less severe, and in what sense, than the costs which national governments would incur from violating the constraints; and
3. Whether they hold a concept of "expert democracy" in any form, a concept that could fit in a stronger, more democratic EU (for core states at least).

If they do hold such a concept, we need to learn how they believe the ECB should and does address popular dissensus about trade-offs between prices and jobs.[47]

Conclusion

This chapter makes two basic points. The first is that political science research on democracy and markets has not addressed important questions about democracy and markets. Macro political economists assert that any room to maneuver in government policies necessarily satisfies public preferences, and that this room to maneuver embodies popular sovereignty. Micro political economists do not ask important questions about democracy and markets, including questions about room to maneuver. Second, both genres are methodologically flawed. The models used by macro political economists rarely include equations for national or international economies; they ignore endogeneity not just between economic and political variables within and between countries, but also the endogeneity that represents popular accountability. The questions used by micro political economists word questions in ways that fail to capture citizens' understandings of the capability of governments to influence economic activity in the face of global market constraints.

To determine if the rise of global markets is compatible with democracy, six specific projects must be completed. In general, we must establish the idea of expert democracy as it applies to monetary technocracy both at the level of national and supranational government. We must also show that citizens have a conception of government capacity vis-à-vis international market constraints and that citizens are content to adhere to these constraints.

Notes

1. Brune, Garrett, and Kogut (2004) report that between 1985 and 1999 there were more than eight thousand privatization transactions worldwide. These transactions peaked in the late 1980s. See also OECD 2001.

2. On the concept of market justice, especially as embodied in the beliefs of Americans, see Lane 1986. Evidence that world growth enhances the welfare of the so-called global south is presented in *The Economist,* October 16, 2004, 67–68.

3. The concept of "authority migration" is advanced by Gerber and Kollman (2004) to describe the transitions upward and downward in political power that are occurring worldwide. The devolution of power in Britain to the Welsh and Scottish parliaments is illustrative. Examples of nation-states that have broken up are Czechoslovakia, Yugoslavia, and the USSR. New nation-states like East Timor also have been created. Scholarly discussions of these and related developments include Rosenau (1990), Ohmae (1995) and Guehenno (1995). Golden shares are shares with special privileges (e.g., the right [of the state] to veto certain takeovers or mergers). The golden share mechanisms used by governments are described in Jones et al. (1999), Biais and Perotti (2002), and Etchemendy (2004).

4. On the idea of democracy as a universal value and its association with nation-states, see Diamond (2003). Anderson (2004) questions the universality of this value as it applies to Arab and other states.

5. The percentages of satisfaction with one's country's democracy come from the Eurobarometer public opinion study. The French figures are for November 1997; the British figures are an average of responses "not very satisfied" and "not at all satisfied" for surveys conducted in January and November 2001. (Note that these responses probably indicate a lack of satisfaction in the practice, not ideal, of democracy. Also, as first wave ["old"] democracies, the responses are less affected by the fortunes of one's preferred party in the most recent election. See also Linde and Ekman 2003). The lack of turnout and importance of the rise of the "awkward squad" are emphasized by *The Economist* in its June 19, 2004, issue (14–15 and 49–50).

6. Lucas (2003) mentions governments primarily as impediments to long-term growth. Markets (trade) are the means by which people avoid diminishing returns from gaining technological skills and from helping their children to do the same. Of course, in the early 1980s, Zysman (1983) and others argued smart governments could promote technological change and growth. But this argument seems to have lost favor in political science.

7. The allocation problem has been known for years. For instance, with regard to the Euromarkets, Dufey and Giddy wrote, "Thus the first two objectives of banking regulation [to properly execute monetary and exchange rate policy and to maintain the soundness of the financial system] are not seriously thwarted [in the 1970s] by the existence of [these markets]. The third, however, clearly is: the Euromarket significantly affects both the international and domestic allocation of credit and hence hinders governments' attempts at domestic credit allocation" (1978, 204). See also Grabbe 1996, 8. Interestingly, the American Bankers Association for many years opposed efforts to regulate international banking on the grounds that such efforts are a disguised effort of governments to determine the allocation of credit, particularly to force banks to hold a larger share of their assests in the form of government debt (Kapstein 1989, 340).

8. On the disparities of tax systems in Europe before Maastricht, see Malinvaud (1989). Examples of capital flight and explanations of how offshore financial markets constrain governments ability to raise taxes can be found in such works as Grabbe (1996, 278–80), and Giovanni (1989). An analysis of the decline in the share of corporate taxes in the rise of payroll and consumption taxes is Tanzi (1996); see also Steinmo (1994). Tanzi and others such as *The Economist* (May 31, 1997, 15–23) predict a marked shift to consumption and property taxes in the years ahead. Whether the composition of taxes has changed in this way is unclear. Estimates of labor, consumption, and corporate tax ratios vary depending on how (if) one measures such things as the deductibility of social security contributions, employer contributions to worker pension funds, and corporate property taxes (Carey and Rabesona 2002, esp. 138–39). Also important is the distinction between the tax rate and the tax base for corporations. A ratio of these variables can be interpreted as a measure of the "corporate tax burden." Using multiple measures of this burden, Stewart and Webb (2006) find little evidence that this burden is increasing in the OECD. They also find only limited, local tax harmonization is occurring in the same countries.

9. In fact, there is in economics a Market Discipline Hypothesis (Bayoumi, Goldstein, and Woglom 1995; Cuddington 1986). In essence, the consensus is that international markets will provide more credit to governments at higher yields, but only up to some threshold. The magnitude of this threshold depends on a number of factors, including a government's ability to extract tax revenue from its economy. For a recent analysis of these issues in the international political economy genre, see Mosley (2000). An important analysis of the discipline that the bond markets impose on subnational (state) governments in the United States is Alt and Lowry (2001).

10. For instance, the IMF regularly discusses regulatory challenges in its publication *International Capital Markets: Developments, Prospects and Key Policy Issues*. Other of its publications also analyzes this issue (e.g., *Global Financial Stability Report: Market Developments and Issues*, 2004).

11. Garrett (1998), for example, argues there is a genuine social democratic alternative. Governments still can choose a mix of relatively high social spending, progressive taxa-

tion, and large budget deficits; this mix produces comparatively lower unemployment, high growth, high interest rates, and high inflation. Steinmo (2002) essentially echoes Garrett in contending that the Swedish experience of the 1980s and 1990s shows that there are multiple "political-economic equilibria" from which countries can choose. Mosley (2000) concludes that her studies of the beliefs and behavior of international bond traders suggest that as long as governments toe the line on inflation and deficits, they have much flexibility to adopt other policies and welfare outcomes.

12. By "golden straitjacket" Rodrik seems to mean limited room to maneuver in terms of policy but outcomes that fully satisfy mass preferences. Concerning fiscal policy, Hays (2003) charts the convergence in capital versus labor tax policies. He argues counterintuitively that partisan politics will be more intense in majoritarian vs. consensual (namely, social democratic) countries.

13. With the exception of Steinmo (1994; 2002), not one of the scholars cited in the text marshals any survey data to show that the public is satisfied with macroeconomic outcomes. We return to Steinmo's work later.

14. Stiglitz (1998) downplays the importance of central banks' fighting inflation at the expense of output and jobs. Tobin's views are expressed in an interview in the December 1996 issue of *The Region,* a publication of the Minneapolis Federal Reserve Bank. A good summary of the competing viewpoints of economists and other academics about central bank independence is McNamara (2002). As I have argued previously regarding the political economy of monetary institutions (Freeman 2002), most political scientists who write on this subject fail to reflect on the implications of central bank independence for democracy.

15. For instance, Mosley (2000, 751) describes the British Election of 1997 as a debate not about the amount of government spending but merely how money should be spent. She does not demonstrate that British citizens conceived of the election in this way, let alone that citizens were *content* with this state of affairs. In fact, the 1986 British Social Survey indicated that about a third of respondents said their government—"of whichever party"—could do "very little" to "keep prices down, to reduce unemployment, or to reduce taxes."

16. Popular sovereignty can be defined as citizens having the "undisputed right to determine the framework, rules, regulations, and policies within a given territory and to govern accordingly" (Held 1991a, 150. Note that Held points out there are various restrictions on popular sovereignty in all democracies including various checks and balances and guaranteed rights. Note also that his definition emphasizes the "input" dimension of democratic legitimacy. See also Schimmelfennig 1996).

17. Rudolph used the question, "Please tell me who you feel is most responsible for the economic conditions of the last few years: the Congress, the President, working people, or business people." My claim is that "most responsible" primes subjects in a way that implies there is room to maneuver in terms of policy when, in fact, in the minds of a substantial number of respondents, no such policy flexibility may exist. It

turns out that only about 1 percent of Rudolph's respondents answered "None of the Agents" listed, and only about 2.5 percent responded "Don't Know" (Tom Rudolph personal communication 2005).

18. For a number of years, with the help of Jon Transue, Jude Hays, and Timothy Hellwig, I have searched surveys for questions about the room to maneuver and its implications for efficacy and political participation. Included in our search are the national election studies of numerous European countries, Program on International Policy Attitudes (PIPA) studies, Eurobarometers, CBS/*New York Times* polls, and the new Comparative Elections Project surveys. Even the International Social Survey Programme (ISSP) surveys on the role of government failed to include questions on the issue. Simply put, with the exception of the surveys mentioned here, we have few questions that address the room-to-maneuver debate. To address this lacunae in the research, the Time Sharing Experiments for the Social Sciences (TESS) Program of the National Science Foundation funded a survey of 514 Americans over the winter of 2005–06. The results are summarized in Hellwig, Ringsmuth, and Freeman 2007. Briefly, we found that a good number of Americans believe that their government retains room to maneuver. However, there also exists a substantial minority that does not. This minority is defined primarily by partisanship and education. In addition, while priming these subjects to think about economic globalization does not affect their responsibility attributions, the choice set matters: when provided the option, a significant number of respondents assign responsibility to market forces rather than to elected officials.

19. Krause (2004) estimates that, under a policy balancing electoral cycle, Democrats produce about a maximum increase of .75 percent in real per capita GDP growth mostly in the immediate two-year aftermath of elections, whereas Republicans engineer at most about a .67 percent increase in the same variable mostly in the year prior to an election. These are point estimates from a single-equation reduced-form model that contains no variables for economic openness. Also, research on the fiscal policies of the American states (Alt and Lowry 2000) finds what are, in my view, minor (4–5 percentage-point estimate) differences in the target levels of revenue Democrats and Republicans seek to collect, and maximum rates of adjustment to these levels of only about one third over two years. (Alt and Lowry consider these effects of partisan transitions substantively significant; I consider them less so, especially when one takes into account the fact they are point estimates.) My own work with Houser (1998) also, in my mind, finds rather small effects of approval shocks on the U.S. macroeconomy.

As I explain below, new work on elections and electoral institutions provides insights about how to probe citizens' understanding of the room-to-maneuver debate. But much of it simply ignores the constraints that markets impose on government. Illustrative are the important new contributions by Kuklinski, Peyton, and Quirk (2004) and Nardulli (2005). The former does not examine how markets constrain "policy correctives" that might be supplied by independent, unsophisticated voters; the latter does not examine the limits that markets impose on the effects of any "electoral jolts" that might occur. Other well-known works in this genre such as Powell (2000) suffer from the same problem of ignoring policy outcomes. Elite-mass congruence is of little import if policy effects are of minor significance vis-à-vis market forces.

20. Recent work in spatial diffusion in international political economy (Franzese and Hays 2004a and 2004b; Basinger and Hallerberg 2004) is a step in the right direction. But note that the respective models account for endogeneity in only one variable and, more important, they do not examine the welfare impact of taxes or any other kind of policy. There are no channels of public accountability in them.

21. For instance, most of Krause's constants in his equations in his final model (2004, Table 6) are statistically significant. But he does not draw any distinction between the short-term effects of elections and long-term trends in growth.

22. This subsection draws from Freeman 2002, esp. 902–5).

23. On the general concept of expert democracy, see such works as Hansen (1989). The idea of technocracy is analyzed in studies like Centeno's (1993). A recent survey of legislative oversight institutions for monetary authorities is Leeper and Sterne (2002).

24. Note that the Hart Teeter survey shows citizens have some sense of the long-term determinants of growth that, according to Lucas, are out of the hands of government. I thank Tom Rudolph for bringing this survey to my attention.

25. McNamara (2002, 58–59) emphasizes the consensus in Germany for price stability and how this consensus helped create support for the Bundesbank's policies.

26. See, for instance, Freeman 1989, ch. 4.

27. Hibbing and Theiss-Morse (2002, 141) note that, when he was at the Federal Reserve, Alan Blinder argued that the bank's legitimacy derived from popular consensus about the goals of monetary policy.

28. To my knowledge, none of the leading political scientists who interviewed central bankers in the past (e.g., Goodman 1992; Bernhard 2002) asked these questions. The Public Opinion Section of the European Commission conducted a survey of top elites in 1996 (see http://ec.europa.eu/public_opinion/index_en.htm), but I have been unable to determine how many of these elites are central bankers or to construct the respective subsample. The German elite study included the opinions of bankers, but, unfortunately, only a small (17 of 100) were bankers who worked for the Bundestag or state governments (Kai-Uwe Schnapp, personal communication, 1997). The Bank of England believes that the new monetary policy framework established in 1997 will be most effective if it is accompanied by wide public support, both for the objective of price stability and for the methods used to achieve it (2001, 164). To this end, it regularly surveys citizens about their knowledge of and expectations for prices and interest rates, and about its own performance in hitting the government's inflation target. The Minneapolis Federal Reserve Office devoted its June 2003 issue of its *Region* to the subject of income inequality in the

United States. Its 2004 essay contest for high school students was on this topic (*Region* June 2004, 28–30). Not surprisingly, the winner argues that "income equality is not a government issue."

29. Austria has intermediate wage bargaining, but due to its history of pegging to the deutsche mark, its monetary institutions are closely intertwined with Germany's. A good comparison with regard to employment performance would have been Austria in the 1980s versus Sweden after the breakdown of peak bargaining (See Iversen 1998, 488). For an extended analysis of the Austrian experience, see Hochreiter and Winckler (1995).

30. Concerning Scheve's (2004a) findings, note that the Bank of England's (2003, 229) question 10 presents the trade-off as one of high(low) interest rates and low(high) inflation, rather than one of high(low) interest rates, low(high) inflation, and *high(low) unemployment.* It thus frames the question in a way that papers over the distributional conflict inherent in monetary policy.

31. In the interest of brevity I do not discuss the issue of whether the identities of central bankers ought to better reflect those of the societies in which they reside—the issue of representative bureaucracy. I also do not discuss the problems of exercising legislative oversight over monetary technocrats. Both matters are addressed in a bit more detail in Freeman (2002). See also Stiglitz (1998, 217).

32. The key table in Steinmo's 2002 article (Table 4) is from a source on Swedish public opinion from 1989. With Sven Steinmo's help I recently contacted two leading Swedish scholars about the availability of data that address the room-to-maneuver debate directly. Unfortunately, neither scholar was able to locate such data.

33. Like most of the works in its genre, it is unclear what "competency" represents in the way of policy choices. In fact, Scheve's model (2004b) treats competency and policy as separate variables. His model also has no linkages between policy choice (competency) and economic processes like price determination. Unlike his other publications, in this study of economic voting Scheve does not supply any survey data to illuminate citizens' conception of "competency."

34. By rewording questions like those Scheve and Slaughter used, Hiscox (2006) finds essentially uniform support for free trade. The trouble with Hiscox's study, as I understand it, is that he essentially gives respondents one half the story about the impact of trade (consumption benefits without employment effects). By using the preferences of "economists" as expert opinion, in effect, he repeats this practice. Nonetheless, Hiscox's investigation points to the need for more careful study of the trade preferences of citizens.

35. Interestingly, in its survey about attitudes toward globalization, PIPA (March 2003) found that many Americans not only support government retraining schemes for workers but also are willing to pay taxes to fund such schemes.

36. The most radical change, according to Iversen and Wren, occurred in Britain, where the conservative governments chose fiscal restraint and employment growth over earnings equality (the neoliberal option). So, British citizens ought to perceive

their polity as having the capacity to make major institutional changes in the face of globalization. But see note 37, below.

37. Interestingly, at the time the neoliberal model was being created in Britain, citizens responded that government has little control over their economy (see also note 15, above). Survey results mentioned above suggest that the neoliberal model of Iverson and Wren has left a large proportion of British citizens in 2001 with the same belief. So, again, the neoliberal alternative seems to amount to the power to relinquish popular sovereignty over economic life.

38. That is, in a model of economic voting with explanatory variables representing long-term growth trends (corresponding to different macroeconomic filters—Peltzman, Beveridge-Nelson, and Hodrick-Prescott) and deviations from these trends, Suzuki and Chappell (1996) find that the former, rather than the latter, explains voting for president and Congress.

39. Note that Hellwig's analysis is based on self-evaluations of the economy, whereas Scheve's analysis is based on actual growth rates. This could explain the inconsistency between Hellwig's and Scheve's results. The concept of "motivated reasoning" (Kuklinski, Peyton, and Quirk 2004) suggests that the more educated ought to credit their governments with the rewards that their skills yield in the global economy. According to Hellwig's findings, the citizens who believe governments still have room to maneuver are less-educated individuals who work in the public sector and in the primary and secondary sectors of the economy. But the implication of Kuklinski, Peyton, and Quirk (2004) is that these less sophisticated citizens are the ones who "know something is not right."

40. On the Spanish case, see Etchemendy (2004). The Austrian privatization "backlog" is described in Belke and Schneider (2003). See also the recent story about the refusal of the Austrian government to privatize various firms in the September 11, 2004, issue of *The Economist* (p. 48). For a more general discussion of the political implications of privatization see Freeman (n.d.).

41. There is evidence that some citizens do not have a good understanding of economic globalization and what it represents in terms of market forces. For instance, in the fall of 2000 the *Washington Post* asked: "The presidential candidates frequently use the word globalization of the world economy. Generally speaking, how well do you understand what that phrase means?" The portion of respondents answering "not too well" or "not at all" totaled more than 40 percent. The European Commission, in its survey on globalization, found that in the United Kingdom and Luxembourg as much as 38 percent of the respondents had not heard of globalization (2003, Q1, p. 7). But we should remember that long before the spread of public education and the mass media, Americans displayed deep understanding of exchange-rate politics and related issues (Frieden 1994). Also, Americans appear able to form expectations about the fiscal policies of different parties and to take into account the institutional context (e.g., unified or divided government) of fiscal policy making (see, for example, Lowry, Alt, and Ferree 1998).

42. Illustrative is the use of a computable political economic equilibrium model of the U.S. political economy to determine, under plausible scenarios, the welfare consequences of increased approval volatility and of government pursuit of higher, more consensual approval levels (Freeman and Houser 1998, 650–55). Sattler, Freeman, and Brandt forthcoming and Sattler, Brandt, and Freeman 2007 employ an alternative approach—Bayesian structural vector autoregression—to study the room to maneuver in Britain. They find that, while British governments were responsive to changes in political evaluations and citizens rewarded their governments for their policy innovations with higher political support, the impact of these same policy innovations on inflation and economic growth were negligible.

43. I focus here on authority migration to institutions "above" the nation-state. This is because, in my mind, the room-to-maneuver debate is based primarily on the issue of government capacity. And authority migration to subnational institutions in almost all cases diminishes this capacity. Most of the well-known works on this question in economics ignore the room-to-maneuver debate. For example, while they include a section on economic integration, Alesina and Spolaore (1997, sect. VI.1) assume that all citizens pay the same tax rate and accrue the same income; moreover, they do not consider the possibility that countries' abilities to increase income by drawing on human capital in the rest of the world—their b2 parameter—depends on their budget balances or on certain features of their local economies, like inflation. The other well-known piece by Bolton and Roland (1997) is more relevant here insofar as its reverse logic explains why countries might adopt Rodrik's "world federalism" or even some unified world government. Bolton and Roland show, for instance, that under perfect capital and labor mobility, neither federalism nor independence are stable outcomes; more specifically, the world's median voter would prefer a single world-jurisdiction over either of these two alternatives (sect. VI). Their analysis of the more realistic condition of capital mobility only (sect. V) is less applicable because, in that case, Bolton and Roland assume independent "regions" can erect barriers to capital mobility and hence enjoy complete room to maneuver; under capital mobility alone, independence connotes a closed economy (see esp. 1073–74). This is not the situation in which nation-states find themselves today.

As for political science, the leading research like Rodden's (2004) and Rodden and Wibbels's (2002) analyze the macroeconomic consequences of competition between subunits *within* countries as well as the existence of international, "market conforming" (515) forces. But they treat the latter as exogenous variables they have to control; international market forces are not incorporated in their analyses in any serious way. Of course, it is conceivable that citizens in new, devolved states might believe that their public authorities have greater room to maneuver than when they belonged to the larger (supranational) state. But the reasoning behind such a belief is difficult, for me at least, to imagine.

44. The logic behind the Tobin tax is illustrative.

45. While there remains writing on the idea of world federalism (Held 1991a and

1991b) and various proposals for world democracy (Connolly 1991), there is no supranational institution yet of this kind. One could argue that a world monetary authority is forming along with an epistemic community of central bankers (Kapstein 1989 and 1992). How this world monetary (financial) authority "fits" in a vision of world federalism is a subject worthy of future study.

46. Duisenberg served as president from the inception of the ECB in June 1998 until the end of 2000. See the opening section of Adolph's piece (2002, 2–3), where Duisenberg's exchange with some social democratic MPs is summarized. Berman and McNamara (1999: 6) report that Duisenberg remarked that "while it [is] 'normal' for politicians to voice their thoughts about monetary policy, it would be 'abnormal if those suggestions were listened to.'"

47. For example, Scheve (2004a) illuminates the different preferences national mass publics in Europe have for inflation and unemployment. His main conclusion is that there are substantial differences in the inflation aversion of these publics.

References

Aberbach, Joel D., Robert D. Putnam, and Bert A. Rockman. 1981. *Bureaucrats and Politicians in Western Democracies.* Cambridge, Mass.: Harvard University Press.

Adolph, Christopher. 2002. "Succession in the Temple: Central Bankers' Careers and the Politics of Appointment." Unpublished manuscript. Cambridge, Mass.: Harvard University.

Alesina, Alberto, Howard Rosenthal, and John Londregan. 1993. "A Model of the Political Economy of the United States." *American Political Science Review* 87:12–33.

Alesina, Alberto, and Enrico Spolaore. 1997. "On the Number and Size of Nations." *Quarterly Journal of Economics* November: 1026–56.

Alt, James E., and Robert C. Lowry. 2000. "A Dynamic Model of State Budget Outcomes under Divided Partisan Government." *Journal of Politics* 62 (4): 1035–69.

———. 2001. "A Visible Hand? Bond Markets, Political Parties, Balanced Budget Laws, and State Government Debt." *Economics and Politics* 13 (1): 49–72.

Anderson, Lisa. 2004. "'Western Institutions' and 'Universal Values': Barriers to the Adoption of Democracy." Paper presented at the conference "Democracy in the Twenty-first Century: Prospects and Problems." University of Illinois, Champaign-Urbana.

Bank of England. 2001. "Bank of England Inflation Attitudes Survey." *Quarterly Bulletin* (Summer): 164–68.

———. 2003. "Public Attitudes toward Inflation." *Bank of England Quarterly Bulletin* 43 (2): 228–34.

Basinger, Scott J., and Mark Hallerberg. 2004. "Remodeling the Competition for Capital: How Domestic Politics Erases the Race to the Bottom." *American Political Science Review* 98 (2): 261–76.

Bayoumi, T., M. Goldstein, and G. Woglom. 1995. "Do Credit Markets Discipline Sovereign Borrowers? Evidence from the U.S. States." *Journal of Money, Credit and Banking* 27 (4): 1046-59.

Belke, Ansgar, and Friedrich Schneider. 2003. "Privatization in Austria: Some Theoretical Reasons and First Results about Privatization Proceeds." Working paper no. 229, Institute for International Economics. Stuttgart: University of Hohenheim.

Berman, Sheri, and Kathleen R. McNamara. 1999. "Bank on Democracy: Why Central Banks Need Public Oversight." *Foreign Affairs* 78 (2): 2–8.

Bernhard, William T. 2002. *Banking on Reform: Political Parties and Central Bank Independence in the Industrial Democracies.* Ann Arbor: University of Michigan Press.

Bernhard, William T., J. Lawrence Broz, and William Roberts Clark, eds. 2003a. *The Political Economy of Monetary Institutions.* Cambridge, Mass.: MIT Press.

———. 2003b. "The Political Economy of Monetary Institutions." In Bernhard, Broz, and Clark 2003a, 1–32.

Biais, Bruno, and Enrico Perotti. 2002. "Machiavellian Political Economy." *American Economic Review* 92 (1): 240–58.

Boix, Carles. 2001. "Democracy, Development and the Public Sector." *American Journal of Political Science* 45 (1): 1–17.

Bolton, Patrick, and Gerard Roland. 1997. "The Breakup of Nations: A Political Economy Analysis." *Quarterly Journal of Economics* November: 1057–85.

Brune, Nancy, Geoffrey Garrett, and Bruce Kogut (2004). "The International Monetary Fund and the Global Spread of Privatization." *International Monetary Fund Staff Papers* 51 (2): 195–219.

Busch, Marc L., and Erik Reinhardt. 2000. "Geography, International Trade, and Political Mobilization in U.S. Industries." *American Journal of Political Science* 44 (4): 703–20.

Carey, David, and Josette Rabesona. 2002. "Tax Ratios on Labour and Capital Income and on Consumption." *OECD Economic Studies* 25 (2): 129–74.

Centeno, Miguel Angel. 1993. "The New Leviathan: The Dynamics and Limits of Technocracy." *Theory and Society* 22 (3): 307–35.

Chappell, Henry W. Jr., and William Keech. 1983. "The Welfare Consequences of the Six-Year Presidential Term." *American Political Science Review* 77:75–91.

Connolly, W. E. 1991. "Democracy and Territoriality." *Millennium* 20 (4): 463-84.

Cuddington, J. T. 1986. *Capital Flight: Estimates Issues and Explanations.* Princeton Studies in International Finance No. 58. Princeton, N.J.: Princeton University.

Diamond, Larry. 2003. "Can the Whole World Become Democratic? Democracy, Development, and International Policies." Paper. Center for the Study of Democracy. Irvine, California.

Dufey, G., and I. Giddy. 1978. *The International Money Market.* Englewood Cliffs, N.J.: Prentice-Hall.

European Commission. 2003. *Globalization.* Flash Eurobarometer 151b, Taylor Nelson Sofres/EOS Gallup Europe.

Etchemendy, Sabastian. 2004. "Revamping the Weak, Protecting the Strong, and Managing Privatization: Governing the Globalization of the Spanish Takeoff." *Comparative Political Studies* 37 (6): 623–51.

Franzese, Robert J. Jr. 2002. *Macroeconomic Policies of Developed Democracies.* New York: Cambridge University Press.

Franzese, Robert J. Jr., and Jude C. Hays. 2004a. "Modeling Spatial Relations in Tax Competition." Paper presented at the annual meeting of the American Political Science Association, Chicago.

———. 2004b. "Empirical Modeling Strategies for Spatial Interdependence." Paper presented at the summer of meeting of the Political Methodology Section of the American Political Science Association, Palo Alto, California.

Freeman, John. R. n.d. "Preface to the Spanish Edition." *Democracy and Markets: The Politics of Mixed Economies.* Political Thought Series. Cordoba, Spain: Editorial Almuzara.

———. 1989. *Democracy and Markets: The Politics of Mixed Economies.* Ithaca, N.Y.: Cornell University Press.

———. 2002. "Competing Commitments: Technocracy and Democracy in the Design of Monetary Institutions." In Bernhard, Broz, and Clark 2003a, 197–218.

Freeman, John R., and James Alt. 1994. " The Politics of Public and Private Investment in Britain." In *The Comparative Political Economy of the Welfare State,* ed. A. Hicks and T. Janoski, 136–65. New York: Cambridge University Press.

Freeman, John R., and Daniel Houser. 1998. "A Computable Equilibrium Model for the Study of Political Economy." *American Journal of Political Science* 42 (2): 628–60.

French National Election Study. 1997. [Computer file]. ICPSR version. Ann Arbor, Mich.: Interuniversity Consortium for Political and Social Research.

Frieden, Jeffry A. 1994. "Exchange Rate Politics: Contemporary Lessons from American History." *Review of International Political Economy* 1 (1): 81–103.

Garrett, Geoffrey. 1998. *Partisan Politics in the Global Economy.* New York: Cambridge University Press.

Gerber, Elizabeth, and Kenneth Kollman. 2004. "Introduction—Authority Migration: Defining an Emerging Research Agenda." *PS: Political Science and Politics* 37 (3): 397–400.

Giovannini, A. 1989. "National Tax Systems and the European Capital Martket." *Economic Policy* 9:346–86.

Goodman, John B. 1992. *Monetary Sovereignty: The Politics of Central Banking in Western Europe.* Ithaca, N.Y.: Cornell University Press.

Grabbe, J. Orlin. 1996. *International Financial Markets.* 3rd ed. Englewood Cliffs, N.J.: Prentice Hall.

Guehenno, Jean-Marie. 1995. *The End of the Nation-State.* Trans. by V. Elliot. Minneapolis: University of Minnesota Press.

Hall, Peter A., and David Soskice, eds. 2001. *Varieties of Capitalism: The Institutional Foundations of Comparative Advantage.* New York: Oxford University Press.

Hanson, Russell. 1989. "Democracy." In *Political Innovation and Conceptual Change*, ed. Terrence Ball, James Farr, and Russell L. Hanson, 68–89. New York: Cambridge University Press.

Hays, Jude C. 2003. "Globalization and Capital Taxation in Majoritarian and Consensual Democracies." *World Politics* 56:79–113.

Heath, Anthony, Roger Jowell, and John Curtice. 2002. British Election Panel Study, 1997–2001. Waves 1–8, UK data archive version, University of Essex, Colchester.

Held, David. 1991a. " Democracy, the Nation-State, and the Global System." *Economy and Society* 20 (2): 139–72.

Held, David. 1991b. "Democracy and Globalization." *Alternatives* 16:201–8.

Hellwig, Timothy. 2001. "Interdependence, Government Constraints, and Economic Voting." *Journal of Politics* 63 (4): 1141–62.

———. 2004 "Political Representation in the Global Economy." Unpublished PhD diss., University of Minnesota, Minneapolis.

Hellwig, Timothy, Eve Ringsmuth, and John R. Freeman. 2007. "The American Public and the Room to Maneuver: Responsibility Attributions and Policy Efficacy in an Era of Globalization." Paper presented at the annual meeting of the Midwest Political Science Association, Chicago.

Hibbing, John R. and Elizabeth Theiss-Morse. 2001. "Process, Preferences and American Politics." *American Political Science Review* 95 (1): 145–53.

———. 2002. *Stealth Democracy: Americans' Beliefs about How Government Should Work*. New York: Cambridge University Press.

Hiscox, Michael J. 2006. "Through a Glass and Darkly: Attitudes toward International Trade and the Curious Effects of Issue Framing." *International Organization* 60 (3): 755–780.

Hochreiter, Eduard, and Georg Winckler. 1995. "The Advantages of Tying Austria's Hands: The Success of the Hard Currency Strategy." *European Journal of Political Economy* 11 (1): 83–111.

Houser, Daniel, and John R. Freeman. 2001. "The Economic Consequences of Approval Management in Comparative Perspective." *Journal of Comparative Economics* 29: 692–721.

Iversen, Torben. 1998. "Wage Bargaining, Central Bank Independence, and the Real Effects of Money." *International Organization* 52 (3): 469–504.

———. 1999. *Contested Economic Institutions: The Politics of Macroeconomics and Wage Bargaining in Advanced Democracies*. New York: Cambridge University Press.

Iversen, Torben, and Anne Wren. 1998. "Equality, Employment, and Budgetary Restraint: The Trilemma of the Service Economy." *World Politics* 50 (4): 507–47.

Jones, Steven L., William L. Megginson, Robert Nash, and Jeffry N. Netter. 1999. "Share Issue Privatization as Financial Means to Political and Economic Ends." *Journal of Financial Economics* 53:217–53.

Kapstein, Ethan. 1989. "Resolving the Regulator's Dilemma: International Coordination of Banking Regulation." *International Organization* 43 (2): 323-47.

———. 1992. "Between Power and Purpose: Central Bankers and the Politics of Regulatory Convergence." *International Organization* 46 (1): 265–87.

Krause, George A. 2004. "Electoral Incentives, Political Business Cycles, and Macroeconomic Performance: Empirical Evidence from Post-war U.S. Personal Income Growth." *British Journal of Political Science* 34:1–25.

Kuklinski, James, Buddy Peyton, and Paul J. Quirk. 2004. "Issues, Information Flows, and Cognitive Capacities: Democratic Citizenship in a Global Era." Paper presented at the conference "Democracy in the Twenty-first Century: Prospects and Problems," University of Illinois, Champaign-Urbana, October 24–26.

Lane, Robert E. 1986. "Market Justice, Political Justice." *American Political Science Review* 80 (2): 383–402.

Leeper, Jonathan, and Gabriel Sterne. 2002. "Parliamentary Scrutiny of Central Banks in the United Kingdom and Overseas." *Bank of England Quarterly Bulletin* 42 (3): 274–83.

Linde, Jonas, and Joakim Ekman. 2003. "Satisfaction with Democracy: A Note on a Frequently Used Indicator in Comparative Politics." *European Journal of Political Research* 42:391–408.

Lohmann, Suzanne. 1999. "What Price Accountability? The Lucas Island Model of the Politics of Monetary Policy." *American Journal of Political Science* 43 (2): 396–430.

Lowry, Robert C., James E. Alt, and Karen E. Ferree. 1998. "Fiscal Policy Outcomes and Electoral Accountability in the American States." *American Political Science Review* 92 (4): 759–74.

Lucas, Robert E. Jr. 2002. "The Industrial Revolution: Past and Future." In *Lectures on Economic Growth,* 109–88. Cambridge, Mass.: Harvard University Press.

———. 2003. "The Industrial Revolution: Past and Future" *The Region* Annual Report Issue. Minneapolis: Federal Reserve Bank.

Malinvaud, Edmond. 1989. "Comment [on Giovannini]." *Economic Policy* 9 (October): 374-77.

McNamara, Kathleen R. 2002. "Rational Fictions: Central Bank Independence and the Social Logic of Delegation." *West European Politics* 25 (1): 46–76.

Mosley, Layna. 2000. "Room to Move: International Financial Markets and National Welfare States." *International Organization* 54 (4): 737–73.

Nardulli, Peter. 2005. *Popular Efficacy in the Democratic Era: A Re-examination of Electoral Accountability in the U.S. 1928–2000.* Princeton, N.J.: Princeton University Press.

Ohmae, K. 1995. *The End of the Nation-State.* Harper Collins.

Olson, Mancur. 1993. "Dictatorship, Democracy, and Development." *American Political Science Review* 87 (3): 567–76.

Organization for Economic Cooperation and Development (OECD). 2001. "Recent Privatization Trends in OECD Countries." *Financial Trends.* Paris: OECD.

Pontusson, Jonas, David Rueda, and Christopher A. Way. 2002. "Comparative Political Economy of the Wage Distribution: The Role of Partisanship and Labor Market Institutions." *British Journal of Political Science* 32 (2): 281–308.

Powell, G. Bingham Jr. 2000. *Elections as Instruments of Democracy: Majoritarian and Proportional Visions.* New Haven, Conn.: Yale University Press.

Rodden, Jonathon. 2004. "On the Migration of Fiscal Sovereignty" *PS: Political Science and Politics* 37 (3): 427–31.

Rodden, Jonathon, and Erik Wibbels. 2002. "Beyond the Fiction of Federalism: Macroeconomic Management in Multitiered Systems." *World Politics* 54 (4): 494–531.

Rodrik, Dani. 2000. "How Far Will International Economic Integration Go?" *Journal of Economic Perspectives* 14:177–86.

Rosenau, J. 1990. "The Relocation of Authority in a Shrinking World." Paper presented at the annual meeting of the American Political Science Association, San Francisco.

Rudolph, Thomas J. 2003. "Who's Responsible for the Economy? The Formation and Consequences of Responsibility Attributions." *American Journal of Political Science* 47 (4): 698–713.

Rueda, David, and Jonas Pontusson. 2002. "Wage Inequality and Varieties of Capitalism." *World Politics* 52:350–83.

Sattler, Thomas, Patrick T. Brandt, and John R. Freeman. 2007. "Economic Policy, Political Accountability, and the Room to Maneuver." Paper presented at the Conference on the Political Economy of International Finance, Federal Reserve Bank of Atlanta.

Sattler, Thomas, John R. Freeman, and Patrick T. Brandt. N.d. "Political Accountability and the Room to Maneuver." *Comparative Political Studies.*

Scheve, Kenneth F. 2004a. "Public Aversion and the Political Economy of Macroeconomic Policymaking." *International Organization* 58:1–34.

———. 2004b. " Democracy and Globalization: Candidate Selection in Open Economies." Unpublished manuscript. New Haven, Conn.: Yale University.

Scheve, Kenneth F., and Matthew J. Slaughter. 2001. *Globalization and the Perceptions of American Workers.* Washington, D.C.: Institute for International Economics.

———. 2004a. "Public Opinion, International Economic Integration and the Welfare State." Unpublished manuscript. New Haven, Conn.: Yale University.

———. 2004b. "Economic Insecurity and the Globalization of Production." *American Journal of Political Science* 48 (4): 662–74.

Schimmelfennig, Frank. 1996. *Legitimate Rule in the European Union: The Academic Debate.* Department of International Relations/Peace and Conflict Research, Institute for Political Science, Eberhard-Karls University, Tübingen.

Steinmo, Sven. 1994. "The End of Redistribution? International Pressures and Domestic Policy Choices." *Challenge* 37 (6): 9-19.

———. 2002. "Globalization and Taxation: Challenges to the Swedish Welfare State." *Comparative Political Studies* 35 (7): 839–62.

Stewart, Kenneth, and Michael Webb. 2006. "International Competition in Corporate Taxation: Evidence from the OECD Time Series." *Economic Policy* January: 153–201.

Stiglitz, Joseph. 1998. " Central Banking in a Democratic Society." *De Economist* 146 (2): 199–226.

Suzuki, Motoshi, and Henry W. Chappell Jr. 1996. "The Rationality of Economic Voting Revisited." *Journal of Politics* 58 (1): 224-36.

Swank, D. 1998. "Funding the Welfare State: Globalization and the Taxation of Business in Advanced Market Economies." *Political Studies* 46 (4): 671–92.

Tanzi, Victor. 1996. "Globalization, Tax Competition, and the Future of Tax Systems." IMF Working Paper WP/96/141. http://www.imf.org/external/pubs/cat/longres.cfm?sk.

Traxler, Franz, Sabine Blaschke, and Bernhard Kittel. 2000. "The Bargaining System and Performance: A Comparison of OECD Countries" *Comparative Political Studies* 33 (9): 1154–90.

———. 2001. *National Labour Relations in International Markets: A Comparative Study of Institutions, Change and Performance.* New York: Oxford University Press.

Wallace, William, and Julie Smith. 1995. "Democracy or Technocracy? European Integration and the Problem of Popular Consent." *West European Politics* 18 (3): 137-57.

Wallerstein, Michael. 1999. "Wage Setting Institutions and Pay Equality in Advanced Industrial Societies." *American Journal of Political Science* 43 (3): 649–80.

Woolley, John T. 1984. *Monetary Politics: The Federal Reserve and the Politics of Monetary Policy.* New York: Cambridge University Press.

Zysman, John. 1983. *Governments, Markets, and Growth: Financial Systems and the Politics of Industrial Change.* Ithaca, N.Y.: Cornell University Press.

10

Economic Globalization and Democracy

MELISSA A. ORLIE

Upon reading the advocates and critics of economic globalization, it does not take long to begin wondering whether they live in the same world.

Advocates of economic globalization claim that the liberalization of markets and expansion of global trade are the best way to foster robust economic growth, and that the resulting rise in national income reduces poverty. Critics claim that economic globalization increases poverty and inequality both within nations and between the global north and south. Advocates of economic globalization argue that the promotion of better labor conditions and wages, improvement in the social position of women, the reduction of child labor, and the protection of the environment are furthered by freer trade and capital mobility. To the contrary, critics claim, economic globalization forces a "race to the bottom" in labor, social, and environmental conditions.

This chapter appraises the current state of political argument about economic globalization. I consider perspectives that represent the current course of economic globalization as, to varying degrees, inevitable and beneficial, as well as perspectives that judge current trends to be detrimental and to require substantial redirection. In section one I explain why representations of the current discourse of economic globalization are usually drawn more narrowly than I do here. I argue that one cost of this truncation of political discourse is a loss of awareness of the range of competing goods that democracies and their citizens must balance. The next two sections consider the arguments in favor of economic globalization and the consensus critique of it. The final section argues that defenders and critics of economic globalization have different conceptions of the political, that is to say, different basic assumptions and commitments that represent competing appraisals of the variety of human goods.

Policy issues relating to markets and democratic governance are often treated as technical matters to be decided by experts. According to the pluralist and political approach I adopt here, however, there is no empirical or normative perspective beyond dispute from which we can decide the most basic political questions. Once we understand the unavoidably political character of our basic assumptions and commitments, we may appreciate the importance of vigorous public debate to the future course of economic globalization and its consequences for democratic governance. A detailed discussion of these competing basic assumptions and commitments clarifies the issues democratic citizens would be advised to cease taking for granted without argument and begin debating.

The Current State of Political Discourse

Popular and academic reflections upon economic globalization tend to be more restrictive than the range I pursue here, and for a number of reasons. The most obvious reason for the representation of only a narrow range of views in popular accounts is that the discourse of economic globalization tends to be highly polemical. Because many statements for and against economic globalization are political in their aim, polemics are not inappropriate. But failure to consider together a wider range of views impoverishes our understanding of what is at stake in economic globalization as well as the quality of public debate about it. One of my aims here is to make a beginning at remedying that situation.

Many scholarly treatments of economic globalization achieve their aim of being evenhanded in their representation of a range of views. Still, more often than not, scholarly representations of the range of relevant issues are drawn more narrowly than I do here. In some cases, this drawing of boundaries is the product of addressing only the leading scholarly accounts (Held and McGrew 2003). However, in some instances, scholarly discussions of economic globalization are characterized by a positivist version of what one finds in more polemical advocacy of current globalist economic policies, namely, a strict limit on what is acknowledged to be practical in the face of what is represented as necessary or inevitable according to the reigning assumptions of economics.[1] For instance, to consider with seriousness the views of those who advocate a turn away from the global and toward the local, as I do here, is likely to provoke some measure of disbelief, condescension, even ridicule on the part of many of one's interlocutors. Why?

GLOBALISM AS THE NEW DOMINANT IDEOLOGY?

Regular reactions of energetic or dumbfounded dismissal in the face of the presentation of substantially alternative views suggests that there may be some warrant for Manfred Steger's claim that globalism is the new dominant ideology. Ideology, as Michael Freeden argues, "attempts to end the inevitable contention over concepts by decontesting them, by removing their meaning from contest" (Steger 2005, 15). When an ideology has achieved some measure of dominance, challenges to its chief tenets are treated as untenable and not to be taken seriously. While Freeden himself thinks that it is too early to pronounce on globalism's status as a dominant ideology, Steger is less reticent.

Steger argues that globalism has six core claims that are increasingly taken for granted as the true meaning of globalization and treated as unarguably true (Steger 2002, 2005):

1. Globalization is about the liberalization and global integration of markets.
2. Globalization is inevitable and irreversible.
3. Nobody is in charge of globalization.
4. Globalization benefits everyone in the long run.
5. Globalization furthers the spread of democracy in the world.
6. Globalization requires a global war on terror (a more recent claim).

As globalism evolves into a mature ideology, it substantially delimits what is regarded as the appropriate and sensible range of debate about what democracy is, about what markets require, and about the possible relationship between politics and economics. In Steger's view, the political role of globalist ideology "consists chiefly in preserving and enhancing asymmetrical power structures that benefit particular social groups" (Steger 2005, 11).

Steger's account is carefully drawn, and he offers compelling empirical evidence in support of it (Steger 2005, 2002). However, I approach political discourse about economic globalization not as a student of ideology but as a political theorist. Accounts of political ideology are a powerful way of explaining the coherence and efficacy of a set of claims that persuade people to support policies without questioning the actual relationship of those policies to their values and interests. But a focus on ideology goes only so far to illuminate what can loosen the hold of such claims upon citizens so as to transform unquestioning acquiescence into productive public debate about a range of worthy political alternatives.

PLURALITY OF GOODS

The pluralist and political approach I adopt here acknowledges, as Isaiah Berlin says, that "there are many different ends that men may seek and still be fully rational . . . capable of understanding each other and sympathising and deriving light from each" (Berlin 1988, 11). Contrary to the dominant philosophical assumption of his day, Berlin became convinced that irreconcilable conflict between equally true ends and equally true answers to the central problems of human life are a distinct possibility. It is ironic that Berlin's (1958) defense of "negative liberty," which arose out of his appreciation for a plurality of goods, is regarded as one of the classic defenses of free market democracy. Since Berlin's life spanned much of the twentieth century, he identified fascists, communists, and nationalists as the chief opponents of the plurality of human goods. But enemies of pluralism in Berlin's sense are found not only among those who oppose markets or democracy. Some critics of the dominant understanding of economic globalization find in Berlin a resource for their critique of what they take to be the latest antipluralist modern ideology, namely, "free market fundamentalism" (Gray 1993, 1998, 2003).

Critics of economic globalization are often represented as antimarket and anticapitalist, even as antidemocratic anarchists with vague gestures made to the sorts found on the streets during the infamous "Battle of Seattle." In fact, a recurring base note of the consensus critique of economic globalization, whether concerned with economic, political, social, or environmental matters, is aimed at its antipluralist tendencies. The most basic claim is that the current regime of economic globalization ignores competing human goods and the diverse ways of life through which they are pursued. The charge is that considerable political and economic power, and in some cases force, is used to undermine, unsettle, and sometimes altogether destroy worthy ways of life in the name of the creation of a global free market.

One could characterize the dispute between advocates of economic globalization and their critics as one between dogmatists and pluralists in Berlin's sense. But such a representation of the dispute is too tendentious if it fails to recognize that the economic globalists themselves advocate worthy human goods, namely, the reduction of suffering and increased material benefits. But a genuine public debate among democratic citizens about the course and consequences of economic globalization cannot occur without acknowledgement of the partiality of even these laudable goods and their purchase at the expense of other competing goods. Following Berlin, I attribute the lack of genuine debate about economic globalization to the prevalence still of the highly dubious operating assumption that there is no conflict between true human ends or that a single model of political and economic development can reconcile the most worthy human goals.

For Berlin, "the notion of the perfect whole, the ultimate solution, in which all good things coexist" (1988, 13) is as conceptually incoherent as it is unattainable, whether the vehicle for achieving the ideal is the philosopher-king, the dictatorship of the proletariat, the rule of the Volk, or, we may add, a world united by a singular model of democracy and markets. Because "some among the Great Goods cannot live together," says Berlin, we are "doomed to choose, and every choice may entail an irreparable loss" (1988, 13). His deep respect for the worthiness of a plurality of human goods, coupled with his awareness that they are not easily reconciled, led Berlin to advocate judicious balancing of various goods. He cautioned against sacrificing worthy goods altogether in favor of the notion that some singular good is of ultimate value or a means of reconciling all goods. When we acknowledge that some worthy human goods are not fully reconcilable, Berlin thinks, the wisdom of achieving a precarious equilibrium among goods may come to recommend itself as the most prudent course for preventing the occurrence of "desperate situations" and "intolerable choices" (1988, 18).

It is in this spirit that I approach a broad range of views about economic globalization. Disputants see empirical reality from different registers of analysis and through the filter of different basic assumptions and commitments. If a genuine public debate about economic globalization is to occur, we must turn our attention to these competing assumptions and commitments.

Defining and Defending Economic Globalization as It Is (or Should Be)

Regardless of the perspective one adopts on current policies of economic globalization, there are certain features of such policies that both its advocates and critics seem to agree define its essence. These are assumptions that critics of globalization aim to challenge. However, that the following assumptions animate economic globalism itself seems to be beyond dispute (Korten 1996, 184):

1. Sustained economic growth, as measured by Gross Domestic Product, is the foundation of human progress and is essential to alleviate poverty and protect the environment.
2. Free markets, that is to say markets free from governmental interference and regulation, result in the most efficient and socially optimal allocation of resources.
3. Economic globalization and market liberalization, that is to say, working toward a single integrated world market in which goods and capital flow freely across national borders, spurs competition, increases economic efficiency and growth, and is generally beneficial to everyone.
4. Localities achieve economic success by abandoning goals of self-sufficiency and aspiring to become internationally competitive in providing conditions that attract outside investors.

Any schematic representation of the underlying assumptions and aims of the current regime of economic globalization is bound to incur the charge from some quarters that one has constructed a straw person. Critics of economic globalization have responded to this objection by pointing out that this artificial person is of the globalists' own making (Steger 2002, 47). In order to make some headway in assessing these claims and counterclaims, let us consider a more extended, if popular, explanation and defense of economic globalization, an account that finds its essence in more and freer global trade.[2]

A RACE TO THE TOP

Jagdish Bhagwati's "In Defense of Globalization" (2004) argues that the economic globalization in the form of ever freer global trade creates a "race to the top" (123, 127–32) rather than, as critics charge, a race to the bottom. In general terms, the liberalization and global integration of markets enhances economic growth, which, in turn, leads to increases in national income and reductions in poverty (51–55). More specifically, freer trade and the increased activity of multinational corporations (MNCs) within countries and in the global market tend to create better conditions for all, but especially in developing countries. MNCs improve conditions in developing countries by introducing economic development, technical and management advances, higher wages, and better labor standards (122–32, 180–82). For reasons of cost efficiency, Bhagwati argues, MNCs are already inclined to use the most advanced technology in production, and new technologies most always reduce environmental pollution. Thus, economic globalization helps the environment by spreading improved technology (135–61). Likewise, because

MNCs require skilled and dependable workers, they pay higher wages than the national average in the countries where they locate production facilities (122–27). For similar reasons, MNCs have little interest in discriminating against women or relying upon child labor (73–91, 68–72).

Because Bhagwati's claims so dramatically differ from often-heard charges against economic globalization, it is worth considering the specific steps of his argument.

WAGES AND LABOR STANDARDS With regard to wages, Bhagwati argues that all empirical evidence suggests that MNCs pay a wage premium over local wages, although he acknowledges that this premium is all but lost when MNCs use subcontractors (172–73). In countries where wages have fallen, especially in the developed world, Bhagwati argues that this fall cannot be blamed on globalization; instead, globalization has moderated that decline by causing technical changes that have actually economized on the use of unskilled labor. Where wages are lower, their real source is laborsaving technical changes rather than competition from workers in poorer countries (122–32).[3] The situation is comparable when it comes to labor standards. There is no evidence that labor standards have been lowered in the United States in response to economic globalization. Bhagwati acknowledges that there may be problems with enforcement inasmuch as there are sweatshops in New York City or Los Angeles. However, sweatshops are a clear violation of national labor law, so there has been no reduction of labor standards attributable to foreign direct investment in the developing world (127–32).

Bhagwati does not explicitly address the phenomenon of plant closings. This may seem an odd omission given the ubiquity of popular discussions of "out-sourcing." For critics of economic globalization sweatshops anywhere are a problem. But as crucial as the presence of illegal and legal sweatshops are plant closings in places like North Carolina. But for Bhagwati, the "ladders of comparative advantage" that explain why there is not a glut of cheap goods on the global market also explain the economic rationality and ultimate long-term benefit of such plant closings. Economists observe a developmental trajectory that begins with labor-intensive production in the first stages of economic development and in the poorest countries. Economies become transformed to more capital-intensive and highly skilled forms of production when countries become more developed, and increased wealth creates a more skilled work force. This ladder of comparative advantage explains why not all countries compete to produce the same goods. Rather, countries at certain levels of development compete among themselves to offer optimal conditions of production that create a win-win situation for the developing country and MNCs. As countries develop, they shift from labor-intensive to more capital-intensive industries. As a result, there is not a piling on of cheaper, labor-intensive goods in the world market; nor is there a depression in their price or in the wages paid to produce them. Rather, what transpires is a continually shifting comparative advantage (124–25). According to this logic, plant closings in North Carolina, while the source of immediate social suffering, represent the shift of production to a location where there is a comparative advantage. Eventually, new job opportunities will arise in the United States in line with its current comparative advantage.

Of course, in moments when the rewards of market liberalization and global trade are less obvious to powerful countries and their citizens, pressure may arise for governments to protect their comparative advantage against poorer countries. It is in this light that Bhagwati views the efforts of rich countries and their NGOs to promote higher labor standards as well as higher social and environmental standards in poorer countries. Although such efforts are represented as humanitarian, Bhagwati regards them as a form of "export-protectionism" designed to undermine the competitive advantage of poorer countries (131–32, 154–58, 182–95). In Bhagwati's view, such anticompetitive measures are not necessary because MNCs have efficiency incentives of their own, which, coupled with the threat of bad publicity, keep them from taking undue advantage of lower standards elsewhere.

LESS INEQUALITY Bhagwati maintains that the claim that inequality is increasing within nations and between nations is simply factually untrue. In fact, he maintains, global inequality has decreased over the past two decades (66–67). But in addition to these statistical facts, Bhagwati argues that inequality is a matter of perception. One of the chief effects on perception is the coexistence of acute poverty and great inequality. Still, the significance of inequality depends upon the particular society and is only meaningful within that society. To compare the income and rates of consumption of people in completely different social contexts, he argues, is completely meaningless. And even within social contexts, he maintains, many people will tolerate greater inequality if their own actual conditions are improved. In other words, people are most concerned that their own income increases than they are about their share of national income or world income (66–67).

CHILD LABOR AND WOMEN What about child labor? Child labor is caused by poverty, not by globalization, says Bhagwati. As freer global trade increases economic growth and reduces poverty, the need for child labor decreases (68–72).

What about the exploitation of women, especially at very low wages by developed industrial standards? Economic progress, Bhagwati says, inevitably breaks down extended families and other aspects of the way of life typical in more traditional, especially rural societies. But he believes it is obvious that life is more difficult and less gratifying in such traditional societies, not to mention unduly restrictive for many of its members, especially women. From the perspective of these women, all things being equal, economic globalization must be far more good than bad. Critics understate the advantages of such social change. The advantages include the greater independence of women and the greater visibility of the economic significance of household labor that their independence reveals (76–89). What about outright prejudice and discrimination against women? Like racial discrimination, Bhagwati thinks that such prejudices are inefficiencies that firms cannot afford in an increasingly competitive global environment (73–76).

PROMOTING DEMOCRACY Bhagwati acknowledges the basic paradox that globalization constrains democracy, but he argues that globalization actually promotes the spread of democracy, both directly and indirectly (92–93). Freer trade directly promotes democratization by enabling rural farmers to bypass bureaucrats to sell directly to the market and thereby to become more independent actors. Moreover, the markets and computer technology that enable this independence are available to them only because of global trade (93–94). The indirect benefit of free trade to the promotion of democracy is that independent economic actors may become more independent political actors.

Whether market liberalization promotes democracy by creating a middle class that seeks political independence or by undermining the impression that authoritarianism is the prerequisite of economic well-being, economic globalization is a force for democratization, not its rival (93–96). To be sure, democratic outcomes are constrained by globalization; global markets punish "radical shifts to the left." However, Bhagwati thinks that this is not due to economic globalization per se but to the fact that leftward shifts are simply bad for economic growth (96–98). To those who argue that economic globalization impairs governments' ability to raise funds for social spending, Bhagwati claims that this is not so, or at the very least that it is a matter of national politics and cannot be blamed on global free trade. There are many countervailing powers to market pressures in the form of existing institutions, labor unions, and social democratic parties that can prevent reductions in social spending (98–102).

Most of these arguments are not unique to Bhagwati (see Wolf 2004). They are standard fare among advocates of economic globalization. Generally speaking, defenders of the current regime of economic globalization want more liberalization of markets, especially in the face of threats they currently see pressing in the opposite direction. The threat they see is not the continued progress of economic globalization but its collapse, as happened early in the twentieth century, with dire consequences for all (Gilpin 2001). What others blame on economic globalization, they attribute to centuries of history. To globalists like Bhagwati, imperialism and colonialism have left parts of the world underdeveloped, exploited, and in a state of profound inequality relative to the powerful nations of the industrial West. In their view, economic globalization is not the continuation of imperialism and colonialism, but their only remedy.

The Consensus Critique of Economic Globalization

It is common to consider critics of economic globalization as simply being "antiglobalization." When represented by other than their friends, one gets the impression of a motley crew who understand little about economics and politics or who have, at best, romantic notions about them (Bhagwati 2004, 3–27). However, what one finds upon investigating an array of critical perspectives on economic globalization is that they come from across the political spectrum, from the traditionally left and liberal to the conservative (Berry 2002; Brown 2003; Cavanaugh and Mander 2004; Daly 2003; Gray 1993, 1998, and 2003; Hawken, Lovins, and Lovins 1999; Mander and Goldsmith 1996; Norberg-Hodge 1991; Roy 2001; Shiva 2000). As a consequence of their political range, critics of economic globalization do not agree about what can or should be done to address its deleterious economic, political, social, and environmental consequences. However, there is a remarkable degree of agreement among its critics about what is wrong with economic globalization. One of my aims here is to establish that such a principled, theoretically coherent consensus critique of economic globalization has emerged.[4]

The consensus critique of economic globalization has four dimensions:

1. A theoretical critique of assumptions that are fundamental to the economic theories underlying the claims of globalists
2. An ecological critique of globalization's impact on the natural environment
3. A social critique of globalization's impact on human communities
4. A political critique of globalization's impact on constitutional governance, political accountability, and democratic power

My aim is to move us beyond a simple restatement of the counterclaims of economic globalism's critics. To simply state, pace Bhagwati, that the current course of economic globalization increases inequality and poverty wreaks havoc upon the social and natural environment and poses a threat to democracy will get us nowhere. Instead, I aim to show that the alternative assumptions and commitments underlying this consensus critique are plausible and worthy of attention. Once we see that there are compelling arguments "against" as well as "for" economic globalization, a genuine debate about these alternatives is more likely to ensue. This then could lead to the judicious balancing of competing goods advocated by Berlin.

ARTICLES OF FAITH AND THE ECONOMICS OF GLOBALIZATION

Critiques of globalization argue that changes in the economic landscape undermine the contemporary application of several fundamental economic concepts, including Ricardo's notion of comparative advantage, Smith's understanding of markets, and the mostly widely used gauge of economic success, Gross Domestic Product (GDP). I argue that differences between advocates' and critics' understanding of economic processes is rooted in differences in contestable assumptions or articles of faith.

COMPARATIVE ADVANTAGE David Ricardo first explicitly formulated the principle of comparative advantage in the early nineteenth century. Ricardo maintained that specialization and export-oriented production would yield the most efficient and prosperous outcomes for all parties under conditions of unregulated free trade. The underlying rationale for this notion lies in technological, cultural, and resource differences that create different costs of production for the same products. When applied to national economies and industries, the principle of comparative advantage prescribes that, even if a community can make every product more efficiently than another community, it should specialize only in what it can produce most efficiently. Each nation specializes so as to achieve the greatest advantage it can. By each country exporting the products in which they specialize, and importing those products in which others specialize, international trade grows. The net result is increases in efficiency and productivity that bring greater prosperity to all.

Critics charge that the trouble with relying on this logic to explain the current conditions of international commerce is that those current conditions contradict one of the basic assumptions underlying comparative advantage: that capital and other factors of production are relatively immobile

(Daly 2003, 230; Morris 2003, 219). Once the factors of production become mobile and the use of subcontractors becomes ubiquitous, critics argue that the logic of comparative advantage turns economic globalization into a race to the bottom. A nation's or locale's comparative advantage is determined by its capacity to offer MNCs conditions that are more profitable than those of their rivals, which they achieve by reforming or suspending labor and environmental regulations and by reducing corporate taxation. Among the consequences is the "outsourcing" of jobs from one locale to another, with the new location maintaining a comparative advantage only so long as another locale does not provide even more profitable conditions by further lowering the "bottom." As a result, critics charge, comparative advantage is more tenuous than Ricardo envisioned. Moreover, its benefits accrue predominantly to the MNCs who shift their sites of production, especially when that shift amounts to little more than replacing one subcontractor with another.

LEVEL OF ANALYSIS AND HISTORICAL ASSUMPTIONS How are we to account for the fact that defenders and critics of economic globalization reach opposite conclusions about the logic of comparative advantage in the current context? Some might argue that the difference is attributable to the fact that the critics do not understand the most elementary matters of economic theory. But the sources of the difference are actually deeper and far more a matter of faith than of fact. The roots of the conflicting positions are the level of analysis and focus each favor, which are founded upon different assumptions about the nature and tendencies of history.

Critics of economic globalization often pay attention to particular people and places. When advocates of economic globalization attend to particular people and places, they analyze the differences between countries. Defenders of economic globalization attend to the differences between nations because many of their conclusions regarding what is beneficial about economic globalization depend upon differences across nations (Bhagwati 2004, 60–66). By contrast, critics of economic globalization typically pay attention to the suffering experienced by particular people and places within countries. For instance, Bhagwati praises India's relatively recent embrace of global trade and the thriving middle class to which it has given rise (64–66). By contrast, critics focus on the plight of failing farmers who are committing suicide in epidemic proportions as cheaper agriculture goods flood their markets, or the rural poor who are displaced from traditional lands and livelihoods, or basic goods made unaffordable by privatization and development projects (Gray 1993, 134: Roy 2001; Shiva 2000).

For defenders of economic globalization, focusing one's concern upon particular people and places is deceptive and obscures the big picture. They argue that while such suffering is unfortunate, prior history is the source of this suffering, not current economic globalization. Moreover, to the extent that this suffering is wrought by economic globalization, the economic development that it alone can provide is the only alternative to the continuation of such suffering. Finally, they argue that dwelling on specifics may lead nations to turn against the only feasible remedy for poverty, thus harming those whom critics of globalization claim they want to help (Bhagwati 2004, 51–67). Critics of economic globalization are not persuaded by these arguments because the arguments rest on contestable assumptions about the nature and tendency of history. Bhagwati, for example, asserts that he is an optimist who believes that technological change generates progress; in contrast, he says, antiglobalizers are pessimists who are nostalgic for the past (115–16).

Bhagwati's faith is certainly the dominant faith of modernity. Fundamental to distinctly modern ideologies and the common ground of Marxist and free market ideology is the modern faith that the future will be better than the past. The sacrifices of the moment, of particular people and places, while unfortunate, will pay dividends in the end (Gray 2003). To these modernists, it is not conceivable that suffering of textile workers in North Carolina or farmers in India is meaningless, purposeless, and avoidable (Gray 1993, 134). The article of faith is that, even if they suffer, their children or their children's children will be better off, or that the majority of Americans and Indians will be better off. Critics, however, ask whether the historical faith of the globalists is any less delusional than that of the now-discredited Marxists (Gray 2003).

SCALE AND SMITH'S INVISIBLE HAND

Critics of economic globalization charge that similar illogical results are derived from Adam Smith's analysis about the ways markets, as if by an invisible hand, balance natural and market prices. Written in 1776, Smith's Wealth of Nations offers a radical critique of government and state protection of business monopolies. Smith's analysis underscores the ways regulation tends to distort or erode the self-corrective mechanisms of the market. Smith's ideal market is comprised of relatively small buyers and sellers, none of whom are large enough to influence the market price of commodities exchanged. Because no enterprise or interest would be large enough to influence pricing artificially, eventually the market price and real costs of production (natural price) would align in ways that support the most efficient production and firms.

It is crucial to Smith's theory that neither sellers nor buyers are large or powerful enough to fix prices artificially or to have sufficient command of the market to manage its self-correcting mechanisms (Korten 1996, 185–88). Yet in a global market of ever-larger firms it is common business practice to employ various means to manage market conditions. Indeed, the structure of today's MNCs suggests that much of their raison d'être is to manage aspects of the market that prevent them from achieving market dominance. More specifically, the growing transnational organization of production and distribution within firms, rather than through markets, suggests that MNCs' efficacy and power is furthered by using markets when advantageous and finding ways to circumvent or control them when necessary (Held, Goldblatt, and Perraton 1999, 256, 260).

Ironically, Smith's ideas are currently invoked to support measures that favor the very sort of concentration of power he criticized. Scale is integral to the functioning of Smith's invisible hand. In today's global economy, governments and international organizations—through laws and subsidies that favor the global over the local—that advantage the large over the smaller scale thereby facilitate the concentration of power Smith found dysfunctional. Thus, in response to those who claim that the large scale is more cost efficient for firms and of ultimate benefit to the consumer, globalization's critics say that those efficiencies are dependent on government support. Were the invisible hand of the market actually allowed to work, critics charge that the playing field between the large and the small scale would be significantly altered. For instance, were the actual costs of national and global transport allowed to operate rather than being externalized and subsidized to manipulate market prices, global trade and MNCs would lose their structural advantage over local communities and smaller business enterprises. Indeed, in some cases the natural price of their goods might prove prohibitive (Cavanaugh and Mander 2004).

As was the case with the questions of level of analysis and concern, the positions that globalization's advocates and critics take here reflect their different attitudes toward history. Advocates of economic globalization generally view the advantages of large-scale enterprises as the inevitable and largely beneficial trend of history rather than as a matter of choice and question of consequences. By contrast, critics see scale as a matter of political decision that becomes self-perpetuating. The concerns of globalization's critics are rooted in the belief, articulated throughout the history of political thought, that the scale of human institutions affects the character of people and the quality of their personal and collective lives. Every human institution has an optimal limit beyond which it cannot grow without becoming something entirely different. As globalists see history as the Darwinian unfolding of progress, their view reinforces notions of necessity and benefit. Where advocates of economic globalization see both inevitability and progress in the elimination of family farms and small retailers, critics make no assumption of historical inevitability or of benefit. Indeed, they see reasons to conclude the opposite, in part because they direct concern at the suffering of particular people and places, and also because they maintain that quantitative indicators of growth can be used to obscure actual quality of life.

QUANTITATIVE INDICATORS THAT OBSCURE QUALITY

The third economic critique concerns the calculation of economic growth by measuring GDP. The critique of GDP goes to the heart of how we measure and debate economic well-being, and it has significant implications for how we assess the effects of economic globalization. The basic claim here is that GDP measures economic activity in ways that distort actual economic conditions and obscure real costs and inefficiencies. As a consequence, we miscalculate the current and future expenses of economic enterprises and inaccurately measure economic improvement. This critique rests on what GDP measures and assumes, as well as what it distorts and obscures.

GDP measures total economic activity by taking account of every monetary transaction within a nation-state. GDP measures a society's well-being by the quantity of services and goods it uses and pays for, or promises to pay for in the future. The trouble with GDP is that it does not make qualitative distinctions among economic transactions. From the perspective of GDP, the building of a prison, the depletion of a natural resource, the clean up after a natural or social disaster, or the increasing reliance upon childcare services outside the home are all economic gains. From the perspective of GDP, every economic transaction is good by definition because GDP does not differentiate between costs and benefits, between productive and destructive activities, or between sustainable and unsustainable economic activities. Critics charge that using GDP as a primary gauge of economic or social progress is at best inadvisable since it obscures social and environmental costs (Halstead and Cobb 1996, 197–206).

Likewise, standard quantitative indicators of income may obscure quality of life. Even many supporters of economic globalization note that income can be a misleading indicator of collective and personal well-being because income is not always an accurate indicator of persons' capabilities and opportunities (Sen 1999, 21–24). Reductions in absolute poverty and rise in per capita income, while notable improvements, may be incomplete gauges of welfare. These statistical improvements may be rendered less significant by increased costs of basic necessities or by persistent dependence of certain subsets of the population in particular locales (Chua 2004). Because critics of economic globalization often direct their analysis and concern at such particular people and places, they see economic globalization as much a story of increasing poverty and inequality as of their diminishment. Whether by design or unintended effect, preoccupation with quantitative indicators can obscure a worsening quality of life (Halstead and Cobb 1996, 204–5).

PURCHASING POWER AND HUMAN HAPPINESS GDP was never intended to be a complete measure of well-being; it is an artifact of the Depression era. This notwithstanding, GDP has become a dominant referent for national economic health, and income is often taken to be a general indicator of both personal and national well being—particularly by globalization advocates such as Bhagwati.[5] There have been notable efforts to seek better quantitative indicators of quality, including Sen's (1999) capability approach and Halstead and Cobb's (1996) notion of Genuine Progress Indicator (GPI). While such efforts to put income in perspective are laudable and welcome, they at best indirectly address the underlying assumptions about human happiness that attach average citizens as much as elite advocates of globalization to preoccupation with monetary transactions and income.

The notion that money is the source of happiness is a principal operating assumption of our modern way of life. We value money because the modern presumption is that the more comfortable we are, the happier we will be. Money is the end as well as the means to such comfort because it enables us to buy what we need and want. This is why we take increases in monetary income to be the key measure of progress. It is quite common to assume that the ability to pay for services that one's forbearers or fellow citizens must perform for themselves is an indicator of the more comfortable life that most modern people associate with happiness. Because this view has diffused throughout the world, it is little wonder that public opinion data indicate that most citizens in developing nations favor economic globalization and its anticipated monetary rewards.[6]

Globalization's critics have scrutinized this confluence in perspectives between elite advocates of economic globalization and ordinary citizens throughout the world. Some critics question whether buying most all of what you need or want is actually a more gratifying way of life. They note the dramatically increased dependence and vulnerability that accompanies full immersion in a monetary economy, especially when one has no means to provide for basic needs such as food, clothing, fuel, and shelter without money. For these critics, the global economy is not a story of greater autonomy as a consequence of greater interdependence, but of the ever-increasing dependence of many upon unseen global forces and their vulnerability to unaccountable global actors (Berry 2002; Norberg-Hodge 1991).

Even if the majority of citizens in the developed and developing world conclude that purchasing power is the key to human happiness, many critics ask whether the social and natural environment can sustain our desire for this sort of happiness? For many critics, the preoccupation with consumer goods is the key to the imbalance between our households and national economies and our natural and social environments, and it helps explain why we give them insufficient care.

DISCOUNTING AND CONSUMING THE NATURAL AND SOCIAL ENVIRONMENT

Central to the consensus critique of economic globalization is the claim that advocates of globalism err in equating quantitative progress with qualitative improvement in the human condition. In other words, globalists tend to view economic and technological progress as ends in themselves, failing to evaluate them in terms of their impact on the well-being of individuals or communities (Gray 1993; Sen 1999; Cavanaugh and Mander 2004). Critics see mounting evidence that the way of life being spread by global trade is ecologically and socially unsustainable. Defenders of the current regime of economic globalization sometimes deny that serious environmental problems exist. When they do acknowledge these problems, they often claim that their severity is overstated. Furthermore, they argue that market incentives will result in timely technological innovations that will address both resource and environmental problems. At the same time, there are issues of environmental and social consequence that Bhagwati and other defenders rarely, if ever, discuss, including the costs of dramatic natural resource use fostered by global trade.

Differences on environmental issues reveal that critics and defenders of economic globalization have profoundly different understandings of the earth. The modern idea of human history as a universal story of progress has fostered views of the earth that are foreign to any ecological understanding of it. Natural ecosystems are characterized by stability rather than by open-ended progress or infinite growth (Gray 1993, 138). Yet critics charge that advocates of economic globalization conceive of the earth as if it provided infinite possibilities. In contrast, most critics of economic globalization subscribe to a more holistic and synthetic view of the earth. This alternative ecological view is perhaps best exemplified by James Lovelock's notion of Gaia, or "the idea of life on the Earth as constituting a single organism, one which regulates the species and environments of which life on Earth is composed so as to maintain stability as a whole" (qtd. in Gray 1993, 138).[7]

According to the consensus critique, the way of life currently being exported around the globe is unsustainable because its aim of unlimited growth is founded upon a basic account imbalance between the environmental ecosystem and economic subsystem. Conventional forms of economic measurement treat natural capital as if it is unlimited and as if the wastes produced by its use are without cost. But natural resources are not unlimited and wastes generate costs. The global ecosystem is the source of all inputs feeding the economic subsystem as well as of all sinks for the wastes produced by the economic subsystem. Since both inputs and sinks are limited, we must attend to the balance between them if we are to avoid exhausting and degrading the ecosystem. Critics charge that what we extract from the ecosystem and what we are requiring it to assimilate are unsustainable. Furthermore, forms of production and markets that actually may be highly inefficient—because they are too costly and wasteful to be sustainable—are viewed as effective mechanisms for enhancing societal welfare (Daly 2003, 62–63; Hawken, Lovins, and Lovins 1999, 57–61). Unfortunately, because standard economic measurement systems treat the liquidation of natural capital as income and fail to include economic waste and environmental problems as costs, this is a short-term mirage (Hawken, Lovins, and Lovins 1999, 5).

SOCIAL INSECURITY

Environmental degradation is not the only detrimental effect of economic globalization on human communities, according to its critics. Both leftist and more conservative critics emphasize how the growing inequality and social insecurity wrought by economic globalization unravel the fabric that binds human communities. As a result, families weaken, crime and violence increase, and civility decreases—sometimes even to the point of civil violence. Obviously, the social effects of globalization vary greatly from society to society, and individual critics give these effects different valences. Generally speaking, however, the consensus critique charges that the current regime of economic globalization, with its emphasis on unlimited increases in economic wealth, generates profoundly disturbing social costs. In the name of liberalization and privatization, it destroys traditional ways of life without providing viable alternatives for those caught in its wake. For example, in some cases, globalization

- impoverishes those who were previously self-subsisting;
- liquidates the public spaces and practices, and distinct cultural conditions and beliefs that make human life bearable and meaningful;
- trades enabling social conditions for detrimental conditions that foster the growth of private and public anti-social behaviors, making the lives of all but the most privileged and protected citizens less safe, less ennobling and less beautiful.

THE CONSENSUS POLITICAL CRITIQUE

If economic globalization has these detrimental effects on the well-being of human communities and nature, then why are there no effective political efforts to put new policies in place? Defenders of the current regime of economic globalization cite widespread acceptance of economic globalization as proof that most people support it (Bhagwati 2004, 102–5). But critics claim that the politics of economic globalization is more complicated.

First, there continues to be substantial resistance around the world to economic globalization and its specific policies and consequences. Millions of people in many nations have mounted massive demonstrations against the institutions and policies of what they call corporate globalism (Cavanaugh and Mander 2004, 1–7, 19).[8] While these mass demonstrations are the most visible form of political action, they are not necessarily the most significant. Across the globe, citizen movements and civil society organizations are working to both resist the changes wrought by economic globalization and develop alternative modes of economic and social organization (Cavanaugh and Mander 2004, 253–67; Hawken 2007).

The political dimension of the consensus critique begins by noting the significant obstacles that global policies and institutions pose to these citizen efforts to expand political and economic democracy. Many use market liberalization as if it were synonymous with democratization. But critics from across the political spectrum agree that economic globalization is antagonistic to democratic self-governance, arguing that it insulates national governments and markets from democratic deliberation and political amendment (Cavanaugh and Mander 2004; Simmons [chapter 8]; Wallach and Woodall 2004).

Critics of economic globalization argue that the trouble here is at least twofold. International economic institutions are, by design, unaccountable.

If one believes that the policy decisions of global economic institutions are purely technical matters, as many of their advocates do, this lack of political accountability is not problematic; indeed, it is regarded as a positive good. But the critics of economic globalization see decisions about economic policy as inherently political and the structure of markets as social and political rather than natural. Thus, the first element of the consensus political critique is that global institutions with ever-increasing power over the lives of citizens are increasingly unaccountable to them (Cavanaugh and Mander 2004; Wallach and Woodall 2004; Simmons [chapter 8]). The second dimension is that the power of constitutional governments to act on behalf of their citizens is increasingly lost or granted to these unaccountable institutions. As a result, even if a nation's citizenry were to reach political agreement about how to address the economic, social, and environmental costs of economic globalization, it is far from clear whether they would be able to transform that political conclusion into action and policy without suffering prohibitive sanction.

For many critics, these two political dimensions of the globalization debate are intimately related; they believe that both may be explained in part by the growing influence of corporate power over national governments. Critics view as irrefutable the notion that state power and initiatives are increasingly beholden to global corporate interests, which influence both electoral and policy-making matters. They note recent trends in law and public policy have had the effect of penalizing ordinary citizens and advantaging corporate interests (Cavanaugh and Mander 2004, 32–74).

A key assertion within the political critique of economic globalization is that the power of corporations in the domestic arena supports the transfer of decision-making power to international economic institutions. Even some defenders of economic globalization, most notably Joseph Stiglitz, argue that commercial and financial interests dominate international institutions such as the IMF and the WTO. In short, limited national constituencies are defining what counts as the "national interest" within these institutions (Stiglitz 2002).[9] For many critics, the dominance of commercial and financial interests within countries and international economic institutions is a product of the excessive legal empowerment of corporations in the domestic political arena, especially within the United States. Although (historically and formally speaking) the power of corporations is publicly granted through charter, this public power to limit corporate activity has been largely abandoned. While the general public takes this corporate power for granted and has been persuaded that it is a matter of right, critics charge that corporate power is a historically contingent, legally defined fiction that could, and should, be reconsidered (Cavanaugh and Mander 2004, 271–300).

To many critics it is the structure of corporations, not the moral failings of individuals, that determines corporate behavior. Key here are corporate imperatives such as profit maximization, continual growth, and control over all aspects of its environment. As a consequence, there is a basic antagonism between corporate structure and its imperatives and the truly democratic organization of power. Corporations prize efficiency, simplification, certainty, and uniformity in order to further their interests. By contrast, democracy, as its etymology (demos [people] + kratia [power]) suggests, requires the collaborative use of power. Democratic power depends on the existence of forms of common life in which power is relatively diffuse so that it can be generated when needed and expanded by being shared. Unlike corporate power, democratic power's legitimacy is heightened by the collaborative and cooperative exercise of power. Indeed, according to a democratic conception of power, it is possible for particular places, people, and institutions to have too much power. Democratic power can sometimes be so maldistributed that the regime's legitimacy is threatened. This democratic conception of power stands in direct contrast to the corporate imperative to accumulate as much profit, power, and control as possible.

From the perspective of its critics, the project of creating a single global free market is not an ally of democracy but its rival. And the rivalry is not that of siblings but of outright opponents (Gray 1998, 17; Cavanaugh and Mander 2004). This does not necessarily mean that critics choose democracy over markets. Rather, they argue that there are forms of market governance that pose a threat to democracy, which they contrast to market forms that are not only compatible with democracy but are one of its preconditions (Gray 1993). Critics insist that corporate political influence and its significant role in advancing the ideal of a single global market is not the essential expression and ultimate end of market economics or the fruit of democratic process; instead, it is a politically constructed economic regime that poses a threat not only to truly free market conditions but also to democracy itself.

EXPANDING POLITICAL DISCOURSE

The consensus critique of the current regime of economic globalization arises among commentators from across the political spectrum. The fact that this emerging arena of consensus cannot be labeled according to traditional ideological dichotomies of "liberal" and "conservative" or "left" and "right" may be a reflection of economic globalization itself. For critics of economic globalization agree that the current regime is neither politically liberal nor conservative. Economic globalization is not politically liberal because it undermines both representative institutions and political accountability, which are essential to the workings of liberal democracy (Brown 2003; Gray 1998; Cavanaugh and Mander 2004). Economic globalization is not conservative because it erodes the fabric that makes human communities cohere and limits the political means of securing social cohesion and protecting the common environment (Gray 1993; 1998). Critics aim to open and expand political discourse that is truncated by overly simple political dichotomies and by unquestioned assumptions that obscure both the particularity of the goods economic globalization favors and the competing goods it discounts. In the absence of such broadening and deepening of political discourse, emendations and alternatives to the current regime of economic globalization that may be politically appealing are largely unknown to many democratic citizens.

The Political: Basic Assumptions and Commitments

That particular assumptions and commitments inform the projects of any particular time and place is as inevitable as the assumptions and commitments themselves being contestable. When it comes to matters of the political, there is no view from nowhere. There is no ground or venue beyond dispute from which we can assess basic political questions such as: Who are we? What do we value? How should we achieve what we value?

Economics came into its own as a scientific and social power when it set its roots in naturalism (Polanyi 1944, 68–76, 111–29). Since then, there has been a recurring tendency to equate the laws governing a market economy with nature itself, as well as to maintain that economy and politics are, and must remain, separate spheres. Scholars of political economy and even many economists may not be so naive as to be market naturalists. But the founding orthodoxy that "human-made" political laws should not interfere with "natural" market laws remains a staple of popular political discourse, at least in the United States. From this perspective, to say that economies are political by nature is likely to sound implausible and perhaps even suspect. But beneath the operation of markets are human, political decisions to invest and subsidize certain modes of economic and social organization rather than others. To say that all economies, even market economies, are political by nature is not to say that they are commanded and controlled by political actors. As is well known, the virtue of markets and their reliance on the price mechanism is that they supply information that no individual person or committee of persons can possess or access. But all governments, even governments that profess to want to let markets run freely, make decisions and invest resources in some forms of development rather than others. They subsidize some forms of economic enterprise rather than others, and those enterprises, in turn, shape markets, society, and politics.

MARKETS AND DEMOCRACY

Markets and the ways of life they encourage are powerfully influenced by policy decisions made and subsidies granted. These decision and subsidies are not determined by nature but by politics. The question, then, is not whether politics will shape our economic way of life but, rather, how politics should shape economics. What sort of economic enterprises and markets should be fostered? What modes of political intervention should be manifested within the economic arena? On behalf of whom? With the aim of accomplishing what? Here, of course, is where the question of markets touches upon the question of democracy: How should markets be regulated, and with what implications for the meaning and practice of democracy? I use the term democracy in a simple and straightforward way and have in mind no specific institutional arrangements or requirements about degrees of participation or representation. We associate being free with democratic governance, as John Dunn argues, because to be free in a most basic sense is the condition of not being under or directly subject to the will of other human beings (Dunn 1996). Stated more affirmatively, the notion of democracy, and the government responsiveness it implies, suggests that human beings should have some means of influencing the major political and policy decisions that affect their lives.

An examination of the historical record reveals that the regulation of markets has varied considerably across locales (Polanyi 1944). This historical and cultural variation in the interaction between markets and government affirms that the relationship between economics and society is inherently political. This historical backdrop underscores the distinctness of the current ideal of creating a uniform, global, free market. The 1944 conference in Bretton Woods, which led to the creation of the World Bank and the International Monetary Fund and, soon after, the General Agreement on Tariffs and Trade (GATT), took as its objective the expansion of global trade, not the establishment of a single global free market. Indeed, the U.S. Senate insisted that GATT's broad trade principles not compromise national sovereignty. But the 1980s and 1990s witnessed a dramatic shift in what U.S. political leaders of both major parties deemed to be in the national interest of the United States (Orlie 2006). When the Uruguay Round of GATT negotiations was completed in 1994, the old GATT trade contract was replaced by the WTO. The WTO was given increased regulatory power to enforce uniform trade rules with the aim of instituting a uniform global market (Gray 1998; Korten 1996).

As even this brief history makes clear, the effort to achieve a single global free market is not the outcome of some natural, historical, or social necessity. It was, from the outset, a political project. To call the current regime of economic globalization a political project, or to say that it is based on certain contestable assumptions, is not to reject it. Viewing economic globalization in this light does, however, underscore the need for political reflection upon it. Indeed, it is of the utmost importance that we have broad-ranging discussions about what the relationship between economics and politics can, and should, be. In much contemporary discourse on these basic political questions we presume too much and debate too little.

Although the need for the political regulation of markets is regularly disputed in popular discourse, few serious advocates of globalism would dispute the importance of regulation.[10] But acknowledging the need for economic regulation is not the same as acknowledging that there are genuine questions about how markets should be regulated, and what interests should be reflected in those regulations. Rather, the current orthodoxy presumes that it is empirically undeniable that export-oriented economies grow most robustly and that such robust growth is a primary and unequivocal good. As a result, it is simply asserted that export-oriented economic development and the range of measures typically associated with it (i.e., privatization, deregulation) are of the greatest benefit to all (Sen 1999).[11] But what the relationship between economics and politics can or should be is not a question that can be determined by reference to empirical reality alone. It would be foolish to ignore the empirical reality created by the extant relationships between political and economic activity. But the judgments that we make about those conditions depend on background assumptions about what is good. And these are normative matters that empirical reality alone cannot decide for us.

COMPETING GOODS AND DEMOCRATIC LEGITIMACY

As we have seen, advocates and critics of economic globalization approach this matter from very different perspectives. They affirm different assumptions about the relevant levels of analysis and concern, and they make different assumptions about the relevance of quantity and quality, as well as about what is unlimited and limited. Along with these relatively modern philosophical concerns, advocates and critics of economic globalization usually adopt competing views about some more traditional philosophical matters, including the tendencies of history, the meaning of progress or improvement, and the nature of human happiness.

The fact that proponents of economic globalization and their critics have such different basic assumptions and visions of the good goes some way toward explaining why there is rarely a genuine debate on the pressing questions this economic order generates. To characterize the debate over globalization in this way is not to embrace some form of relativism or to presume that those who have the most power will necessarily prevail. Rather, it should reinforce our determination to conceive of competing arguments about the current state and future of economic globalization as arguments about basic human goods and aims—the very sort of questions that a vital democratic citizenry should engage. To the extent that a democratic community ignores these emphatically political questions, or treats them as a matter of technocratic administration, we may rightly worry. Such a state of public discourse can generate a crisis of democratic citizenship, governance, and legitimacy.

Notes

1. As Amartya Sen (1999) notes, the current assumption in economics is that the "virtues of the market mechanism" are "so pervasive that qualifications seem unimportant." But it was not so long ago that pointing to the defects of the market mechanism was as in fashion as it is out of fashion today. In Sen's view, current views of the market suggest that one set of prejudices has given way to another opposite set of preconceptions so that "yesterday's unexamined faith has become today's heresy, and yesterday's heresy is the new superstition." Sen concludes that the "need for critical scrutiny of standard preconceptions and political-economic attitudes has never been stronger" (111–12).

2. For purposes of simplicity and clarity I am going to leave aside the regulation of finance capital and focus on free trade.

3. Bhagwati explains the fate of American labor by the decline in unionization. The explanation for this decline is not globalization, however, but the Taft-Hartley antilabor legislation that severely constrains the efficacy of the strike. Unionization is meaningless without the capacity to wage an effective strike. But the state of American labor is the product of domestic politics, not economic globalization (2004, 126–27).

4. The consensus presented here is my synthesis of a range of views drawn from a variety of quarters. I do not claim that all upon whom I draw would affirm all aspects of what I call the consensus critique. For a comparable effort from which I have learned much, see Gray 1993, 124–77.

5. It should be noted that Bhagwati (2004) does acknowledge the need to measure environmental costs in arriving at more accurate appraisals of economic growth.

6. For example, see the poll released by the Center on Policy Attitudes and the Center for International and Security Studies at the University of Maryland (June 4, 2004, and April 25, 2007), available at http://www.worldpublicopinion.org/pipa/articles/btglobalizationtradera.index.

7. It would be a serious error to confuse this holistic view with some sort of romantic picture of the earth as a loving mother. Quite the contrary, says Lovelock: "Gaia, as I see her, is not a doting mother, tolerant of misdemeanours, nor is she some fragile and delicate damsel in danger from brutal mankind. She is stern and tough, always keeping the world warm and comfortable for those who obey the rules, but ruthless in her destruction of those who transgress. Her unconscious goal is a planet fit for life. If humans stand in the way of this, we shall be eliminated with as little pity as would be shown by the micro-brain of an intercontinental ballistic missile in full flight to its target" (qtd. in Gray 1993,173).

8. Critics point to developments in India, the Philippines, Indonesia, Brazil, Bolivia, the United Sates, Canada, Mexico, Argentina, Venezuela, France, Germany, Italy, the Czech Republic, Spain, Sweden, the United Kingdom, New Zealand, Australia, Kenya, South Africa, Thailand, Malaysia.

9. This is where the consensus critique would part ways with Beth Simmons's analysis of international economic organizations (see chapter 8), namely, in her assumption that national governments serve the general interests of their constituencies rather than the interests of distinct, if powerful, minorities within those constituencies. If Stiglitz as well as the consensus critique are right, international economic institutions pose problems of democratic accountability not only for countries in a relatively weak political economic bargaining position, as Simmons argues, but also for the constituencies of even relatively powerful countries like the United States if the interests of their financial and commercial sectors are at all at odds with the interests of the broader national population.

10. This acknowledgment of the need for political regulation of markets is what distinguishes neoliberalism from nineteenth century classical liberalism.

11. Because his topic is the current academic discourse of political economy, John Freeman's chapter in this volume takes these assumptions for granted, even as he worries about the implications of these assumptions for democratic governance.

References

Berlin, I. 1958. "Two Concepts of Liberty." In *Four Essays on Liberty,* 118–72. New York: Oxford University Press.

———. 1988. "The Pursuit of the Ideal." In *The Crooked Timber of Humanity,* 1–19. Princeton, N.J.: Princeton University Press.

Berry, W. 2002. "The Idea of a Local Economy." Orionmagazine.org/index.php/articles/article/299.

Bhagwati, J. 2004. *In Defense of Globalization.* New York: Oxford University Press.

Brown, W. 2003. "Neo-liberalism and the End of Liberal Democracy." *Theory & Event* 7:1.

Cavanaugh, J., and J. Mander, eds. 2004. *Alternatives to Economic Globalization: A Better World Is Possible; A Report of the International Forum on Globalization.* San Francisco: Berrett-Koehler.

Center on Policy Attitudes and the Center for International and Security Studies at the University of Maryland. http://www.worldpublicopinion.org/pipa/articles/btglobalizationtradera/index.

Chua, A. 2004. *World on Fire: How Exporting Free Market Democracy Breeds Ethnic Hatred and Global Instability.* New York: Anchor.

Daly, H. E. 2003. "Sustainable Economic Development: Definitions, Principles, Policies." In Wirzba 62–79.

Dunn, J. 1996. "How Democracies Succeed." *Economy and Society* 25 (November): 511–28.

Gilpin, R. 2001. *Global Political Economy.* Princeton: Princeton University Press.

Gray, J. 1993. *Beyond the New Right: Markets, Government and the Common Environment.* London: Routledge.

———. 1998. *False Dawn.* New York: New Press.

———. 2003. *Al Qaeda and What It Means to Be Modern.* New York: New Press.

Halstead, T. and C. Cobb. 1996. "The Need for New Measurement of Progress." In Mander and Goldsmith, 197–206.

Hawken, P. 2007. *Blessed Unrest: How the Largest Movement in the World Came into Being and Why No One Saw It Coming.* New York: Viking.

Hawken, P., A. Lovins, and L. H. Lovins. 1999. *Natural Capitalism: Creating the Next Industrial Revolution.* Boston: Little Brown.

Held, D., A. McGrew, D. Goldblatt, and J. Perraton. 1999. *Global Transformations: Politics, Economics and Culture.* Stanford, Calif.: Stanford University Press.

Held, D., and A. McGrew, eds. 2003. *The Global Transformations Reader: An Introduction to the Globalization Debate.* Malden, Mass.: Polity.

Korten, D. C. 1996. "The Mythic Victory of Market Capitalism." In Mander and Goldsmith, 183–91.

Mander, J., and E. Goldsmith. 1996. *The Case against the Global and for a Turn Toward the Local.* San Francisco: Sierra Club.

Morris, D. 2003. "Free Trade: The Great Destroyer." In Wirzba 218–28.

Norberg-Hodge, H. 1991. *Ancient Futures: Learning from Ladakh.* San Francisco: Sierra Club.

Orlie, M. A. 2006. "Mass Support for Power Politics." *South Atlantic Quarterly* 105 (1): 217–40.

Polanyi, K. 1944. *The Great Transformation: The Political and Economic Origins of Our Time.* Boston: Beacon.

Roy, A. 2001. *Power Politics.* Cambridge, Mass.: South End.

Sen, A. 1999. *Development as Freedom.* New York: Anchor.

Shiva, V. 2000. *Stolen Harvest: The Hijacking of the Global Food Supply.* Cambridge, Mass.: South End.

Steger, M. B. 2002. *Globalism: The New Market Ideology.* Lanham, Mass.: Rowman.

———. 2005. "Ideologies of Globalization." *Journal of Political Ideologies* 10 (1) (February 2005): 11–30.

Stiglitz, J. 2002. *Civilizations and Its Discontents.* New York: Norton.

Wallach, L., and P. Woodall. 2004. *WTO: Whose Trade Organization?* New York: New Press.

Wirzba, N, ed. 2003. *The Essential Agrarian Reader: The Future of Culture, Community and the Land.* Lexington: Kentucky University Press.

Wolf, M. 2004. *Why Globalization Works.* New Haven, Conn.: Yale University Press.

Contributors

LISA ANDERSON is the James T. Shotwell Professor of International Relations in the Departments of Political Science and of International and Public Affairs at Columbia University. From 1997 until 2007, she served as the dean of Columbia's School of International and Public Affairs. A scholar of state formation and regime change, particularly in the Middle East and North Africa, she is the author or editor of numerous books and articles, including *The State and Social Transformation in Tunisia and Libya, 1830–1980* and *Transitions to Democracy.* She serves as the chair of the board of directors of the Social Science Research Council, is a past president of the Middle East Studies Association, and served on the governing council of the American Political Science Association. An emeritus member of the Board of Human Rights Watch, where she was a co-chair of Human Rights Watch/Middle East, she was awarded an Honorary Doctor of Laws from Monmouth University in 2002.

LARRY DIAMOND is a senior fellow at the Hoover Institution. At Stanford University he is also a professor of political science and sociology and the coordinator of the Democracy Program of the Center on Democracy, Development, and Rule of Law. Diamond has been co-editor of the Journal of Democracy, published by the National Endowment for Democracy (NED), since the journal was launched in 1990. He also serves (since 1993) as co-director of the NED's International Forum for Democratic Studies. From January to April 2004, he served as a senior advisor to the Coalition Provisional Authority in Baghdad. His book on that experience is *Squandered Victory: The*

American Occupation and the Bungled Effort to Bring Democracy to Iraq. He is also the author of *Developing Democracy: Toward Consolidation* and *The Spirit of Democracy: The Struggle to Build Free Societies throughout the World.* He has edited or co-edited more than twenty-five books on democracy.

ZACHARY ELKINS is an assistant professor of political science at the University of Illinois, Urbana-Champaign. He received his BA from Yale University and his PhD from the University of California, Berkeley. His research focuses on issues of democracy, nationalism, and institutional reform, with an emphasis on cases in Latin America. He is currently completing a book manuscript entitled "Designed by Diffusion: Constitutional Reform in Developing Democracies," which examines the design and diffusion of democratic institutions. His articles have appeared in journals such as the American Political Science Review, American Journal of Political Science, and International Political Organization. Professor Elkins is also a co-director of the Comparative Constitutions Project at the Cline Center for Democracy at the University of Illinois.

JOHN R. FREEMAN is the Distinguished McKnight University Professor of Political Science at the University of Minnesota. Among his honors is the Morse-Alumni All-University Distinguished Teaching Award. Freeman is the author of *Democracy and Markets: The Politics of Mixed Economies*, which won the International Studies Association's Quincy Wright Award, and the co-author of *Three-Way Street: Strategic Reciprocity in World Politics.* Freeman has also edited three volumes of *Political Analysis* and (co)authored numerous research articles in North America and Europe. Several of Freeman's research projects have been supported by the National Science Foundation. Freeman has held many professional posts, including the presidency of the American Political Science Association's section for political methodology. In addition, he has been a member of the National Science Foundation's political science research panel and of seven major editorial boards. Freeman currently is engaged in two research projects. The first analyzes the implications of market globalization for democracy; the second applies Bayesian time series methods in the study of international conflict dynamics.

BRIAN J. GAINES is an associate professor of political science at the University of Illinois and has an appointment in the Institute of Government and Public Affairs. His research focuses on elections and public opinion, and his work has appeared in more than a dozen journals. Between February 2005 and January 2007, Gaines ran marathons on all seven continents.

JAMES H. KUKLINSKI is the Matthew T. McClure Professor of Political Science at the University of Illinois, Urbana-Champaign. His current research focuses on the nature and quality of citizen decision making. His work has appeared in the *American Political Science Review, American Journal of Political Science, Journal of Politics,* and *Political Analysis,* as well as in other disciplinary journals. He co-edited *Information and Democratic Processes* and edited *Citizens and Politics: Perspectives from Political Psychology* and *Thinking about Political Psychology.*

PETER F. NARDULLI is a professor of political science and law at the University of Illinois, Urbana-Champaign, and the founding director of the Cline Center for Democracy. He has been on the faculty at UIUC since 1974 and served as the head of the Political Science Department from 1992 until July 2006. Nardulli is the author of six books on various aspects of the American legal process and empirical democratic theory. His most recent book is *Popular Efficacy in the Democratic Era: A Re-examination of Electoral Accountability in the U.S., 1828–2000.* Nardulli has edited another five books. He has authored a number of articles in journals such as the *American Political Science Review, Public Choice, Political Communication, Political Behavior,* and a number of law reviews. Nardulli is currently directing a global study, the Societal Infrastructures and Development Project, which uses a number of innovative methodologies to examine the impact of democracy, free enterprise, and the rule of law on a wide range of societal development indicators (economic growth, environmental quality, human rights, societal stability, etc.).

MELISSA A. ORLIE is an associate professor of political science and criticism and interpretive theory at the University of Illinois, Urbana-Champaign. She is the author of *Living Ethically, Acting Politically;* has published essays in *American Political Science Review, South Atlantic Quarterly, Political Theory, Philosophy & Social Criticism, and International Studies in Philosophy;* and has written invited essays for leading collections on the thought of Hannah Arendt, Charles Taylor, and Sheldon Wolin. Orlie is a political theorist who works primarily in normative and democratic political theory. She is currently finishing two projects: a collection of essays on the politics of the good after Nietzsche and a book on the new local citizen politics emerging in response to economic globalization from which her chapter in this volume is drawn.

BUDDY PEYTON is a PhD student at the University of Illinois, Urbana-Champaign. His current research revisits Philip Converse's findings on issue stability among members of the American citizenry.

PAUL J. QUIRK is the Phil Lind Chair in U.S. Politics and Representation at the University of British Columbia. Since receiving his PhD at Harvard University, he has been a research associate at the Brookings Institution and a faculty member at several U.S. universities, including, from 1990–2004, the University of Illinois, Urbana-Champaign. His articles have appeared in the *American Political Science Review, American Journal of Political Science, Journal of Politics,* and *Political Analysis,* among others. His books are *Industry Influence in Federal Regulatory Agencies, The Politics of Deregulation* (co-authored with Martha Derthick), and *Deliberative Choices: Debating Public Policy in Congress.* He is a co-editor of *The Legislative Branch* and *The Republic Divided.* His awards include the Louis Brownlow Book Award of the National Academy of Public Administration and the Aaron Wildavsky Enduring Achievement Award of the public policy section of the American Political Science Association. He currently serves on the editorial board of the *American Political Science Review.*

WENDY RAHN is an associate professor in the Department of Political Science and an adjunct associate professor of psychology at the University of Minnesota. Before joining the Minnesota faculty, Rahn held faculty positions at Ohio State University, the University of Wisconsin, and Duke University. She served on the board of overseers for the National Election Studies from 1996 to 2004, and she recently completed an eight-year term as a co-editor of Political Psychology. In 1999 she received the Erik Erikson Award for Distinguished Early Career Contribution to Political Psychology. Also in 1999, she received the Emerging Scholar Award from the American Political Science Association's organized section on elections, public opinion, and voting behavior. Her research interests include the role of emotions in political thinking and behavior, citizen participation in politics, the origins and consequences of political and social trust, and national identity. Her articles have appeared in the *American Political Science Review, American Journal of Political Science, Public Opinion Quarterly,* and *Political Communication.*

BRUCE RUSSETT is the Dean Acheson Professor of Political Science at Yale University and editor of the *Journal of Conflict Resolution.* He has held visiting appointments at Columbia University, the University of Michigan, the

University of North Carolina, Harvard University, the Free University of Brussels, the Richardson Institute in London, the Netherlands Institute for Advanced Study, the University of Tel Aviv, and the Tokyo University Law School. A past president of the International Studies Association and of the Peace Science Society (International), he is a fellow of the American Academy of Arts and Sciences and holds an honorary doctorate from Uppsala University. His most recent books are *New Directions for International Relations* (co-edited with Alex Mintz), *Purpose and Policy in the Global Community,* and *International Security and Conflict.*

BETH SIMMONS is the Clarence Dillon Professor of International Affairs at Harvard University. She received her PhD from Harvard University's Department of Government. She has taught international relations, international law, and international political economy at Duke University, the University of California at Berkeley, and Harvard. Her book *Who Adjusts? Domestic Sources of Foreign Economic Policy during the Interwar Years, 1924–1939* was recognized by the American Political Science Association in 1995 as the best book published in 1994 in government, politics, or international relations. She has worked at the International Monetary Fund with the support of a Council of Foreign Relations fellowship, was a senior fellow at the United States Institute of Peace, and spent a year in residence at the Center for Advanced Study in the Behavioral Sciences at Stanford University. She currently serves as director of the Weatherhead Center for International Affairs at Harvard and is finishing a book on the effects of international law on human rights practices.

Index

Page numbers in italics are either figures (*f*) or tables (*t*).

DEMOCRACY, FREE ENTERPRISE, AND THE RULE OF LAW

Domestic Perspectives on Contemporary Democracy
Edited by Peter F. Nardulli
International Perspectives on Contemporary Democracy
Edited by Peter F. Nardulli

The University of Illinois Press
is a founding member of the
Association of American University Presses.

Composed in 10.5/13 Adobe Minion Pro
with Meta display
by Jim Proefrock
at the University of Illinois Press
Manufactured by Sheridan Books, Inc.

University of Illinois Press
1325 South Oak Street
Champaign, IL 61820-6903
www.press.uillinois.edu